The International Trafficking of Human Organs

A Multidisciplinary Perspective

Advances in Police Theory and Practice Series

Series Editor: Dilip K. Das

The International Trafficking of Human Organs: A Multidisciplinary Perspective
Leonard Territo and Rande Matteson

Police Reform in China
Kam C. Wong

Mission-Based Policing
John P. Crank, Dawn M. Irlbeck, Rebecca K. Murray, Mark Sundermeier

The New Khaki: The Evolving Nature of Policing in India
Arvind Verma

Cold Cases: An Evaluation Model with Follow-up Strategies for Investigators
James M. Adcock and Sarah L. Stein

Policing Organized Crime: Intelligence Strategy Implementation
Petter Gottschalk

Security in Post-Conflict Africa: The Role of Nonstate Policing
Bruce Baker

Community Policing and Peacekeeping
Peter Grabosky

Community Policing: International Patterns and Comparative Perspectives
Dominique Wisler and Ihekwoaba D. Onwudiwe

Police Corruption: Preventing Misconduct and Maintaining Integrity
Tim Prenzler

The International Trafficking of Human Organs

A Multidisciplinary Perspective

Leonard Territo and Rande Matteson

CRC Press
Taylor & Francis Group
Boca Raton London New York

CRC Press is an imprint of the
Taylor & Francis Group, an **informa** business

CRC Press
Taylor & Francis Group
6000 Broken Sound Parkway NW, Suite 300
Boca Raton, FL 33487-2742

© 2012 by Taylor & Francis Group, LLC
CRC Press is an imprint of Taylor & Francis Group, an Informa business

No claim to original U.S. Government works

Printed and bound in Great Britain by TJI Digital, Padstow, Cornwall
Version Date: 20110824

International Standard Book Number: 978-1-4398-6789-1 (Hardback)

This book contains information obtained from authentic and highly regarded sources. Reasonable efforts have been made to publish reliable data and information, but the author and publisher cannot assume responsibility for the validity of all materials or the consequences of their use. The authors and publishers have attempted to trace the copyright holders of all material reproduced in this publication and apologize to copyright holders if permission to publish in this form has not been obtained. If any copyright material has not been acknowledged please write and let us know so we may rectify in any future reprint.

Except as permitted under U.S. Copyright Law, no part of this book may be reprinted, reproduced, transmitted, or utilized in any form by any electronic, mechanical, or other means, now known or hereafter invented, including photocopying, microfilming, and recording, or in any information storage or retrieval system, without written permission from the publishers.

For permission to photocopy or use material electronically from this work, please access www.copyright.com (http://www.copyright.com/) or contact the Copyright Clearance Center, Inc. (CCC), 222 Rosewood Drive, Danvers, MA 01923, 978-750-8400. CCC is a not-for-profit organization that provides licenses and registration for a variety of users. For organizations that have been granted a photocopy license by the CCC, a separate system of payment has been arranged.

Trademark Notice: Product or corporate names may be trademarks or registered trademarks, and are used only for identification and explanation without intent to infringe.

Visit the Taylor & Francis Web site at
http://www.taylorandfrancis.com

and the CRC Press Web site at
http://www.crcpress.com

Dedication

To the thousands of men and women throughout the world who have devoted their professional and personal lives to combating the illegal activities associated with the trafficking of human organs.

Table of Contents

Series Preface — xi
Acknowledgments — xv
Preface — xvii
About the Editors — xxi
Key Terms — xxv

Section I
A CRIMINAL JUSTICE PERSPECTIVE

1 Trafficking in Body Parts — 3
LEONARD TERRITO, EdD AND RANDE MATTESON, PhD

2 China Profit$ from Prisoners: Organ Procurement and the Ethical Issue of Consent — 13
JESSICA NEAGLE, MA

3 Trafficking in Human Organs in Europe: A Myth or an Actual Threat? — 23
SILKE MEYER, PHD

Section II
A BUSINESS AND ECONOMIC PERSPECTIVE

4 A Free Market for Human Organs — 49
MEGAN CLAY, MA AND WALTER BLOCK, PhD

5 Karnataka's Unabating Kidney Trade — 59
VIDYA RAM, MS

6	**To Solve a Deadly Shortage: Economic Incentives for Human Organ Donation**	71
	CURTIS E. HARRIS, MS, MD, JD AND STEPHEN P. ALCORN, JD	
7	**A Free Market for Kidneys: Options, Futures, Forward, and Spot**	95
	WILLIAM BARNETT II, PhD AND MICHAEL SALIBA, PhD	

Section III
A MEDICAL, ETHICAL, AND PHILOSOPHICAL PERSPECTIVE

8	**Medical Tourism: Organ Trafficking and Kidney Transplantation**	117
	SNEZANA (ANA) MIJOVIC-DAS, MD, FASN	
9	**Body Values: The Case against Compensating for Transplant Organs**	131
	DONALD JORALEMON, PhD AND PHIL COX, PhD	
10	**Autonomy, Constraining Options, and Organ Sales**	143
	JAMES STACEY TAYLOR, PhD	
11	**Markets and the Needy: Organ Sales or Aid?**	161
	T. L. ZUTLEVICS, PhD	
12	**Selling Bits and Pieces of Humans to Make Babies: The Gift of the Magi Revisited**	169
	CYNTHIA B. COHEN, PhD, JD	

Section IV
A THEOLOGICAL PERSPECTIVE

13 A Catholic Perspective on Organ Sales   189
NICHOLAS CAPALDI, PhD

14 Body Parts and the Marketplace: Insights from Thomistic Philosophy   203
MARK J. CHERRY, PhD

15 The Commercialization of Human Body Parts: A Reappraisal from a Protestant Perspective   227
LARRY TORCELLO, PhD AND STEPHEN WEAR, PhD

Index   245

Series Preface

While the literature on police and allied subjects is growing exponentially its impact upon day-to-day policing remains small. The two worlds of research and practice of policing remain disconnected even though cooperation between the two is growing. A major reason is that the two groups speak in different languages. The research work is published in hard-to-access journals and presented in a manner that is difficult to comprehend for a lay person. On the other hand the police practitioners tend not to mix with researchers and remain secretive about their work. Consequently, there is little dialogue between the two and almost no attempt to learn from one another. Dialog across the globe, amongst researchers and practitioners situated in different continents, are of course even more limited.

I attempted to address this problem by starting the IPES, www.ipes.info, where a common platform has brought the two together. IPES is now in its 15th year. The annual meetings which constitute most major annual event of the organization have been hosted in all parts of the world. Several publications have come out of these deliberations and a new collaborative community of scholars and police officers has been created whose membership runs into several hundreds.

Another attempt was to begin a new journal, aptly called *Police Practice and Research: An International Journal*, PPR, that has opened the gate to practitioners to share their work and experiences. The journal has attempted to focus upon issues that help bring the two on a single platform. PPR is completing its 10 years in 2009. It is certainly an evidence of growing collaboration between police research and practice that PPR which began with four issues a year, expanded into five issues in its fourth year and, now, it is issued six times a year,

Clearly, these attempts, despite their success, remain limited. Conferences and journal publications do help create a body of knowledge and an association of police activists but cannot address substantial issues in depth. The limitations of time and space preclude larger discussions and more authoritative expositions that can provide stronger and broader linkages between the two worlds.

It is this realization of the increasing dialogue between police research and practice that has encouraged many of us—my close colleagues and I connected closely with IPES and PPR across the world—to conceive and implement a new attempt in this direction. I am now embarking on a book series, Advances in Police Theory and Practice, that seeks to attract writers from all parts of the world. Further, the attempt is to find practitioner contributors. The objective is to make the series a serious contribution to our knowledge of the police as well as to improve police practices. The focus is not only in work that describes the best and successful police practices but also one that challenges current paradigms and breaks new ground to prepare a police for the twenty-first century. The series seeks for comparative analysis that highlights achievements in distant parts of the world as well as one that encourages an in-depth examination of specific problems confronting a particular police force.

Although there are numerous books on the topic of organ trafficking, none view it from a multidisciplinary perspective. In order to fully appreciate and intelligently understand the problem of organ trafficking one must examine it from a broad perspective, and this is exactly what the editors have done in *The International Trafficking of Human Organs: A Multidisciplinary Perspective*.

For example, it does little good to deal with the problem of organ trafficking from a moral or ethical perspective without examining the economics that drive individuals who are desperate to seek out those who would pay them for their organs, or for that matter criminals who attack and drug victims, subdue them, and steal their organs (typically a kidney). In the final analysis there is no one perspective that is more important than the other in understanding the problem. Thus, in keeping with this philosophy, this book has been organized into the following four parts:

Section 1—A Criminal Justice Perspective
Section 2—A Business and Economic Perspective
Section 3—A Medical, Ethical, and Philosophical Perspective
Section 4—A Theological Perspective

This book has the unique distinction of being applicable across a number of academic disciplines as well as being useful to a number of government agencies. The academic disciplines include:

Criminal Justice/Criminology
Business and Economics
Medicine
Philosophy
Theology

Some of the primary government agencies include:

The Centers for Disease Control
Health and Human Services

Series Preface

Justice Department
Immigration and Customs Enforcement
Food and Drug Administration

In addition this book also has the unique feature of having an Instructor's Manual, which is not typically developed for edited volumes. The Instructor's Manual has been divided into the following six sections:

SECTION I—Learning Objectives
SECTION II—End Article Discussion Questions and Answers
SECTION III—Test Bank of Multiple-Choice Questions
SECTION IV—Web sites Dealing with the International Trafficking of Human Organs
SECTION V—DVDs Dealing with the International Trafficking of Human Organs
SECTION VI—United States Federal Statutes Dealing with the Issue of Organ Trafficking

It is hoped that through this series it will be possible to accelerate the process of building knowledge about policing and help bridge the gap between the two worlds—the world of police research and police practice. This is an invitation to police scholars and practitioners across the world to come and join in this venture.

Dilip K. Das, PhD
Founding President,
International Police Executive Symposium, IPES, www.ipes.info

Founding Editor-in-Chief, Police Practice and Research:
An International Journal,
PPR, www.tandf.co.uk/journals

Acknowledgments

We wish to express our thanks and indebtedness to the following distinguished scholars who allowed us to use their research papers in this book. Without their dedicated efforts this book could never have come to fruition: Stephen P. Alcorn, JD, Oklahoma County, Oklahoma, District Attorney's Office; William Barnett, II, PhD, Loyola University, New Orleans; Walter Block, PhD, Loyola University, New Orleans; Nicholas Capaldi, PhD, University of Tulsa; Mark J. Cherry, PhD, Saint Edwards University, Austin, Texas; Megan Clay, MA, Loyola University, New Orleans; Cynthia B. Cohen, PhD, JD, The Kennedy Institute of Ethics, Georgetown University; Phil Cox, University of Massachusetts at Dartmouth; Curtis E. Harris, MD, JD, University of Oklahoma School of Medicine; Donald Joralemon, PhD, Smith College; Silke Meyer, PhD, Centre of Excellence in Policing and Security (CEPS) at the Institute for Social Science Research (ISSR); Snezana (Ana) Mijovic-Das, MD, FASN, Albany Medical College; Jessica Neagle, MA, Georgetown University, and her mentor, Gladys White, PhD; Vidya Ram, MS, in Bangalore, India; Michael Saliba, PhD, Loyola University; James Stacey Taylor, PhD, Louisiana State University; Larry Torcello, PhD, State University of New York at Buffalo; Stephen Wear, PhD, State University of New York at Buffalo, and T. L. Zutlevics, PhD, Philosophy Department, Flinders University, Adelaide, Australia.

Typing and other numerous clerical and research services were also provided by our hardworking secretary, Sharon Ostermann, whose constructive comments and long hours of work are very much appreciated. She has a wonderful attitude, and it is always a pleasure working with her. We also want to thank her trusty assistant, Shari Allen, for her numerous hours of typing. She, too, was a pleasure to work with.

Lastly, we want to thank our publisher, Carolyn Spence, for sharing our conviction that this book will make a significant contribution toward the understanding and prevention of the illegal international trafficking of human organs.

Preface

The World Health Organization (WHO) reported a few years ago that organ trafficking and transplantation pose new challenges because the international illicit trade in human organs is on the increase, fueled by growing demand as well as unscrupulous traffickers. The rising trend has prompted a serious reappraisal of current legislation, while the WHO has called for more protection for the most vulnerable people, who might be tempted to sell a kidney for as little as $1,000.

Increasing demand for donated organs, scarce resources, contaminated donors, high economic profitability, uncontrolled trafficking, fragmented laws and nonenforcement practices, corruption, and the challenges of transportation between closely related species have prompted a serious reevaluation of international guidelines and given new impetus to the role of the WHO in gathering epidemiological data and setting basic normative standards.

There are no reliable data on organ trafficking—or, indeed, transplanting activity in general—but it is widely believed to be on the increase, with brokers reportedly charging between $100,000 and $200,000 to organize a transplant for wealthy patients, Donors—frequently impoverished and ill educated—may receive as little as $1,000 for a kidney, although the going price is more likely to be about $5,000. There is ample evidence to find a global network of organized criminal cartels engaged in the trade of human organs, skin, bone, and tissue.

The WHO has also urged governments "to take measures to protect the poorest and most vulnerable groups from 'transplant tourism' and the sale of tissues and organs, including attention to the wider problem of international trafficking in human tissues and organs."[1] Just recently, the police broke up an international trafficking ring that arranged for Israelis to receive kidneys from poor Brazilians at a clinic in the South African port city of Durban. But such high-profile successes merely scratch the surface.

Countries such as Brazil, India, and Moldova—well-known sources of donors—have all banned the buying and selling of organs. But this has come at the risk of driving the trade underground.

Behind the growth in trafficking lies the increasing demand for transplant organs. In Europe alone, there are currently 120,000 patients on dialysis treatment and about 40,000 people waiting for a kidney, according to a recent report by the European Parliamentary Assembly. The waiting list for a transplant in 2010 was 10 years. With the potential for this delay resulting in death, the desperation of sick people increases dramatically and gives enormous advantage to the traffickers, who are motivated only by greed.

In Asia, South America, and Africa, there is widespread resistance—for cultural and personal reasons as well as due to the high cost—to using cadaveric organs, or those from dead bodies. The failure to adequately screen cadaveric organs, skin, bone, and tissue from nations such as African ones with high rates of communicable diseases adds more public health concerns to the problem.

In China, the organs of executed prisoners are harvested without their permission and distributed in rank order to (1) high-ranking government officials, (2) members of the military, (3) wealthy Chinese and foreigners, and (4) common citizens.

The majority of transplanted organs come from live, often unrelated donors. Even in the United States, the number of renal or kidney transplants from live donors exceeded those from deceased donors for the first time in 2001. Yet the "Guiding Principles" on human organ transplantation, adopted by the World Health Assembly in 1991, state that organs should "be removed preferably from the bodies of deceased persons," and the live donors should in general be genetically related to the recipient. They also prohibit "giving and receiving money, as well as any other commercial dealing."

There are numerous books on the topic of organ trafficking, but none view the problem from a multidisciplinary perspective. In order to fully appreciate and intelligently understand the problem of organ trafficking, one must examine it from a broad perspective, and this is exactly what we have done in this edited volume. For example, it does little good to deal with the problem of organ trafficking from a moral or ethical perspective without examining the economics that drive individuals who are desperate to seek out those who would pay them for their organs, or for that matter physicians who illegally remove a kidney from poor or otherwise socially marginal hospital patients during routine and minor surgeries for other medical problems. In the final analysis there is no one discipline that is more important than the other in understanding the problem, but in combination they provide a perspective that is missing in any single source. Thus, in keeping with this philosophy, we have organized this book into the following four sections:

Section I: A Criminal Justice Perspective
Section II: A Business and Economic Perspective
Section III: A Medical, Ethical, and Philosophical Perspective
Section IV: A Theological Perspective

Each section of the book will be preceded by a brief annotated summary of each research paper to assist readers in identifying which ones might be of particular interest to them.

Note

1. World Health Organization, "Organ Trafficking and Transplantation Pose New Challenges," http://www.who.int/bulletin/volumes/82/9/feature0904/en/index.html.

About the Editors

Dr. Leonard Territo is presently a distinguished visiting professor in the Department of Criminal Justice at Saint Leo University, Saint Leo, Florida, as well as professor emeritus in the Department of Criminology at the University of South Florida, Tampa, Florida. He has previously served first as a major and then as chief deputy (undersheriff) with the Leon County Sheriff's Office, Tallahassee, Florida. As chief deputy, he was responsible for the daily operation of the Leon County Sheriff's Department. While serving with the Leon County Sheriff's Office, he was a major homicide investigative advisor on the murders committed by Theodore Robert (Ted) Bundy on the Florida State University campus in Tallahassee, Florida. This investigation eventually led to the arrest, conviction, and execution of Bundy. He also served for almost nine years with the Tampa, Florida, Police Department and had assignments as a patrol officer; motorcycle officer; homicide, rape, and robbery detective; internal affairs detective; and member of the police academy training staff. Dr. Territo is the former chairman of the Department of Police Administration and director of the Florida Institute for Law Enforcement at St. Petersburg Junior College (now St. Petersburg College), St. Petersburg, Florida.

He is a graduate of the U.S. Secret Service's Dignitary Protection Seminar, the nationally recognized University of Louisville's National Crime Prevention Institute, and the Saint Leo University Institute for Excellence in Criminal Justice Administration's Non-Verbal Communications/Detecting Deception.

He has coauthored some of the leading books in the law enforcement profession, including *International Sex Trafficking of Women and Children: Understanding the Global Epidemic*; *Criminal Investigation*, 11th ed., which is by far the bestselling book of its kind in the United States and has recently been translated into Chinese for use by the Chinese police and Chinese criminal justice students; *Police Administration*, 8th ed.; *Crime and Justice in America*, 6th ed.; *Stress Management in Law Enforcement*, 2nd ed.; *Stress and Police Personnel*; *The Police Personnel Selection Process*; *Police Civil Liability*; *Hospital and College Security Liability*; and *College Crime Prevention and Personal Safety Awareness*. He has also had his first novel published titled *Ivory Tower Cop* which is a chilling, suspenseful thriller inspired by a true story. His books have been used in over 1000 colleges and universities in all 50 states, and he has had numerous articles published in nationally recognized law enforcement and legal journals. His books have been used and referenced by both academic and police departments in the following 16 countries: Australia, Barbados, Belarus, Canada, Chile, China, Czechoslovakia, England, France, Germany, Israel, the Netherlands, Poland, Saudi Arabia, South Korea, and Spain.

He was selected for inclusion in *Who's Who in American Law Enforcement*; selected as Florida's Outstanding Criminal Justice Educator by the Florida Criminal Justice Educators Association; cited for 10 years of meritorious service by the Florida Police Chiefs Association; given the Outstanding Teacher Award by the College of Social and Behavioral Sciences, University of South Florida, Tampa, Florida; cited for 25 years of teaching and meritorious service to the Tampa Florida Police Academy; and awarded the Saint Leo University, Saint Leo, Florida, Outstanding Publication Award.

He has also been qualified as a police policies and procedures expert in both state and federal courts in the District of Columbia as well as the following states: Alaska, Arizona, Florida, Georgia, Illinois, Iowa, Kansas, Kentucky, Louisiana, Michigan, New Jersey, Ohio, Oregon, Pennsylvania, Tennessee, Virginia, Washington, and Wisconsin.

Dr. Territo has served as a lecturer throughout the United States and has instructed a wide variety of police subjects to thousands of law enforcement officials.

Dr. Rande Matteson has served as the department chair and is currently an associate professor of criminal justice at Saint Leo University, Saint Leo, Florida, as well as a retired federal agent. Dr. Matteson is a 32-year career law enforcement officer having served progressively responsible leadership and operational positions in local, state, and federal investigative agencies.

He is a graduate of the DEA Basic Special Agent Academy at the Federal Law Enforcement Training Academy, and has completed numerous training programs on a wide range of domestic and international topics. Dr. Matteson initiated and managed numerous special covert operations with significant and successful operational outcomes in domestic and global venues.

As a federal agent, Dr. Matteson has actively investigated the illicit trade in human organs, skin, bone, and tissue in the global marketplace. Organized criminal cartels dominate the trade and are found in all regions of the world. In order to be successful, the leaders, organizers, and managers of these transnational crime groups conceal their activities from authorities and operate with the cooperation of corrupt foreign officials who violate the Foreign Corrupt Practices Act with private sector partners. These cartels amass considerable wealth from these illicit enterprises and as such engage in international money-laundering schemes. Dr. Matteson has provided subject matter expertise on trafficking in human organs to federal and state prosecutors, law enforcement officials, and private sector organizations.

During his career, he was assigned to domestic and foreign legal attaché and headquarters offices as a supervisory special agent, policy maker, covert operations special agent, pilot, clandestine-covert special operations manager, educator, and multi-agency task force manager. Dr. Matteson has traveled extensively during his career and conducted sensitive criminal investigations abroad. While assigned overseas, he served as the backup DEA pilot to the CIA flying operational missions abroad.

His geographic duty assignments have included the Miami Field Division; Dallas Field Division; Pakistan Country Office; Mexico Country Office; FBI-DEA Training Academy at Quantico, Virginia; and Headquarters—Office of Science and Technology, San Juan, Puerto Rico, and Tampa, Florida. He earned his doctorate in corporate leadership, is a certified fraud examiner and certified hostage negotiator, and is certified in international marine maritime security.

Dr. Matteson began his career serving as a uniformed police officer and was later promoted into various positions, including the criminal investigation division, where he worked on crimes against persons (homicide) and property offenses.

His breadth of experience ranges from street crime to complex international and corporate crime. During his career, Dr. Matteson has been qualified in federal and state courts as an expert witness and recognized for his investigative contributions and awards/commendations in numerous high-profile investigations.

At the FBI-DEA Academy, Dr. Matteson served as a new basic agent-training coordinator, counselor, and subject matter expert, and was permanently assigned to the FBI-DEA Academy serving as a senior instructor and course developer and manager in the Leadership—Field Management Training Unit, which made him responsible for leadership training of all DEA and international partner agency managers.

His background includes complex transnational clandestine investigative operations inclusive of violations of federal and state statutes and securing intelligence vital to national security. He was selected as the agency representative and served for an extended assignment at the Counter-Terrorism Operations Center coordinating proactive terrorism operations at the U.S. Winter Olympics in Salt Lake City, Utah.

Dr. Matteson holds various memberships in professional associations, lectures, has published numerous scholarly articles and several books, and presents at academic conferences frequently on a wide variety of transnational topics related to criminal and social justice.

Key Terms

Normally when key terms are incorporated into an edited volume, they are inserted either after each chapter or in the back of the book. However, we believe it makes better sense for the reader to become familiar with these "key terms" prior to reading each of the papers or for that matter having to constantly go to the back of the research paper or the back of the book to check the key terms. Thus we have chosen to put the key terms at the very beginning of this book. We would strongly recommend readers become familiar with the key terms before they start to read this book.

Altruism: The principle or practice of unselfish concern for or devotion to the welfare of others.
American Medical Association (AMA): An organization of U.S. physicians. It was founded in 1847 "to promote the science and art of medicine and the betterment of public health." It has about 250,000 members, about half of all practicing U.S. physicians. Its publications include *Journal of the American Medical Association, American Medical News*, and journals on medical specialties.
Bellagio Task Force on the International Traffic in Organs: This task force examined the ethical, social, and medical ramifications for the trafficking, donation, and sale of human organs and evaluated strategies to ameliorate them. The task force's report recommended steps that could be taken to promote public trust in organ donation and to protect the well-being of all participants.
Bioethicists: These are individuals and groups who examine a variety of ethical issues, including the procurement of organs, the voluntary sale of organs by the poor, and all the problems associated with it, including relevant philosophical, ethical, and medical issues.
Brain Death: The irreversible end of all brain activity (including any involuntary activity necessary to sustain life) due to total necrosis of the cerebral neurons following loss of brain oxygenation. It should not be confused with a persistent vegetative state.
Cadaveric Organ Donation: These are organs legally harvested from individuals who are already deceased. In most cases, the decedent has given permission to harvest their organs prior to death or family members have given permission.

Caritas: Latin for charity, the Christian concept of spiritual and brotherly love, which is love for all people.

Center for Organ Recovery and Education (CORE): A regional not-for-profit organ procurement organization serving Pennsylvania, New York, and West Virginia. CORE is one of 58 federally designated agencies in the United States known as a not-for-profit organ procurement organization (OPO).

Commodification of Human Organs: This is the buying and selling of human organs as one would any other commodity on the free market. It is based upon the assumption that compensation for the purchase of organs is no different from any other permissible forms of body commodification.

Council of Europe: Traditionally, this has been the most active European institution in fighting organized crime. However, in the past 10 years it has been addressing issues in the field of biomedicine, which focuses on guidelines for organ and tissue removal and transplantations.

Cyclorosporine-A: A drug that controls a recipient's immune response and reduces the possibility of the body rejecting the transplanted organs.

Debt Peonage: This involves individuals who are in debt or in some kind of financial crisis. In many cases, the donors are women who are primarily low-paid domestic workers whose families have run out of credit and have money lenders knocking at the door. Thus, the decision is made by the woman or perhaps her husband to sell an organ in order to pay for this debt.

Dermalogan: A product made of processed human skin and skin-based gel that is sold to plastic surgeons for use in operations to enlarge the lips and smooth wrinkles.

Economic Failure: This occurs in cases of an acutely inefficient use of capital and labor and/or when there is an exceedingly unjust distribution of basic goods and services for subsistence.

Economic Failure Hypothesis: This is a hypothesis that concludes that the level of predatory organized crime is directly and positively correlated with the failure of the attainment of general material well-being by the population under the economic system.

End-Stage Renal Disease (ESRD): A final stage of kidney impairment that is irreversible, cannot be controlled by conservative management alone, and requires dialysis or kidney transplantation to maintain life.

Extortion–Protection Trap: The paradoxical condition in which a criminal organization is capable of providing effective protection simply because it poses a credible threat of illegal violence.

Falun Gong: This is an international group based in China with transnational membership that has allegedly been targeted for procurement of organs because of their political and religious beliefs, which are contrary to that of the Chinese Communist Party.

Forward Market: This is a system in which individuals could sell the future rights to one or both of their kidneys for money to be received at the time of such sale. Organ brokers or financial intermediaries can make one payment buying the rights to one or both organs for a lifetime or annual payments of lesser amounts, in leasing the rights for a year.

Free Market for Human Organs: The legalization of the sale of body parts as a legitimate free market activity in which the donor has complete rights regarding the sale of his or her body parts.

Hemodialysis: A medical procedure that uses a special machine (a dialysis machine) to filter waste products from the blood and to restore normal constituents to it.

Hemophilia: A group of inherited bleeding disorders in which the ability of blood to clot is impaired.

Human Gametes: These are reproductive cells that unite during sexual reproduction to form a new cell called a *zygote*. In humans, male gametes are sperm and female gametes are ova (also called *oocytes* or *eggs*).

Human Immunodeficiency Virus (HIV): A retrovirus that causes immune system failure and debilitation. HIV is spread through direct contact with bodily fluids and can also be transmitted via organ transplant if the donor is HIV positive.

Karnataka Authorisation Committee: This was a committee set up under the Transplantation of Human Organs Act of 1984 in India to insure that no buying and selling of human organs take place.

Kidney Belts: These are countries that appear to be disproportionately providing kidneys to wealthier countries. The kidney belt countries include the Philippines, Iraq, Turkey, Romania, Moldova, and Georgia.

Kidney Colonies: These are geographic locations within a country in which a disproportionate number of citizens sell their kidneys. An example of this would be Tamil Nadu, a state in India in which more than 10 percent of the population has sold kidneys for financial gain.

Kidney for a Dowry: A fairly common strategy for poor parents to arrange a comfortable marriage for an otherwise economically disadvantaged or "extra daughter," essentially a spare kidney for a spare daughter.

Kidney Theft: This form of theft often involves allegations of kidney theft from poor and otherwise socially marginal hospital patients during routine and minor surgeries for other medical problems.

Mandated Choice: This is a choice in which individuals would be required on a regular basis to indicate whether they are willing to donate an organ or not. It can be included on tax forms or when a person renews a driver's license.

National Organ Transplant Act of 1984 and the Uniform Anatomical Gift Act of 1987: These acts explicitly prohibit payment for organs and marketing any type of financial compensation or market for organs in the United States.

Nonvital Organs: An example would be the removal of a kidney, which can be considered nonvital if the other is functioning properly.

Nucleic Acid Amplification: This is a research initiative in selected blood banks that allows for direct testing of the genetic material of viruses such as hepatitis and HIV, which eliminates having to wait for the body's immune system to respond to the antigen. Thus the virus can now be identified immediately, closing the 2-month gap that previously existed.

OKT3: A drug that has greatly increased the success rate of organ transplants because of its ability to reduce the body's immune response to organ transplants.

Oocytes (Eggs): A female gametocyte or germ cell involved in reproduction. These are human eggs, typically either donated or sold for reproductive purposes.

Operation Scalpel: This was the name given to a police operation performed by Brazilian federal police officers in a sting that resulted in key organ brokers being convicted and sent to prison, where they are now serving long sentences for their crimes.

Organ Harvesting: The systematic removal of vital organs for transplantation.

Organ Procurement and Transplantation Network (OPTN): The national transplant waiting list and organ allocation system established by the National Organ Transplant Act of 1984.

Organ Procurement Organization (OPO): Regional, nonprofit organizations responsible for coordinating organ and tissue donations at hospitals throughout the United States; all OPOs are designated by the federal government to serve specific regions.

Organ Tourism: This generally involves wealthy tourists traveling to parts of the world where they can purchase organs from donors living in poverty.

Presumed Consent: Assumes consent that the individual would donate his or her organs unless they register to opt out of the donation.

Primum Non Nocere: This is the basic Latin tenet of the medical profession, which means "First, do no harm."

Regenerative Organ: The best example of a regenerative organ commonly donated is human blood because it continues to replenish, allowing a person to give blood and leaving the donor in no significantly worse condition than before the donation. This also includes skin, bone, nerve, fascia, tendon, heart valve, derma, bone marrow, and dedicated stem cells lines.

Rules concerning the Utilization of Corpses or Organs for the Corpses of Executed Prisoners: This is a Chinese law that allows the use of prisoners' bodies and organs for medical research and scientific studies.

Spot Markets: In this system, those living individuals who desire to sell one of their kidneys, assuming the price and other relevant factors are satisfactory, would make this known through a listing with one or more brokers.

Stem Cell: This is one of the human body's master cells, which has the ability to grow into any one of the body's more than 200 cell types. While these are primitive undeveloped cells that have the potential to be used for the production of in vitro replacement organs, their most promising short-term use is in immunology and the treatment of immunological disorders.

Tissue Banks: These are unregulated international multimillion-dollar businesses involved in the sale of body parts, including heart valves, pituitary glands, corneas, skin grafts, bone, and other body parts, which are removed for research, teaching, product testing, and sale to biotech companies.

Trans-Atlantic Organ Trade Triangle: This was an operation that brought together an unlikely group of Israeli and U.S. buyers, Brazilian and Moldovan kidney sellers, South African doctors, and transnational brokers from Israel.

Transplant Tourism: This generally involves wealthy tourists traveling to parts of the world where they can purchase organs from donors living in poverty. This also includes access to an organ while bypassing the laws, rules, or process of any or all countries involved.

Uniform Anatomical Gift Act of 1968: This act allows individuals to indicate their desire to donate their organs upon death.

United Network for Organ Sharing (UNOS): Located in Richmond, Virginia, the United Network for Organ Sharing (UNOS) is a nonprofit, scientific, and educational organization established by the U.S. Congress in 1984 that administers the nation's only Organ Procurement and Transplantation Network (OPTN).

Vital Organs: Those organs that cannot be removed without loss of function necessary to life. Examples are the heart, lungs, liver, pancreas, stomach, and both kidneys.

World Health Organization (WHO): This is a group within the United Nations system whose mission is to be the directing and coordinating authority for health worldwide. It is responsible for providing leadership on global health matters, shaping the health research agenda, setting norms and standards, articulating evidence-based policy options, providing technical support to countries, and monitoring and assessing health trends.

Xenotransplantations: Transplantation from an organism other than human.

A Criminal Justice Perspective[1]

I

Trafficking in Body Parts. The researchers have provided a few case studies of some of the more despicable crimes committed in the United States and Mexico as they relate to the illegal trafficking of body parts. Every case discussed is motivated by greed with little or no concern about the safety and health of the recipients, their family members, or the family members of those whose bodies have been systematically dismembered and sold. The researchers also provide some specific recommendations regarding how such crimes can be effectively investigated and the U.S. laws that are most applicable for both enforcement and prosecution.

China Profit$ from Prisoners: Organ Procurement and the Ethical Issue of Consent. This research paper discusses the rise of the Chinese security system and how this has led to unusually high numbers of arrests and executions in China. These executed prisoners have become the primary source of human organs used for medical transplantation in China. Organ procurement from prisoners violates the principle of voluntary consent because of the very nature of incarceration. In addition, this research paper also discusses the role of the medical professionals who are secretly involved in the process of removing organs from prisoners who are also tortured and abused before being executed. A close examination of the Chinese prison system reveals how laws in China permit the removal of organs from prisoners.

Trafficking in Human Organs in Europe: A Myth or an Actual Threat? This research paper focuses on whether the phenomenon of trafficking in organs exists in Europe or countries accessible and relevant to European citizens, and to what extent it can be considered as organized crime. The author attempts to identify supplier and destination countries, as well as the actors involved in this business and the prevailing circumstances smoothing the way for the commerce in organs. In relation to these issues, difficulties that scientific research faces in this field when it comes to the accessibility and reliability of data are also discussed. The author also elaborates on regulations, legislation, and operational measures to prevent or combat the illicit donation and transplantation of human organs.

Note

1. The majority of the abstracts presented at the beginning of Sections 1 through 4 were, with slight modifications, taken directly from the original research papers and were written by the author(s).

Trafficking in Body Parts

LEONARD TERRITO, EdD
Department of Criminal Justice, Saint Leo University, Saint Leo, Florida

RANDE MATTESON, PhD
Department of Criminal Justice, Saint Leo University, Saint Leo, Florida

Contents

Case 1	4
Case 2	5
Case 3	6
Case Origination	7
The Law Applied	8
The Global Network	9
Discussion Questions	10
Endnotes	10

> The pound of flesh which I demand of him is dearly bought and I will have it.
>
> **—William Shakespeare,** *The Merchant of Venice,* **Act IV, scene I**

Every reported case involving the illegal harvesting and sale of body parts is motivated by money with little or no concern about the safety and health of the recipient, their family members, or the family members of those whose bodies have been systematically dismembered and sold one piece at a time.

As one reads through many of the research papers that comprise the chapters of this book, they will be exposed to descriptions of deceit, greed, and cruelty, but very few are more "despicable" than the following three cases reported in the United States and Mexico.

Case 1

The first case emanated in Fort Lee, New Jersey, and involved a business called Biomedical Tissues Services, Ltd. (BTS), which shipped bones, skin, and tendons to tissue processors to be used as transplants for medical patients in need. Also involved in this case were embalmers and others from dozens of funeral homes in New York City.

At the time the case finally came to the attention of the authorities, it was estimated that the organs from 10,000 people had been harvested by BTS. The principal individual involved in this case was a highly regarded dentist and oral surgeon who had lost his license to practice because of drug abuse. His name was Michael Mastromarino. At the conclusion of the investigation, it was estimated that Mastromarino did all the harvesting with a crew of assistant cutters. Many of the organs harvested were obtained without the permission of family members. The funeral directors who provided the bodies in many cases were paid $1,000 per corpse. But when the bones and tissues were sold, they had a value of approximately $13,000. They were sold to tissue-processing companies. In the process, Mastromarino had forged medical histories and causes of death, and in many cases the corpses were individuals who had died of hepatitis, cancer, HIV, and other highly contagious diseases. Federal regulations prohibit transplants from such corpses.[1]

This case started to develop in 2004 as a result of a complicated disagreement over the sale of a funeral home in Bensonhurst, Brooklyn. A couple operating the funeral home approached the police and prosecutors in 2003 with accusations of fraud. An offhand remark developed into an accusation that the embalmer was returning bodies with parts missing, and the embalmer's business connection to a dentist led to questions about the possibility of sales of improperly obtained tissues. That dentist, as it turns out, was Michael Mastromarino.

It was learned during the investigation that one of the best-known victims of this illegal harvesting was a well-known PBS star, Alistair Cooke. His daughter had requested his body be cremated. It was learned during the investigation that when his body was turned over to the funeral home, his arms and legs were removed, as well as his pelvis and other tissues. Eventually his remains, or something purported to be the remains, were cremated, and the ashes were turned over to his daughter. It was also learned that there was falsification of the information regarding Mr. Cooke. His age was listed as 85, but he was actually 95. The wrong time of death was indicated, which is important because of the onset of decomposition. The cause of death was also incorrect. He had actually died of lung cancer.

The falsification of documents was a common element in many of the cases investigated, because if they had been accurately reported, the body parts would not have been acceptable.

It was finally determined by prosecutors that Mastromarino had netted $4.6 million in 3 years as a result of his work. He paid undertakers $1,000 each for providing access to the dead, paid the assistant cutters $300 to $500 for extracting the most marketable parts, and according to his lawyer managed to take home up to $7,000 per body. A former employee of Mastromarino contends that Mastromarino was actually making double that. The New York Police Department later interviewed the families of 1,077 people's bodies who were harvested for spines, bones, tendons, and other tissues. BTS had arranged with funeral homes in New York City and Rochester, New York, Philadelphia, Pennsylvania, and New Jersey to get these bodies.

The company's work was characterized as amateurish at best, and dangerous at worst. For families who planned an open-casket funeral, BTS cutters would patch up the corpses as best they could. Investigators found legs stuffed with PVC piping of the kind found in hardware stores. An employee said that he had used rolls of socks for the same purpose.

And police found surgical gloves sewn inside hastily repaired remains.[2]

Mastromarino subsequently pled guilty to all the charges and was sentenced to 18 to 54 years in prison. All the men involved with him also pled guilty and received lengthy prison sentences.

Case 2

This case involved not only the illegal harvesting of body parts but also very likely murders committed in order to obtain body parts.

In March 2004, UCLA's director of the Willed Body Program, Henry Reid, was arrested and a criminal investigation launched into the action of him and others at the University of California for the illegal sale of body parts. Once again, this crime, like all others in this category, was motivated purely by monetary gain. For example, one body can be dismembered and sold in parts for over $200,000 to pharmaceutical and medical institutes.

The probe of the UCLA Medical Center went back as far as 1998. Also arrested in March 2004 was Ernest Nelson, a body parts dealer who claimed to have paid Reid over $700,000 for permission to enter the UCLA body freezer and literally chop up some cadavers and harvest their parts.

The cadavers stored at the university were supposed to be used exclusively by medical students for study. Nelson provided documentation to authorities that allegedly proved high-level UCLA administrators had knowledge of and approved the secret sale of the body parts.

Reid, employees under his supervision, and others at the UCLA Medical Center appeared to have avoided detection by keeping some of the donated cadavers "off the books" and by possibly accepting cadavers that were never recorded.

At that time, there had been numerous reports of homeless persons vanishing from the downtown Los Angeles "Skid Row" area located close to UCLA. There had been unexplained disappearances of UCLA students as well. One of these students was 18-year-old freshman Michael Negrete, who vanished from his dormitory on December 10, 1999, and has never been found. Although it could never be proven, there was serious suspicion in the criminal justice community that there was somehow a connection between these disappearances and the illegal sale of human organs.

The pharmaceutical and medical industries, as already indicated, pay very well for a host of body parts including skin, scalps, fingernails, tendons, heart valves, skulls, and bones, which then find their way into research, drug manufacturing, and replacement surgery. Medical device and instrument manufacturers often use these harvested body parts in training seminars for doctors.

In 2004, Johnson & Johnson was named in court documents as having contracted with Nelson for certain human tissue samples.

One of the serious problems with this illegal trafficking is that it circumvents all screening and testing procedures set up and maintained to ensure recipients will not receive diseased or otherwise contaminated tissue or organs. With the possibility that dozens of unsuspecting patients could receive tissue or bone from a single diseased cadaver, the potential for a medical catastrophe cannot be minimized.

All one needs to do is to consider the fact that, within the past few years, nine people have died as a result of receiving transplanted organs from only two donors infected with a rodent virus known as lymphocytic choriomeningitis virus (LCMV).[3]

Prosecutors said Nelson and Reid devised the scam in 1999. Nelson said he thought the sales were authorized by the university.

Nelson used cashier's checks to pay Reid a total of $43,000 in 1999. Other payments were made in cash and were not documented.

The plan unraveled after a state health investigator became concerned about a sale in 2003 and contacted UCLA.

Reid has pled guilty to conspiracy to commit grand theft and was sentenced to more than 4 years in prison.

The scandal led to the suspension of UCLA's cadaver program for a year in 2004 and forced the University of California system to reexamine its donation rules.[4]

Case 3

On occasion the trafficking and harvesting of human organs start in another country but wind up in the United States. One of the most notorious cases involved the kidnapping of children from Mexico in order to harvest their organs for American children.

One of the cases involved a Mexican infant believed to be abducted in Tijuana by an American man and woman that the news media characterized as "baby organ snatchers." The criminals were operating in various cities along the U.S.-Mexico border. One of the children kidnapped belonged to a Mixtec Indian mother from Tijuana, who informed the FBI authorities that an American couple had abducted her 20-day-old daughter and taken her to California. The FBI confirmed that they had every reason to believe that the child was in fact abducted and that the agency had previously received reports about a woman spotted in Tijuana looking for babies. The FBI reported that both they and the Mexican federal agents get numerous cross-border child abduction cases each year and countless cases of child disappearance in Tijuana. Most of these children are very poor and of Mexican Indian descent. Most of the mothers speak very little English and are afraid of the authorities.

It was suspected by children's rights groups in Mexico that these babies and young children were being abducted for their organs and transplantable tissues. They report that there are many children in the United States waiting for organs in order to survive. Therefore, dozens of Mexican midwives, nurses, doctors, lawyers, judges, and even clerics participate as accomplices in the theft of Mexican children from whom organs are harvested at clandestine clinics on the U.S.-Mexico border. The organs are then transplanted to the children of rich Americans. It is estimated that one baby can bring as much as $10,000 and that corrupt government officials are known to take part in it. One of the largest rings is allegedly headed by a top Mexican government official. Attempts to prosecute him have failed because of his parliamentary immunity and his influence over the court system and its judges. The existence of a U.S.-Mexican "organ mafia" and threats by them have silenced journalists in Mexico, but one courageous member of the Mexican Congress, Hector Ramirez Cuellar, has stated he knows a child in his district who was kidnapped, had a kidney removed, and then was returned home with $2,000. Mr. Cuellar said that he has information that points to a U.S.-Mexico connection and that the rings deal in children's livers, hearts, corneas, kidneys, pancreas, and other body parts. During the same period, it was verified by the president of the Geneva-based World Organization Against Torture that there are in fact international rings that kidnap children not only for illegal adoptions, pornographic activities, and child prostitution, but also for the purpose of trafficking in organs.[5]

Case Origination

It is interesting to note that in almost all cases in the United States where the illegal harvesting of body parts has been discovered, they generally result from information provided by individuals outside of the criminal justice system who are either directly or indirectly involved with the harvesting operation. This would seem to suggest that somehow there are major systemic failures in the regulatory and oversight responsibilities of various governmental agencies. Florida is one of the very few states that criminalizes the sale of anatomical matter by state statute. The activity can be found at local venues, which makes this topic of interest to local authorities. However, there are numerous federal laws (discussed later in this chapter) that can be applied to this type of activity as enforcement options.

We should point out that unless actionable information is developed and furnished to law enforcement and regulatory agencies, it is not likely that this conduct can be effectively policed.

It is common for law enforcement officials to lack the requisite information and knowledge necessary to understand and investigate cases involving the illegal trafficking of human organs and tissue. There are, however, certain things that can be done to improve and develop technical expertise in this scientific criminal enterprise.

The authors have underscored some investigative tools that can be applied to this important sociological issue. First off, we propose establishing contacts and liaison with a variety of institutional and governmental contacts; however, this is only a basic starting point. As will be seen, this issue is complex and global in nature and difficult to investigate from a local perspective. The investigation phase will require the participants to learn as much as possible about the trade of human organs, as well as understanding the laws that can be applied.[6]

The Law Applied

One of the most significant enforcement tools to combat this activity is the law of conspiracy. In summary, any individual or business that conspires to engage in any unlawful conduct violates this law.

The U.S. Public Health Service Title 42 is the primary area of law that controls for the importation of human anatomical matter. One of the key highlights to conspiracy law includes those overt acts in furtherance of the conduct and does not require the conduct to be illegal; simply any conduct in furtherance of the intent to violate the law, whether completed or not, we define as overt acts in furtherance of the crime.

Violating the law of conspiracy is a separate crime. The second most important key area of the law of conspiracy incorporates those acts by known and unknown co-conspirators regardless of their geographical location, which legally binds all participants to the crime regardless if the conduct is fully carried out. In other words, a group of people located around the world who are participants in trafficking in human organs, bone, or tissue can each be charged as co-conspirators with the manner and means to carry out this scheme. To further illustrate the benefit of this investigative tool would include a co-conspirator making a telephone call to a source to facilitate the overall enterprise.

Another important investigative tool includes using a communications device to have communication that facilitates the crime. As creative as electronic communications is today, any transmission of messages or data can apply to violating wire and mail fraud laws. A simple analogy would include paying a credit card charge for using an internet service that is used to communicate with others to facilitate trafficking in human organs, bone, and tissue. Another important investigative tool includes knowledge of a felony crime. Under federal law, any person or corporation that has knowledge of a felony crime is required to report that conduct to authorities; failure to do so is a federal felony offense.

Providing false information or false oral statements made to private or government agencies is also a federal felony offense and includes false or misleading statements with respect to invoicing, customs, freight forwarders, commercial shipping businesses such as UPS or Fed Ex, commercial air freight, and the USPS or other express mail services.

It is common for importers to utilize the numerous foreign trade zones located around the world to facilitate this business by repacking and invoicing the products to disguise them from law enforcement. In addition, internet service providers may find medical tourism and local bone and tissue banks actively utilizing their services to facilitate this trade. The assets derived from this enterprise are generally found to have been laundered and may be subject to seizure and forfeiture by the U.S. government and/or foreign governments under treaties providing for mutual assistance.

Together, various local, state, federal, and international governmental partnerships can provide the necessary resources to investigate and apply enforcement options to the trade in human organs, bone, and tissue.

The Global Network

Few would disagree that our world has become a vast network of global electronic business networks where digital masked bandits can be found lurking. A simple keyword search for "kidney for sale" returns thousands of electronic responses in this global market bazaar offering body parts for sale. The instant access to people and information will likely continue to expand well into the twenty-first century and beyond.

A simple keyword search delivers a plethora of worldwide contacts that will assist interested parties in securing human organs, bone, tissue, and more anatomical matter. Because of the ease of these electronic communications, the effective monitoring of these activities can become complex for authorities primarily because many are located offshore and local police have no jurisdiction.

As the authors point out in this book, the demand for human organs, tissue, and bone far exceeds the available demand, and this void drives the market. One of the nations with the largest demand for organs, bone, and tissue is the United States, and this is unlikely to change in the near future.

On balance, as already discussed, U.S. federal law provides for adequate criminal penalties for violations of these laws. We think it is important to note that interstate commerce is regulated by federal law and that the movement of any article in interstate commerce creates governmental oversight and regulation. So, we recommend that public sector officials and others familiarize themselves with individual state and federal statutes regulating this conduct.

Discussion Questions

1. Who is Michael Mastromarino?
2. What role did Michael Mastromarino play in the business called Biomedical Tissues Services, Ltd. (BTS)?
3. What was it that brought the BTS case to the attention of officials?
4. How much money was made by Michael Mastromarino and his accomplices in the illegal trafficking in body parts?
5. What eventually happened to Michael Mastromarino?
6. What was the major source of organs harvested in the UCLA case?
7. Who was the principal person involved in the UCLA case, and what was the outcome of his conviction?
8. What is the demographic profile of the babies abducted from Mexico and transported to the United States for the purpose of harvesting their organs for transplantation?
9. What is the demographic profile of the Mexican mothers whose children were abducted and transported to the United States for the purpose of harvesting their organs for transplantation?
10. What types of individuals were involved in the Mexican "baby snatching" cases?
11. According to the Geneva-based World Organization Against Torture, international rings were involved in what types of crimes against children?
12. How have most of the cases of the trafficking in body parts been discovered by authorities?

13. What is one of the most significant enforcement tools to combat the illegal trafficking in human organs, bones, tissues, and other anatomical matter?

Endnotes

1. Michael Brick, "A Funeral Home Investigation Considers the Macabre," *New York Times*, October 31, 2005.
2. Terry Howley, "Big Business in Body Parts," *Reason*, March 2007.
3. Steven Dijoseph, "Illegal Harvesting and Sale of Body Parts, Tissue, and Organs: Dr. Frankenstein Would Have Been Proud," *News Inferno*, 8 April 2006, http://www.newsinferno.com/archives.
4. FOX News, Thursday, 14 May 2009. It was estimated Ernest Wilson made $1.5 million from these harvesting operations. He was found guilty of eight counts, including grand theft and tax evasion. He was sentenced to 10 years in prison. Reid pled guilty earlier and was sentenced to 4 years in prison.
5. Hector Carreon, "The Corruptive Influence of the Dollar: The Shameful Trade in Mexican Baby Organs!" *La Voz de Aztlan*, http://www.aztlan.net/organs.htm.
6. There are numerous information resources available for both researchers and criminal investigators. These include Organs Watch, the United Nations, the World Bank, the U.S. Public Health Service, the U.S. Food and Drug Administration, the Center for Disease Control, the U.S. Department of Justice, and U.S. Immigration and Customs Enforcement.

China Profit$ from Prisoners
Organ Procurement and the Ethical Issue of Consent*

JESSICA NEAGLE, MA
Georgetown University, Washington DC

Contents

Organ Procurement of Executed Chinese Prisoners	13
Confidentiality or Concealment?	15
Lack of Consent	16
Medical Doctors' Involvement	17
The Brain Death Criterion	18
Acknowledgments	20
Discussion Questions	20
Endnotes	20

Organ Procurement of Executed Chinese Prisoners

In 1984, the Chinese Supreme People's Court, Supreme People's Procuratorate, Ministry of Public Security, Ministry of Justice, Ministry of Public Health, and Ministry of Civil Affairs established the Rules Concerning the Utilization of Corpses or Organs from the Corpses of Executed Prisoners, which allows the use of prisoner's bodies and organs for medical research and scientific studies.[1] The rules allow the use of dead bodies and organs *if and only if* they are "1) the uncollected dead bodies or the ones that family members refuse to collect; 2) those condemned criminals who volunteer to give their dead bodies or organs to medical institutions; 3) upon approval of the family members."[2] Essentially, the "uncollected" dead bodies stated in the first rule are prisoners left "unclaimed" or "unidentified" after execution. Many are left unclaimed by family members because they are often not informed until the day before execution, if at all, and thus are unable to either make the trip in time to refuse or have the finances to make it in time to claim the

---

* Dissertation, 2009, Georgetown University.

body and by that time organs are extracted regardless. "They also set execution dates and ensure that the family will not be notified until after the execution is already carried out."[3] In addition, prisoners are also marked as "unidentified" because they refuse to identify themselves to officials when initially arrested because of fear that their family members will be subject to the same arrest and torture, which usually occurs. Therefore, many prisoners choose to remain "unidentified" and thus, by law, become a legal source for organ procurement.

The second rule allows the use of prisoners' bodies and organs if the condemned criminals "volunteer" to give their dead bodies or organs to medical institutions. However, the idea that a prisoner is in a position to actually "volunteer" is questionable. "But even in the apparent minority of cases where the consent of prisoners is sought as required by law, the abusive circumstances of detention and incarceration in China, from the time a person is first accused of a capital offense until the moment of his or her execution, are such as to render absurd any notion of 'free and voluntary consent.'"[4] However, even *if* prisoners did consent, are death row prisoners really in a position to make free voluntary decisions? Prisoners are not in a legal capacity or position to be fully informed about their decision as to what happens to the disposition of their body after death.

The third rule requires the "approval" of the family members; however, there are numerous reports of families testifying they were not informed and did not approve of the procurement of organs from their sibling or loved one before they were removed and then "donated" to medical institutions. In some cases, family members were even given cash payments to remain silent; if not, they were threatened with arrest. "In other cases, not only are families not informed but they are offered cash sums in advance—anything from several hundred to a few thousand Yuan, to authorize use of the condemned person's body. Refusal to grant permission, however, may reportedly result in the families being presented with unauthorized bills for large sums of money by the police, covering everything from the cost of the prisoner's food and 'board' while in detention to the price of the bullet used for the execution (about six cents) plus onerous cremation charges."[5] In addition, officials are required by regulations to cremate the body immediately after execution, allowing any evidence of illegal organ procurement to vanish. Many family members have reported that the body was already cremated prior to their arrival, and thus they have no way of predicting whether or not organs had been removed without their approval. If the body has not been cremated, it is usually covered with a sheet and family members are not allowed to view the body or request an autopsy.

Perhaps what is most concerning regarding the 1984 provisions is the declaration that the primary recipients of these organs should first be government officials, the military, and then the wealthy. The official document states that the recipients of the organs extracted from prisoners to be used for transplantation should be "1) high ranking government officials; 2) members of the military; 3) wealthy Chinese and other foreigners; 4) the common citizen."[6] The very fact that this has been ranked in a particular order indicates that the incentive to remove organs from prisoners is not necessarily to save the lives of the common folk, but only those who can afford to receive an organ or enhance research. In addition, what is most disturbing about the 1984 provisions is that they require secrecy during the *entire* process. "The use of the corpses or organs of executed criminals must be kept strictly secret, and attention must be paid to avoiding negative repercussions.… A surgical vehicle from the health department may be permitted to drive onto the execution grounds to remove the organs, but it is not permitted to use a vehicle bearing health department insignia or to wear white clothing. Guards must remain posted around the execution grounds while the operation for organ removals is going on."[7]

Confidentiality or Concealment?

The 1984 regulations also require that the use or "utility" of the dead bodies and organs of prisoners must be kept strictly "confidential" and in supreme "secrecy." "Use of the dead bodies or organs from condemned criminals must be kept strictly confidential, attention must be paid to the effect, and they should in general be used within the units. Only in real need, upon the approval of the Peoples Court executing the death penalty, can the operation from medical institutions be allowed entry into the execution grounds to remove organs, but vehicles with the logo of medical institutions are not to be used, and white clinic garments are not to be worn."[8] Securing organs from prisoners in a way that requires a hidden process is subject to abuse. "Were consent meaningful, there would be no need to set for elaborate procedures for concealment and to exempt minorities from the law."[9] In addition, the provisions in the law require absolute secrecy and confidentiality regarding the actual procedure for procurement between health personnel and public security officials. The issue here is that often "confidentiality" in this case is not used to "protect" the prisoner's privacy; but instead is used to conceal participants' involvement in the process.

The relationship between secrecy and confidentiality tests the limits that ought to be allowed especially if the restrictions are harmful, deceitful, and misleading. Instead of "lying," secrecy and silence comprise the preferred option or alternative when police and medical doctors are questioned by prisoners. "But the limits are uncertain where these strong personal and professional bonds are present. And so lies to protect confidentiality come to be pitted against the restrictions on harming innocent persons. Practices, some legitimate, others shoddy, persist and grow behind the shield of confidentiality."[10] Is it really ever all right to uphold confidentiality if it is harmful or deceptive? Perhaps there would be no need to keep such a practice secret if there were an established legal donor program within the nation.

Lack of Consent

The consent of prisoners for the use of their bodies and organs for transplantation, medical advancement, or scientific research, although required by law, is rarely sought. Perhaps the real reason why the government relies on prisoners as a source is because the idea of separation of the body after death goes against the traditional Chinese belief system. "In the case of Chinese prisoners, the issue of consent becomes even more contentious as Buddhist and Confucian beliefs dictate that the bodies are to be kept whole after death, meaning that voluntary donations are rare, if they occur at all."[11] Therefore, prisoners serve as the primary source of organ supply in China because there are no willing donors, nor are there systems established where a citizen can actually volunteer to give his or her organs anywhere in the nation. "There is no national registry for people to sign for donation of their organs after they die."[12] Regardless of this fact, somehow China is miraculously able to supply organs and bodies to meet the international demand and do so more than any other nation. "According to the report in the *Chinese Journal of Organ Transplantation*, over 25,000 kidney transplants have been completed in China in the past 20 years."[13] Since there are very few donors in China, if any at all, the medial institutions and the judicial court feel pressured to extract organs from prisoners even if they break the rules of the 1984 provisions, and they do so because they know prisoners would not "volunteer" or consent otherwise. "According to a former judge directly familiar with pre-execution procedures in Shenzhen, condemned prisoners would typically be taken, still in leg irons, into individual interrogation rooms at the jail around 10:00 P.M. on the night before their execution. At no point, according to this informed source, were prisoners asked if they were willing to allow their organs to be removed after execution."[14] Such coercive pre-execution procedures as these preclude all meaningful possibility of "free consent" being given. In addition, the character behind these activities of torture truly belittles the claim that voluntary consent is actually obtained from the prisoner. "The notion that someone on death row can give meaningful consent to a procedure—particularly when death row is a miserable hovel in a local jail and the prisoner is kept shackled—is in itself very difficult to accept; add to that the exceptional secrecy that envelops the process, and the claims for consent become still weaker."[15] In addition, medical professionals are involved in organ retrieval prior to and after execution. The World Medical Association (WMA) in 1994 noted "the increasing number of reports of physicians participating in the transplantation of human organs or tissue taken from the bodies of prisoners executed in application of a death sentence without previously obtaining their consent or giving them the opportunity to refuse."[16] Medical doctors should not participate in determining the fitness of the prisoner's bodies for organ donation as their involvement creates incentives to schedule the prisoner's death sentence for the *sake* of their organs.

Medical Doctors' Involvement

Before an execution takes place and not soon after a criminal is convicted, medical workers are allowed to visit prisons, usually let in by guards, so that they can begin to perform blood tests to determine if the prisoner is healthy and suitable to be an organ donor. The tests are usually performed days before the actual execution; however, medical personnel are forbidden to inform the prisoner of the reason for the tests. If the prisoner proves to be a perfect match and is healthy, the execution date is usually set sooner rather than later. "Hospitals are notified ahead of time when the execution is to be held so they may arrange a donor-patient match and prepare to make the transplant."[17] Medical professionals are an intricate part of the process of the removal of organs from prisoners and are usually on the execution site to assist. They are also present on the execution ground so that at the moment of "death," they can begin to immediately remove the organs, store them on ice, and rush back to the hospital in secret vans. "Immediately after the prisoner was shot (in the head), the physician stemmed the blood flow, put the prisoner on the respirator, and injected compounds to raise blood pressure and cardiac output so as to keep the organs perfused. In this way, the physician becomes an intimate participant in the execution process, functioning not to preserve life but to manipulate death in the service of transplantation."[18] Thus, the killing and saving of lives become intermingled in the process. "It is a contravention of medical ethics for health personnel, particularly physicians, to be involved in any professional relationship with prisoners or detainees for the purpose of which is not solely to evaluate, protect or improve their physical and mental health."[19]

In addition, with medical advancements such as "lethal injections," a medical specialist is almost always required in the process. "With the advent of lethal injections as a method of execution it is likely that more executions will take place in hospitals or clinics linked to prisons or police facilities."[20]

Although execution by gunshot is required by the 1984 provisions, if the prisoner happens to be a perfect match and it is too risky to damage the organs by gunshot, officials sometimes bypass the rule and instead illegally use lethal injection to induce death instead since it minimizes trauma to the body and it is the most convenient method for organ procurement. However, if a gunshot is used, it must be done in the back of the head to preserve the organs, or if cranial injury destroys desired body parts, such as the corneas, prisoners are illegally shot in other parts of their bodies, such as the heart, in order to preserve the needed part. "Obviously, the role played by health personnel in the execution and organ transplantation process in no way furthers the health of the prisoners involved. Instead, it converts state-sponsored killing into a grotesque, quasi-medical operation. Indeed the physician's primary duty to safeguard life and health is fundamentally corrupted by the practice of using executed prisoners as a source of organs."[21] What is even more disturbing is that medical doctors even go so far as to keep the body "alive" after execution in order to remove the organs prior to death so that the transplantation of the prisoner's organ is more viable, since a kidney or a liver, for example, must be properly stored within minutes prior to the actual death of the prisoner. "A very few localities, in order to be able to use particular organs from the criminals bodies, even go so far as to deliberately avoid killing them completely when carrying out the death sentence, so as to preserve live tissue. In other words, vivisection sometimes occurs."[22] The issue is that doctors are involved in the removal of organs prior to death and begin extracting while the prisoner is still "alive." Perhaps this has to do with the fact that "dead on arrival" cases are unusable for most procurement purposes and with China's nonrecognition of the "brain death" criterion.

The Brain Death Criterion

China's current legal definition of death is when the "heart stops beating." However, the majority of other nations have adopted the *brain death* definition as a more accurate criterion for the standard of clinical "death." In China, there are increasing reports that executions are actually prolonged in order to postpone brain death to assist in the retrieval of organs while the blood is still circulating. In addition, at the actual execution site it is required that a coroner be present to monitor the precise moment of "death." "Two coroners, one from the court and another from the procuracy, are required to be present at the execution ground to certify the prisoner's death, which is measured as the time at which the heart stops beating. According to a former judge of the Shenzhen Municipal Intermediate Court who has witnessed executions, the coroners sometimes ignore the requirement altogether and proclaim the prisoner dead based only upon the fact that he or she has duly received a bullet in the head."²³ Doctors play a dual role, that of a surgeon preparing to "save lives" through transplantation and another of assisting in the actual execution and "killing" of the prisoner. This creates conflicts of interest in which there are incentives to prematurely diagnose or even falsify death.

Regardless, even if the nation did recognize and adopt a brain death criterion, it would only assist by providing wider access to organs in China, which may be why many in the medical profession are advocating for the adoption of this new standard. "According to a typical view, China should quickly formulate a law using the 'brain death' (*nao siwang*) concept in order to broaden the supply and safeguard the quality of organs. This is really the key to developing China's organ transplantation work; one might even say that whether or not corpses can be readily used for medical treatment and research constitutes the standard and measure of whether a country is modern."²⁴ The issue is that "brain death" is very difficult to measure and can be costly as it requires complex medical technology to determine particular brain waves. Even if a new brain death standard were implemented, there are too many incentives for medical professionals to extract the organs without much concern if the prisoner is either "brain dead" or "heart dead." There is pressure to expedite death and falsify pronouncements of death to ensure success of the organ transplant. "At the place of execution there are no adequate facilities for the diagnosis of brain death, and at the same time the recipient (of a transplant) may be in a hurry."²⁵ In addition, because of the government's totalitarian nature, there is political pressure to increase the amount of organs available, and doctors or coroners feel rushed in their decision in the pronouncement of death. "In a totalitarian country a judge is not immune to political pressure. Those high up in the system may say we need more transplant organs, and even those in the medical profession are subject to such political pressure."²⁶

In addition, the People's Liberation Army (PLA) actually runs the majority of the medical institutions and hospitals in China. The close relationship that the PLA has with the prisons and the justice system ensures that a great number of victims will be individuals who are condemned for their political and religious beliefs, but convicted under other pretenses. The issue is that this population is convicted more often than any other group because their religious beliefs become politically "sensitive" according to the Chinese Communist Party (CCP). In fact, one particular group known as Falun Gong is currently under close investigation. There have been numerous reports by medical doctors from China confessing that they have been witnesses to or participants in the procurement of organs from this particular group because they are the "healthiest" prisoners. In fact, the U.S. Congress' Committee on International Relations recently published a report entitled "Falun Gong: Organ Harvesting and China's Ongoing War on Human Rights."

Acknowledgments

Jessica Neagle is a recent graduate of Georgetown University. A portion of her thesis, titled "China Profit$ from Prisoners: Organ Procurement and the Ethical Issue of Consent," is the basis for this chapter. Jessica would like to sincerely thank her mentor, Gladys White, PhD, who supported this endeavor and research during the entire process.

Discussion Questions

1. What are the Rules Concerning the Utilization of Corpses or Organs of the Corpses of Executed Prisoners in China?
2. What is the reason many prisoners choose to remain unidentified when they are arrested?
3. What is the preferential order of recipients for organ transplants in China?
4. What role do medical professionals play in the intricate process of organ removal at the time of a prisoner's execution?
5. Why is the role played by health professionals in contravention to medical ethics?
6. Under what circumstances might a decision be made by medical personnel to execute a prisoner by the use of lethal injection rather than a gunshot to the head?
7. Although a gunshot to the back of the head is required for execution, there might be a decision made to shoot the prisoner in another part of the body. Why is this so?
8. What dual and conflicting role do surgeons play in the organ retrieval process?
9. What conflict arises because of the close relationship of the People's Liberation Army (PLA) and the prisons and justice system?

Endnotes

1. Jessica Neagle, "China Profits from Prisoners: Organ Procurement and the Ethical Issue of Consent" (master's thesis, Georgetown University, 28 April 2009), 18–29.
2. U.S. Congress, House Committee on International Relations, Subcommittee on International Operations and Human Rights, "Organs for Sale: China's Growing Trade and Ultimate Violation of Prisoners Rights" (hearings before the Subcommittee on International Operations and Human Rights of the Committee on International Relations, Serial no. 107-29, 107th Cong. 1st Sess., 27 June 2001). Retrieved from http://www.foreignaffairs.house.gov.archives/107/73452.pdf.

3. U.S. Congress, "Organs for Sale."
4. Human Rights Watch, "Organ Procurement and Judicial Execution in China," *Human Rights Watch on China*, August 1994. Retrieved from http://www.hrw.org/legacy/reports/1994/china1/china 948.htm.
5. Human Rights Watch, "Organ Procurement."
6. Ibid.
7. Bellagio Task Force, "Transplantation, Bodily Integrity and the International Traffic in Organs," *The Bellagio Task Force Report on Organ Trafficking*, January 1997. Retrieved from http://www.icrc.org/Web/Eng/siteeng0.nsf/iwpList302/87DC95FCA3C3D63EC1256B66005B3F6C.
8. U.S. Congress, "Organs for Sale."
9. Bellagio Task Force, "Transplantation, Bodily Integrity and the International Traffic in Organs."
10. Sisella Bok, *LYING: Moral Choice in Public and Private Life* (New York: Random House, 1978), 149.
11. U.S. Congress, "Organs for Sale."
12. Ibid.
13. Ibid.
14. Human Rights Watch, "Organ Procurement and Judicial Execution in China."
15. Bellagio Task Force, "Transplantation, Bodily Integrity and the International Traffic in Organs."
16. Ibid.
17. Human Rights Watch, "Organ Procurement and Judicial Execution in China."
18. Bellagio Task Force, "Transplantation, Bodily Integrity and the International Traffic in Organs."
19. Human Rights Watch, "Organ Procurement and Judicial Execution in China."
20. Amnesty International USA, "The Death Penalty: Unprecedented Rise in Death Sentences and Executions," *The Amnesty Report on China*, June 1999. Retrieved from http://www.amnestyusa.org/document.php?id=4E6461682F7A3B0B80256A110057000&lang=e.
21. Human Rights Watch, "Organ Procurement and Judicial Execution in China."
22. Ibid.
23. Ibid.
24. Ibid.
25. Ibid.
26. Ibid.

Trafficking in Human Organs in Europe
A Myth or an Actual Threat?*

3

SILKE MEYER, PhD
Centre of Excellence in Policing and Security (CEPS) at the Institute for Social Science Research (ISSR), Tempe, Arizona

Contents

Introduction	24
Trafficking in Organs as a Face of Organized Crime?	24
The Problem of Defining Organized Crime	25
Definition by Criminals Involved	26
Definition by the Crimes Committed	26
The Problem of Gathering Reliable Data: Scientific Sources versus "Suspense Articles"	27
Aspects and Methods Involved in the Business of Trafficking in Organs	29
Short Overview of Main European Supplier (or So-Called Donor) and Destination (or So-Called Demanding) Countries	29
Which Circumstances in Donor and Demanding Countries Smooth the Way for the Commerce in Organs, Predominantly Kidneys?	30
Supplying the Black Market with the "Illicit" Good and Services	32
Actors Operating This Business	32
Different Methods Applied by Actors	33
Who Are the Victims of Trafficking in Organs?	34
The Donor as a Victim	34
The Recipient as a Victim	35
Discussed and Developed Measures to Tackle the Phenomenon	35
European Legislations and Conventions to Combat the Phenomenon	35
Convention on Human Rights and Biomedicine[80]	36
Additional Protocol to the Convention on Human Rights and Biomedicine concerning Transplantation of Organs and Tissues of Human Origin[82]	36
Increasing the Number of Available Transplants as a Preventive Measure	37

---

* First published in *European Journal of Crime, Criminal Law and Criminal Justice*, 14(2), 208–229, 2009.

Conclusion 39
Discussion Questions 41
Endnotes 41

Introduction

An unsuspecting tourist was supposedly drugged in his hotel room by a prostitute and woke up the next morning in a bathtub full of ice, minus a kidney. It is a scenario that has been passed around the world in different versions via email to a countless number of people, and it is what many people believe to be the phenomenon of trafficking in human organs, while police as well as organ transplant foundations have tried to stop it several times already.[1] Several internet sources as well as several national and international tabloids offer horrifying stories about organ snatchers operating throughout the world. These crime rings supposedly take organs from human beings without their consent and sell them on the black market for enormous amounts of money.

But what is trafficking in human organs really about? Is it a phenomenon that really exists? Or is it just a myth the public wants to believe because mass media and tabloids sell it so well? When talking about trafficking in organs, we first of all have to move away from the idea of crime rings snatching people to take out any kind of transplantable organ available in order to sell it on the black markets because this business is mainly based on living donations. The only similarity between the *suspense version* and the phenomenon being worked on in this chapter is the profit-oriented attitude of the actors in the business of trafficking in organs. The forms this phenomenon actually takes are far different from the crime legend just described. Still, this phenomenon does include victims as well as organized criminals that get together due to certain socioeconomic circumstances as well as fateful decisions to improve their living conditions.

Trafficking in Organs as a Face of Organized Crime?

Just like in cases of any other form of so-called organized crime, such as trafficking in women, drugs, arms, and so on, it is difficult to define whether trafficking in organs can actually be categorized as organized crime. Many approaches have been made to define *organized crime*, and there is no agreement on a valid international definition yet. While some scientists defined organized crime by the form of crime involved or the economic motives, others tried to define it by the structure of the criminal group behind the operation.² The difference between traditional forms of trafficking in illicit goods (e.g., drugs, and trafficking in organs) can be seen in the fact that while trafficking in drugs for example includes harmful consequences for those receiving and consuming them, this is usually not the case for recipients of illicitly donated organs. Trafficking in organs is helpful rather than harmful for the recipients, and the goods can and are actually supposed to be received on a licit market to a certain extent.³ Following, we will show if and to which extent trafficking in organs can be categorized as organized crime.

The Problem of Defining Organized Crime

Organized crime is often associated with Mafia-type crimes. Even though different Mafia organizations are still operating a high amount of organized crime in Europe, this is not the case for all forms and occurrences of this phenomenon.⁴ While organized crime used to be marked through a rather monopolistic structure, it is today characterized by a competitive and less visible low-profile structure.⁵

Trends in defining organized crime have changed throughout the past three decades. In the 1970s, it was a rather new phenomenon to most European countries, and the leading role in defining this phenomenon was then played by the United States, which was already more familiar with it due to existing crime groups on their territory, such as the Cosa Nostra in New York City.⁶ In the late 1980s, a more international discussion about the definition of organized crime flourished among leading scientists and the confusion about a generally accepted definition reached its peak.⁷ Several different criteria to categorize organized crime were introduced during the following decade. The most common ones were the hierarchic structure, monetary interests, involvement in illicit business, laundering the proceeds, the use of corruption on the level of official authorities, and internal systems of punishment for group members.⁸

Even today, there is no definition that holds international general validity. While some definitions require a certain number of group members involved (e.g., three), others require a certain period of time over which criminals have to operate within that group. In addition, most definitions still include the use of violence and/or corruption to advance the illegal business.⁹ One definition often used in scientific research is the definition developed by the German Federal Criminal Office (BKA). It also includes the monetary means, the organizational structure, and its systematic involvement in illicit activities as well as the involvement of corruption and/or violence.¹⁰

Two key elements that remained after all the diverse discussions about an adequate definition and that are still used to define organized crime are *crimes* and *criminals*.

Definition by Criminals Involved

This approach refers mainly to the structure of organized crime groups as well as their methods. According to Bovenkerk, one criterion for organized crime is that criminals, operating in the underground economy, are organized to make money through criminal methods.[11] This is the case when it comes to trafficking in organs because the organs are supposedly transplanted in private hospitals, usually by internal medical staff, where medical records are not being checked on by the government and often the transplantations take place at night—aside from the licit daily business of the hospitals.[12] Due to the growing shortage of donor organs, there is a growing demand for the underground economy of organ transplantations in which buyers as well as sellers are trying to circumvent national laws and to remain undetected.[13]

Trafficking in organs requires a well-organized network due to the complex nature of this business. It requires highly qualified medical professionals to carry out the transplantation, as well as intermediaries or brokers who recruit willing donors, usually out of poor communities, and find well-paying recipients, in many cases supposedly via the internet.[14] In addition, the "exchange" of the illicit good cannot take place anywhere, as it is possible in other forms of trafficking in illicit goods, because it requires a setting which provides the entire necessary medical instruments (e.g., an operating theater).[15]

Besides disposing of well-organized networks, organized crime is often said to involve violence and corruption. While corruption is involved in most cases of organized crime in order to facilitate the trade and transport in illicit goods, violence is more common when it comes to the abuse or infiltration of legitimate businesses or the attempt to control or monopolize a market.[16]

Definition by the Crimes Committed

Often crimes are typified by the nature of activity and the harm they cause in order to classify them as organized crime. The two main types of activity are the provision of illicit services and goods (e.g., trafficking in human beings, trafficking in narcotics, gambling, and prostitution) and the abuse or infiltration of legitimate businesses (e.g., labor racketeering or extortion). While the first category is based on consent between the supplying and demanding parties,[17] the second category involves nonconsensual activities, such as threat, coercion, or violence.[18] Trafficking in human organs fits into the first category because it supplies black markets with illicit organ donations and in most cases is based on mutual consent between donors and recipients. In addition, it fulfills the main criteria for organized crime, included in the BKA definition, because it involves illicit goods systematically traded by well-organized criminal networks that are profit oriented and use corruption at certain points (e.g., border control) in order to facilitate the movement of donors across borders.[19]

Still, the business involves not only organized crime but also white-collar crime. While the business as a whole is mainly dominated by organized crime, a smaller, but very important, part is mainly operated by white-collar crime. Once again, there exists a definition problem. While some scientists consider white-collar crime to be the same as organized crime, others see an overlap between these two forms, and again others draw a clear line between these two phenomena.[20] From my point of view, there is an overlap when it comes to the monetary interest and the violation of national legislations, but a clear line should be drawn between the two forms of crime when it comes to the criminals and their methods. The criminal activity, operated by white-collar crime in the field of trafficking in organs, is the transplantation procedure itself. According to Maltz, who agrees with Sutherland in that case,[21] white-collar crime is considered to be a form of crime, where a legitimate business—such as organ transplantation—turns into an illegitimate one due to circumventions and violations of national transplant legislations (e.g., the prohibition of transplanting organs for financial gain). This is the case where medical and nursing staff involve themselves in transplanting unregistered and sold, respectively purchased, organs, such as kidneys.[22]

The Problem of Gathering Reliable Data: Scientific Sources versus "Suspense Articles"

When it comes to trafficking in organs, hardly any official or reliable data exist.[23] As mentioned in this chapter, many reports about trafficking in organs can rather be considered as crime legends than as empirically proven and scientifically documented publications.[24]

It is interesting to see how persistent and effective these stories are. Horrifying stories promoted by mass media reach far more people than scientifically documented facts about this phenomenon. The problem is that scientifically documented and reliable data are rare in the field of organized crime and therefore also in this area. Adequate proof of committed crimes can be either given by the victims or by criminals themselves. In the field of organized crime, the latter are rarely caught, and the victims are often scared of testifying or—as it is in this case—not interested in official authorities finding out about their own violation of laws regulating organ donations.[25] We usually find out about organized crime at a level where the ones running the business are not visible anymore. Mainly, organized crime gets visible when illegal immigrants or drug traffickers are caught. The problem is that these people are usually not involved in planning and organizing the business. As a consequence, the information they can provide on the ones behind the scheme is rather poor.[26]

So how do we know that certain incidents fit into the larger picture of the business of organized crime? In order to find out more about a criminal organization and its methods, further investigation is necessary. In comparison to information provided by bystanders and victim-witnesses, information provided by the real offenders, who are involved in planning and organizing the business, is much richer. There are three ways of getting offender information—surveillance, undercover investigation, or offenders as informants.

Surveillance can be either physical or electronic. It has a long tradition in police investigations but is often complicated by a lack of reliable pre-information and proof of planned criminal activities that are needed under some governments' regulations in order to launch a surveillance investigation. In addition, private spaces, to which criminals can conceal without being kept under surveillance, can further complicate this kind of investigation.[27]

Undercover observation is rarely used in organized crime cases due to the long-term investigation necessary to get accepted by criminal organizations and to get access to relevant information about them.[28]

The most common investigative tool is an informant. This can be either a noncriminal or a criminal informant, whereas the latter is the most common. While noncriminal informants are usually people who just want to report criminal behaviour without any personal interest, criminal informants usually cooperate with the police in exchange for criminal immunity or at least for a reduced sentence. While informants mean a great advantage in data gathering for the police, they also cause further caretaking. These witnesses require anonymity in order to guarantee their physical safety.[29]

The problem of gathering reliable data in the field of trafficking in organs results from the complex business itself. Many countries are aware of the existence of this phenomenon, but it is hard to prove it.[30] Neither donors nor recipients are interested in making the transplantation public—and some donors do not even seem to be aware of the fact that they are violating legislations on organ transplantation. Since the business is not as expanded as other businesses of trafficking, it is less visible.

The ones carrying out the transplantation itself usually operate in a semilegal business, such as a private hospital at night or a developing country where legislations prohibiting the selling and purchasing of organs do not exist or have not entered into force yet.[31] It is therefore less obvious that these particular transplantations are illicit and the ones running the business are operating in the background and are therefore rarely caught. The ones that do get caught and prosecuted every once in a while are members of the medical staff,[32] but then again they are only able to provide the information they have on the criminal organization, which is, again, just as much information as a bystander or a member without influence in the criminal activities can have.

Aspects and Methods Involved in the Business of Trafficking in Organs

The business of trafficking in organs is far different from the idea of organ-snatching criminals, who are willing to kill people in order to sell their organs on the black market. While this phenomenon is rather new and shows a relatively modest scale in European countries, worldwide it has been an issue ever since the 1980s. Back then, experts became familiar with the so-called *organ tourism* or *transplant tourism*, which included wealthy Asians traveling to Southeast Asia (e.g., India) to purchase organs from donors living in poverty.[33] Meanwhile, the lucrative opportunity of trafficking in organs in some European countries, or at least to European customers, has been identified by international criminal organizations. The disproportion between available transplants and needed organs offers a niche for this kind of business.[34]

Trafficking in organs is about donations from people living in very low socioeconomic standards. These people are willing to sell an organ—usually a kidney because it is the most common organ received from living donors[35]—in order to improve their living standards.[36] This phenomenon meets the needs of many people from industrialized countries who are desperately waiting for a kidney donation. Just like any other form of trafficking, this business is demand driven, and the demand is not only high in Europe[37] but also worldwide.[38]

Short Overview of Main European Supplier (or So-Called Donor) and Destination (or So-Called Demanding) Countries

While trafficking in organs started out in developing countries (e.g., India) in the 1980s, today it has reached several European countries as well. As mentioned before, most illicitly donated and transplanted organs originate from people living in poverty. Therefore, the main donor countries are the ones with very low socioeconomic standards, high unemployment rates, and few chances to cover living expenses through legitimate work.[39] It can be said that the poorest countries are the ones most likely to be confronted with their citizens selling kidneys to organized criminals, who procure them to people supposedly willing to pay prices as high as $100,000–200,000.[40] Within the European context, the countries most often associated with trafficking in human organs are Moldova, the Ukraine, and Turkey, whereby the latter is the one where most transplantations are carried out while the first two countries are those where most donors originate from.[41] Beyond these countries, Bulgaria, Georgia, Romania, and Russia have also reported the recruitment of donors for the traffic in organs.[42]

There are other countries outside of Europe that play a major role as well when it comes to this phenomenon, such as India and Israel. In India, kidneys from living donors used to be sold more or less openly due to a lack of national legislations regulating transplantations. Recipients are mainly affluent Middle Easterners and Europeans who arrange the transplant procedure and hospital stay with Indian agents—or so-called brokers.[43] Meanwhile India and Moldova have banned the formerly legal selling and purchasing of organs within their territory or among their citizens. Still, this business has not vanished. It has just moved further to the underground and become less visible.[44]

In Israel, the majority of the recipients are Israeli citizens, while the donors again are mainly Eastern European citizens, such as from Ukraine, Moldova, Estonia, Russia, Georgia, Romania, and Turkey.[45] Furthermore, several allegations about human rights violations were made against the Chinese government in the 1990s for selling the organs of executed prisoners. One of the main discussion points of human rights activists in this field—besides the alleged financial profit gained by the government through selling other people's body parts—was the question of whether prisoners, awaiting execution, are able to give voluntary consent as required by Article 19, chapter VI, of the Convention on Human Rights and Biomedicine of 1996.[46]

While the phenomenon of organ trafficking observed in China did not concern Europe when it came to receiving those transplants, the other locations associated with trafficking in organs did. According to a survey conducted by the Steering Committee on Bioethics and the European Health Committee, both committees of the Council of Europe (COE), some European countries are aware of the fact that their citizens travel to so-called donor countries, such as the ones mentioned here, in order to receive a transplant from the black market. Among these are citizens from Belgium, Cyprus, Croatia, France, and the United Kingdom.[47]

Which Circumstances in Donor and Demanding Countries Smooth the Way for the Commerce in Organs, Predominantly Kidneys?

As mentioned before, the market of illicit organs is not only demand driven but also supply driven. While supply is guaranteed by citizens of the donor countries, demand is guaranteed by the shortage of organs all over Europe. These are the main circumstances smoothing the way for the commerce in organs.

The willingness of people to agree on a living donation for financial profit can be understood if one takes a look at their living standards. Moldova—being the main European donor country—is one of the poorest in Europe.[48] The average monthly salary in Moldova lies below EUR50,[49] and its unemployment rate is estimated to be higher than 50 percent.[50] Many people still live without running water, heating, and adequate food supply.[51] Sums ranging from $2,500 to $3,000 are offered by organized criminals for the donation of a kidney.[52] Considering that this is more than many of these people will be able to earn within the next few years, no further incentives are needed to convince people to sell an organ such as a kidney.

This business is smoothened not only by donor countries but also by demanding countries, being different European ones. The involvement of European citizens can be best explained by the major shortages of transplants in Europe. In most European countries, transplantations are strictly regulated by transplantation centers that administer the active waiting list for organs that are allowed to be transplanted in Europe, the most common ones being kidneys, livers, and hearts, followed by lungs and pancreas.[53] In addition, certain forms of tissue (e.g., cornea) can be transplanted as well.[54] In order to receive an organ from the licit market, one has to be registered on the official waiting list and wait until a suitable organ becomes available.[55]

Currently, about 40,000 people are supposedly waiting for a kidney transplant in Europe, and 15-30 percent die while on the waiting list due to the shortage of available organs. The average waiting time for kidney transplantations in Europe is 3 years, and in Germany even 5,[56] and it is estimated to have increased by 10 years in 2010.[57] These numbers are discouraging, especially for those desperately awaiting a kidney donation. In addition to long waiting times, some people are not eligible to get on the waiting list and to receive an organ that way at all. That is the case if someone's general health condition is poor; if life expectations—even with the new organ—are rather short; and/or if the success of the transplantation is not indicated.[58] For these reasons people turn to illicit measures because for many, accepting an illicitly donated and transplanted organ can be life-saving.[59]

As indicated the business of trafficking in organs—predominantly kidneys—is based on despair. On the one end of the *trading business* there are human beings driven by the desperate need for money in order to cover their living expenses, while on the other end there are human beings driven by the desperate need for a donor organ in order to guarantee their survival in the long run. It can therefore be said that the success of this business is built on people's desperate wish for survival—either from a financial or from a medical point of view.

Even though donors and recipients are those influencing the success of the business, it could not flourish without those who notice that exploitation of this despair can be quite lucrative—the organized criminals procuring the organs and arranging the transplantation procedure as well as the ones carrying out the latter, being medical staff who are willing to circumvent or violate national transplant legislations.

In addition to the demand and supply smoothing the way for this kind of business, a lack of antitrafficking legislations criminalizing the sale or purchase of organs in certain European countries, such as Bulgaria, Ireland, Lithuania, and Malta,[60] additionally facilitates the business. According to national law, foreigners are granted the same rights as citizens when it comes to selling or purchasing an organ in these countries. Even though it might be prohibited to sell one's organ in the country of origin, there still exists the niche of doing it in another country. First measures against these gaps in legislations have been taken by some European countries and are discussed later in this chapter.

Supplying the Black Market with the "Illicit" Good and Services

The main illicit goods in the business of trafficking in organs are kidneys. The improvement of medical technology has turned organ, and especially kidney transplantation, into a routine medical practice. Increased life expectations after kidney transplantations have caused an increased demand for transplants as well.[61] Due to the growing demand of transplants, it has been easier for organized criminals to establish the lucrative supply of illicitly donated organs. In addition to providing the illicit goods and illicit services, the transplantation procedure itself has to be provided as well since the goods are of no use to the recipients if they do not come with the necessary medical service. Therefore, this business involves several different actors as well as methods, which will be examined next. In addition, attention will be paid to the different kinds of victims involved as well.

Actors Operating This Business

Trafficking in organs requires different kinds of professionals in order to carry out the whole operation—from the recruitment of potential donors all the way to the successful transplantation of organs into a new human system. Therefore, different kinds of actors are involved.

Starting out with the recruitment or broking process, people who approach potential donors and get into contact with interested recipients are needed. Contact with donors and recipients is usually established through advertisements on the internet or in local newspapers,[62] but it is also common for desperate donors to approach medical facilities known for their involvement in the illicit transplantation business, of their own accord.[63] In some cases, depending on where the donors are recruited from and where the transplantation will take place, people arranging and carrying out transportation to and from the hospital are needed as well. Recipients usually travel there themselves. Once at the hospital, highly skilled medical and nursing staff is required because transplantations of human organs cannot be carried out by just anyone.[64]

Furthermore, the ones operating this business are often suspected to have excellent connections to official authorities (e.g., the police or customs services) to facilitate the movement of people across borders[65] (e.g., in cases where donors come from Moldova but transplantations are carried out in Turkey). In addition to those involved in the practical procedure itself, people are operating in the background. Those are usually the ones taking care of the criminal proceeds (e.g., through money laundering).[66]

Different Methods Applied by Actors

Even though stories of organized criminals traveling to poor countries and snatching people's organs against their will and at the expense of their lives, putting the transplants on ice, and transporting them back to where the transplantation will take place still occur in mass media reports every once in a while, this scenario is said to be rather unlikely to take place.[67] In general, those donating an organ for the black market are lured rather than forced into selling an organ. According to the COE, organized criminals offer potential donors between $2,500 and $3,000 for one of their kidneys.[68] The World Health Organization (WHO) has published numbers ranging from $1,000 to $5,000, with the latter one supposedly being more common.[69]

Either way, these are offers that someone living in extreme poverty can hardly resist. In addition to the practice of luring donors through financial means, there also exist reports of people being lured through false promises of work in the first place. According to these reports, young Moldavians were promised work in Turkey. Due to the fact that the business of trafficking in organs is known in Moldova, many of these men suspected they will be asked to sell their organs once arriving in Turkey. Still, coming from a country where the monthly income is below EUR 50,[70] if one has an occupation at all, makes people want to believe in promises of work abroad because for many it is the only way out of a life in poverty.[71]

While organized criminals only pay between $1,000 and $5,000 to those selling a kidney on the black market, they charge those who purchase them afterward enormous amounts of money. According to the COE and the WHO, amounts paid for a kidney on the black market range from $100,000 to $200,000.[72] Both prices, the one being paid by organized criminals in the first instance as well as the ones being paid by the final recipients in the second instance, are regulated by the supply and demand. The higher the number of donations for the black market, the lower the prices for transplants—in the first instance as well as in the second.[73]

Once donors and recipients are located, more or less solid examinations of both kinds of patients are carried out in order to match the criteria of a donated and needed transplant. The quality of pre-examinations and the matches of required and offered transplant criteria depend on how professional and thorough an organized crime group operates in this field.[74] It has been reported the transplantations carried out in Turkey are usually of high professional quality.[75]

While those paying high amounts of money for receiving a transplant enjoy a rather good aftercare, those donating their organ receive less adequate aftercare. Transplantations in Turkey foresee an approximate stay of 5 days at a local private hospital, and afterward the donors receive their money and are sent back to their country of origin, such as Moldova. At this stage, their health condition is often still unstable, and they require further medical assistance to gain full recovery. Since this is not available in many Moldovan villages, many cannot recover as necessary.[76]

Who Are the Victims of Trafficking in Organs?

The definition of *victims* depends on the point of view. While some consider those buying organs on the black market as criminals or at least offenders, they could be categorized as victims as well. Therefore, there are two different kinds of victims, the donors and the recipients—both for different reasons.

The Donor as a Victim
People who sell their kidneys—a part of their system—come from very poor backgrounds where life is cheap and sometimes even worthless. They originate from countries marked by high unemployment rates and low socioeconomic standards where the trade in human beings as well as human body parts is no rarity. Life has its price, and if one is willing to sell at least parts of it, it can be a lucrative deal, considering that the opportunities of earning a decent salary are rather poor or nonexistent in these areas.[77]

What is being ignored or forgotten about by the donors, mostly due to a lack of information, is the risk to their own health condition. Coming from and returning to an environment where medical support is lacking causes most donors health damage due to the lack of aftercare. In addition, an unhealthy way of life (e.g., due to alcohol abuse or a lack of rest after the transplantation) slows down the healing process and weakens their own organs, which causes the dependence on dialysis or a transplant in the long run for some donors themselves.[78]

People who have been victimized through economic failure of their governments get revictimized through criminals, interested in using their body parts but not providing them with the necessary aftercare. Profits in this field of organized crime are thus gained at human expenses.

The Recipient as a Victim

Recipients of illicitly donated organs are usually wealthy people who can afford the enormous amounts charged for an organ on the black market. Even though they violate national transplant legislations and receive an organ at someone else's physical expenses, they can also be regarded as victims. As mentioned before, waiting lists for receiving a kidney on the licit market are long, and for many people receiving an organ as soon as possible can make a difference between life and death. People going through dialysis for years make the decision to buy an organ on the illicit market out of despair and personal necessity, rather than decadence or cold-blooded calculation.[79] In addition, they get into a kind of victim status, where organized criminals take advantage of their health condition and charge them enormous amounts of money, just so the recipients can secure their survival.

Although it should be an ethical matter that wealthy citizens should not improve their health conditions at poor people's physical expenses, both parties involved can be regarded as victims in this case. It is the type of victimization that differs rather than the status of the different parties.

Discussed and Developed Measures to Tackle the Phenomenon

Following, we will give an overview of measures developed in the field of policy making and the complications arising when it comes to implementing operational measures. Furthermore, different ideas and developments regarding the increase of available transplants will be elaborated.

European Legislations and Conventions to Combat the Phenomenon

As realized by several countries, the phenomenon of trafficking in human organs has become a relevant issue, even for industrialized Western European countries. Even though it still ranges on a rather modest scale, different regulations and recommendations addressing the phenomenon have been developed in the field of policy making. The COE, being the most active European institution in this field of combating organized crime, has passed a convention and additional protocols and recommendations within the past 10 years. Among these, the most relevant documents in the effort to prevent trafficking in organs are the following.

Convention on Human Rights and Biomedicine[80]

This convention was adopted by the Committee of Ministers in November 1996 and, among other issues in the field of biomedicine, it focuses on guidelines for organ and tissue removal and transplantations. Within this context it includes guidelines to prevent trafficking in organs, such as the prohibition of organ and tissue removal without expressed consent in Chapter VI, Articles 19 and 20, and the prohibition of financial gain through organ and tissue donation under Article 21. The latter is constantly violated by everyone involved in the business of trafficking in organs.

Countries that signed this convention by 1999, and additional ones that signed in 2001, include those that have been identified as some of the main donor and demanding countries earlier in this chapter (e.g., Cyprus, Croatia, Estonia, France, Georgia, Moldova, Romania, Turkey, the United Kingdom, and the Ukraine).[81]

Additional Protocol to the Convention on Human Rights and Biomedicine concerning Transplantation of Organs and Tissues of Human Origin[82]

This protocol, made in January 2002, supplements the convention and emphasizes some more detailed regulations regarding transplantations. In Chapter II, Article 3, it states that organs should only be allocated "among patients on an official waiting list." In the same chapter, Article 5 states the right to adequate information of risks and consequences involved in donations and transplantation and Article 7 foresees the provision of adequate medical aftercare for recipients as well as donors. As earlier discussed, all three articles are violated by the procedure involved in trafficking in organs. In addition, Chapter III, Article 10, of this protocol solely foresees living donations to people having a "close personal relationship as defined by law" or "with the approval of an appropriate independent body" in lack of this relationship. This article is also violated in cases of trafficking in organs because this relationship usually does not exist between donors and recipients.

In addition to the convention and its protocols, established on an international level, there exist national transplant acts and legislations on transplantations within most national criminal codes of European countries, regulating the procedure of transplantations and criminalizing violations of these regulations.[83] The fact that some countries, such as Bulgaria, Ireland, Lithuania, and Malta, do not prohibit the sale or purchase of an organ within their territory, neither by their own citizens nor by foreigners, constitutes a niche for trafficking in organs. Due to this gap in legislation in some countries, first steps have been taken to prevent the sale and purchase or organs abroad by many European countries, such as Belgium, Bulgaria, Croatia, Cyprus, Czech Republic, France, Germany, Hungary, Italy, Latvia, Romania, Russia, Slovakia, Slovenia, Sweden, Switzerland, Turkey, and Ukraine, through implementing legislations that criminalize the sale or purchase or organs abroad.[84] Furthermore, recommendations have been directed at the Committee of Ministers by the Parliamentary Assembly of the COE, pointing out the deplorable state of affairs in some European countries, such as Recommendation 1611, which points out the alarming situation in Eastern Europe.[85]

Despite the convention and all other legislations, trafficking in human organs keeps on being an issue in Europe, which shows that in some countries the implementation of legislations and operational measures to ensure their obedience still needs to be improved, extended, and intensified. As with all forms of organized crime, the implementation of detection and prosecution measures is rather complicated because this business takes place in an *invisible niche*. In addition, the detection is complicated through the fact that neither party involved in this business has an interest in uncovering the criminal process. While other forms of organized crime involve victims that may press charges and/or cooperate in the criminal proceedings at some point (e.g., trafficking in human beings), this business involves parties who to a certain extent all benefit from the criminal process, and who at some point all have violated one legislation or another related to the market of illicit transplants. Another difficulty, when it comes to a sufficient enforcement of antitrafficking legislations, is the fact that it often collides with medical regulations such as the right to medical confidentiality and the inaccessibility of medical records. Even though many countries may be aware of the fact that their citizens may donate or receive an organ abroad, it is often hard to trace back the medical history of recipients and donors as well as the medical data of institutions carrying out transplantations, which complicates the enforcement of prosecution measures.

Increasing the Number of Available Transplants as a Preventive Measure

The shortage of transplants in Europe is unlikely to change in the near future, unless the field of biomedicine develops xenotransplantations (transplants from an organism other than human)[86] that will be possible to be transplanted into the human system and in addition will be agreed on by the relevant commission on ethics, for example in Germany by the Central Commission on Ethics (Zentrale Ethikkommission).[87] Awareness-raising campaigns on the situation in Europe as well as information about improved medical technology and decreased risks for living donors on the other hand might not increase available donor organs right away but could increase people's willingness to donate in the long run.

Standardization in national transplant legislations, from expressed consent to presumed consent, might increase the number of donations but is currently still highly controversial. About half of the European countries, such as Denmark, Germany, Ireland, Iceland, Malta, the Netherlands, Romania, the United Kingdom, and the former Yugoslavia, still operate on expressed consent, meaning organs can only be removed from deceased persons if they have expressed their consent while still alive or if the next of kin agree on a donation in case the deceased person has expressed neither consent nor objection during his or her lifetime.[88] While Bulgaria is the only country operating on a regulation where organs can be removed from a deceased person, no matter if the decedent objected during his or her lifetime, approximately the other half of European countries operate on presumed consent, a regulation where organs can be removed from a deceased person unless he or she objected during his or her lifetime. In some countries, such as Cyprus, Liechtenstein, Lithuania, Norway, and Sweden, the presumed consent is restricted, meaning that the next of kin have to be informed and asked about a possible donation or multi-organ explantation[89] (a form where all transplantable and usable organs, tissues, etc., are being removed).[90] As long as the controversial discussion about a standardization of presumed consent continues, no increase in available transplants can be expected either.

Another highly controversial idea on how to increase the number of available donor organs is the legalization of payment for transplants. According to this idea, transplantations would still be regulated by official transplantation centers and in accordance with official waiting lists, but it foresees a financial incentive for donors. Advocates of this idea expect that this would result in an increased number of willing donors and therefore in a decreased number of people dying on the waiting lists, while opposing parties regard financial incentives as incompatible with basic human values, such as human dignity or the spirit of altruism.[91] Advocates further argue that other donations, such as blood or semen for example, are subject of financial interests, so why should organs and tissues not be treated in the same way?[92] The answer seems rather simple. According to national and international regulations and legislations, reproducible parts of the human system, such as semen, blood, DNA or bone marrow, are excluded from the list of parts that are not allowed to become subjects of financial interest. It is therefore legal for institutions, operating in the field of science, medical treatment, donations of blood, and so on, to sell or purchase those excluded parts of the human system.[93] In addition, the financial interests involved in this field do not constitute a relevant financial benefit to individuals, such as donors. Even if some individual decisions on sperm or blood donations were influenced by the financial compensation some institutes pay, it does not encourage a decision involving health risks because what is donated in this case is automatically being reproduced by the human system. It is therefore no convincing argument that these parts can be the subject of financial interest while donor organs cannot.

Since ideas on increasing the number of donor transplants (e.g., through changing regulations from confirmed to presumed consent or through introducing financial incentives) are still highly controversial, a relevant increase of donations cannot be expected in the near future.

Conclusion

As it can be derived from different sources used for this chapter, stories of organ-snatching criminals, killing people in order to sell their organs to affluent people from industrialized countries, are more an urban legend than anything close to reality. Maybe this form of unscrupulous trafficking in organs did occur in individual cases, but since there does not exist any kind of official confirmation through judicial authorities or any form of scientific evidence, it is rather unlikely that trafficking in organs generally takes place in this form. However, it does take place in another form, and even though this one does not include selling people's organs at the expense of their lives, it does include exploiting people's vulnerable situation and gaining significant financial profits.

In addition, trafficking in human organs constitutes different violations of national legislations as well as human rights. As shown before, it is a phenomenon that works through the existing difference between living standards, especially between industrialized and developing countries. On the one hand, there are still countries with very low socioeconomic standards in Europe, where life is cheap and people are willing to sell it or at least risk it in order to make some money. On the other hand, there are affluent societies where pretty much everything can be purchased with money. One thing that is not purchasable unconditionally is health.

Even though affluent societies possess highly skilled medical staff and advanced medical technology, a shortage of transplants and a waiting list that has by far outgrown the demand drive those in desperate need of a donor organ to illicit measures. Since organized criminals have spotted the situation on both sides of the phenomenon, an illicit market for organs, specifically kidneys, was possible to establish. Poverty and prosperity get linked by brokers at the point where some people are willing to pay a fortune to improve their health, while others are willing to accept what seems like a fortune to them at the expense of their health. Taking a look at the consequences of trading organs for money might explain the widespread controversial attitude toward legalizing payments for organs. Payments would constitute an ethical conflict because organ donations are supposed to be altruistic and no profits should be gained through giving away organs or tissues. Once people receive financial benefits through donating an organ, the matter of consent should be questioned. Would those selling a kidney also consent to donations if no financial means were involved? And would decisions on donations not be influenced by socioeconomic standards then? Legalizing payments for organs is in fact likely to result in an increased number of donors because, even in industrialized countries, there will always be a considerable number of people that would do anything for money—no matter if needed for survival or simply out of greed. In addition, wealthy people can be expected to take advantage of donors' situations, once purchasing organs becomes legal. Legalizing the sale of one's own body parts would degrade the human system to a commodity and therefore result in an infringement of human dignity.

Since the demand for illicit transplants will remain, measures against the illicit supply need to be taken in order to combat the trafficking business efficiently. Legislations criminalizing this activity are a first and important step, but that will not keep those from violating these legislations who live on the verge of society and do not have anything to lose. Measures against economic failures, resulting in an extremely high level of poverty, as is for example the case in Moldova, need to be taken in order to improve the citizens' living standards. These people need to be given the opportunity of earning money and supporting their family through legitimate means in order to prevent them from participating in illegitimate businesses. Therefore, *donor countries*, as well as the European member states supporting them, need to focus on combating poverty and high unemployment rates first before the problem of trafficking in organs can be tackled efficiently.

Trafficking in human organs might not pose a threat to monetary means of the licit markets because donations of organs are supposed to be altruistic and therefore without financial gain. It also does not affect the medical business and its profits in the demanding countries since it does not diminish the demand for licitly donated organs because patients in need of an organ still outnumber available transplants by far. Still, trafficking in organs poses a threat to humanity and the well-being of several people being trapped in the illicit donation procedure. Therefore, it needs to be taken seriously and tackled sufficiently.

When it comes to policy making, personal situations of donors and recipients should be taken into account when prosecuting cases of trafficking in organs. Criminalization of selling and purchasing organs and therefore threat of punishment for donors and recipients comprise one essential measure to disrupt the illicit markets. Hence, punishment for those exploiting the vulnerable position of both donor and recipient, and gaining the main financial profits in this business should definitely be harsher than for those who should actually be protected by legislations against trafficking in organs. Therefore, organized criminals (e.g., brokers) and white-collar criminals (e.g., medical staff participating in illicit transplantations or hospital staff manipulating official waiting lists in exchange for financial benefits from patients buying their way up on the waiting list, as was allegedly the case in the United States in the mid-1980s)[94] should receive higher sentences than donors and recipients.

Last but not least, further scientific research will have to be conducted on this phenomenon in order to replace crime legends through scientific facts. Only then will this issue be taken seriously by all governments affected, and the results will constitute a solid ground for the field of policy making.

Discussion Questions

1. Why is it difficult to define whether trafficking in organs can actually be categorized as organized crime?
2. What are the necessary requirements for trafficking organs?
3. Why is it a problem to gather reliable data in the field of trafficking organs?
4. What does the term *organ tourism* or *transplant tourism* mean, and which group was first involved as recipients?
5. Where do most illicitly donated and transplantable organs come from?
6. Why is Moldova the main European donor country?
7. What do the statistics look like for those who are waiting on registered organized transplant waiting lists in Europe?
8. Who are the actors operating in the organ transplant business?
9. Who are the victims of trafficking in organs?
10. What ways were recommended to increase the number of available transplants as a means to prevent the illegal sale of organs?

Endnotes

1. P. Donovan, "Crime Legends in a New Medium: Fact, Fiction and Loss of Authority," *Theoretical Criminology* 6 (2002): 189–215.
2. F. Allum and J. Sands, "Explaining Organized Crime in Europe: Are Economists Always Right?" *Crime, Law and Social Change* 41 (2004): 133–60; C. Fijnaut, *Organized Crime in the Netherlands* (New York: Springer, 2000), 10f.; C. Fijnaut and L. Paoli, eds., *Organised Crime in Europe: Concepts, Patterns and Control Policies in the European Union and Beyond* (Berlin: Springer, 2004), 25; and M. D. Maltz, "On Defining 'Organized Crime': The Development of a Definition and a Typology," *Crime & Delinquency* 22 (1976): 338–46.

3. U. Schroth, "Das Organhandelaverbot—Legimitat und Inhalt einer paternalistischen Strafrechtanorm," in *Festschrift fur Claus Roxin zum 70. Geburtstag*, ed. B. Schtinermann, H. Achenbach, W. Bottke, et al. (Berlin: Walter de Gruyter, 2000), 869–90.
4. E. W. Plywaczewski, "The Russian and Polish Mafia in Central Europe," in *Global Organized Crime, Trends and Developments*, ed. D. Siegel, H. van de Bunt, and D. Zaitch (Berlin: Springer, 2004) 63–72; and Allum and Sands, "Explaining Organized Crime in Europe," 137.
5. P. Arlacchi, "The Dynamics of Illegal Markets in Combating Transnational Crime: Concepts, Activities and Responses," in *Combating Transnational Crime: Concepts, Activities and Responses*, ed. P. Williams and D. Vlassis (London: Routledge, 2001), 5–12.
6. Fijnaut, *Organized Crime in the Netherlands*, 8, 14.
7. Ibid., 11ff.
8. Ibid., 17f.
9. A. A. Aronowitz, "Smuggling and Trafficking in Human Beings: The Phenomenon, the Markets That Drive It and the Organisations That Promote it," *European Journal on Criminal Policy and Research—Illegal Markets and Practices* 9 (2001): 163–95; R. Godson and P. Williams, "Strengthening Cooperation against Transnational Crime: A New Security Imperative," in *Combating Transnational Crime: Concepts, Activities and Responses*, ed. P. Williams and D. Vlassis (London: Routledge, 2001), 321–55; and T. Obokata, "EU Council Framework Decision on Combating Trafficking in Human Beings: A Critical Appraisal," *Common Market Law Review* 40 (2003): 917–36.
10. Fijnaut, *Organized Crime in the Netherlands*, 23f.
11. F. Bovenkerk, "Organized Crime and Ethnic Minorities: Is There a Link?" in *Combating Transnational Crime: Concepts, Activities and Responses*, ed. P. Williams and D. Vlassis (London: Routledge, 2001), 109–26.
12. R. G. Vermot-Mangold, "Der Organhandel nutzt extreme Armut aus," *Soziale Medizin, Hintergrund Transplantation, Gesprach mit Ruth-Gaby Vermot-Mangold* 1 (2004): 20–23.
13. T. W. Foster, "Trafficking in Human Organs: An Emerging Form of White-Collar Crime?" *International Journal of Offender Therapy and Comparative Criminology* 41 (1997): 139–50; Schroth, "Das Organhandelaverbot," 877f.; and H. E. Sung, "State Failure, Economic Failure, and Predatory Organized Crime: A Comparative Analysis," *Journal of Research in Crime and Delinquency* 41(2004): 111–29.
14. The methods involved in this business will be discussed in the first and second main sections of this chapter.
15. Foster, "Trafficking in Human Organs," 144; and Vermoth-Mangold, "Der Organhandel nutzt extreme Armut aus," 22.
16. J. S. Albanese, "The Prediction and Control of Organized Crime: A Risk Assessment Instrument for Targeting," in *The Prediction and Control of Organized Crime: The Experience of Post-Soviet Ukraine*, ed. J. O. Finckenauer and J. L. Schrock (New Brunswick, N.J.: Transaction, 2004), 11–42.
17. It might sound odd to talk about consent in cases of trafficking in human beings, especially for sexual exploitation, but *mutual consent* refers only to the demanding party (e.g., brothel owners) and the supplying party (e.g., traffickers).

18. Albanese, "The Prediction and Control of Organized Crime," 21; and C. Fijnaut, "Transnational Organized Crime and Institutional Reform in the European Union," in *Combating Transnational Crime: Concepts, Activities and Responses*, ed. P. Williams and D. Vlassis (London: Routledge, 2001), 276–302.
19. Council of Europe, *Trafficking in Organs in Europe. Report of the Social, Health and Family Affairs Committee* (2003), http://assembly.coe.in/Documents/WorkingDocs/doc03/ EDOC9845.htm, sec. II, no. 15; and Schroth, "Das Organhandelaverbot," 883.
20. Fijnaut, *Organized Crime in the Netherlands*, 28f.; Maltz, "On Defining 'Organized Crime,'" 340; and P. J. Ryan and G. E. Rush, *Understanding Organized Crime in Global Perspective: A Reader* (Thousand Oaks, Calif.: Sage, 1997), 10f.
21. Maltz, "On Defining 'Organized Crime," 339.
22. Foster, "Trafficking in Human Organs," 139.
23. World Health Organization (WHO), *Organ Trafficking and Transplantation Pose New Challenges* (2004), http://www.who.int/bulletin/volumes/82//9/feature0904/en0print.html.
24. Donovan, "Crime Legends in a New Medium,"190.
25. Albanese, "The Prediction and Control of Organized Crime," 12f.
26. Ibid., 12.
27. Ibid., 15f.
28. Ibid., 15.
29. Ibid., 13.
30. Council of Europe, *Replies to Questionnaire for Member States on Organ Trafficking* (2004), http://www.who.int/ethics/en/ETH_CDBI_CDSP_questionnaire_Ogan_Trafic.pdf, 58f.
31. Vermot-Mangold, "Der Organhandel nutzt extreme Armut aus," 22; Foster, "Trafficking in Human Organs," 146; and Council of Europe, *Trafficking in Organs in Europe*, sec. II, no. 7.
32. Council of Europe, *Replies to Questionnaire for Member States on Organ Trafficking*, 60f.
33. Council of Europe, *Trafficking in Organs in Europe*, sec. II, no. 9.
34. Council of Europe, *Recommendation 1611: Trafficking in organs in Europe* (2003b), http://assembly.coe.int/Documents/AdoptedText/TAO3/erec1611.htm, no. 1; and V. Ram, "International Traffic in Human Organs," *Frontline* 19 (2002): http://www.frontlineonnet.com/fl1907/19070730.htm (2002).
35. Eurotransplant International Foundation, *Preliminary Procurement Activities* (2005), http://www.eurotransplant.nl/files/statistics/procurement_activities.html; and Foster, "Trafficking in Human Organs," 145.
36. Council of Europe, *Trafficking in Organs in Europe*, sec. II, no. 11; and Donovan, "Crime Legends in a New Medium," 100.
37. Council of Europe, *Recommendation 1611*, no. 9; and World Health Organization, *Organ Trafficking and Transplantation Pose New Challenges*.
38. Schroth, "Das Organhandelaverbot," 877.
39. E. Tomiuc, "Analysis: Council of Europe Examines Problem or Organ Trafficking," *The Ukrainian Weekly*, electronic version (2003): http://www.ukrweekly.com/Archive/2003/330305.shtml.

40. Council of Europe, *Trafficking in Organs in Europe*, sec. II, no. 11; World Health Organization, *Organ Trafficking and Transplantation Pose New Challenges*; and Tomiuc, "Analysis."
41. Tomiuc, "Analysis"; and Council of Europe, *Trafficking in Organs in Europe*, sec. II, no. 11.
42. Council of Europe, *Trafficking in Organs in Europe*, sec. II, no. 15.
43. Foster, "Trafficking in Human Organs," 146.
44. World Health Organization, *Organ Trafficking and Transplantation Pose New Challenges*.
45. Tomiuc, "Analysis."
46. Foster, "Trafficking in Human Organs," 147.
47. Council of Europe, *Replies to Questionnaire for Member States on Organ Trafficking*, 58f.
48. Tomiuc, "Analysis."
49. Ibid.
50. Council of Europe, *Trafficking in Organs in Europe*, sec. II, no. 23.
51. Ibid., sec. II, no. 13.
52. Ibid., sec. II, no. 6.
53. Eurotransplant International Foundation, *Preliminary Procurement Activities*.
54. Medicine-Worldwide, *Mogliche Transplantationen* (2005), http://www.medicine-worldwide.de/kontrovers/organspende_organhandel.html?page=3#moegliche_transplantationen.
55. Council of Europe, *Additional Protocol to the Convention on Human Rights and Biomedicine concerning Transplantation of Organs and Tissues of Human Origin* (2002), http://www.who.int/en/ETH_EC_Protocole_transplantation.pdf, chap. II, art. 3; Medicine-Worldwide, *Rechtliche Grundlagen und Voraussetzungen* (2005), http://www.Medicine-worldwide.de/kontrovers/organspende_organhandel.html?page=2#rechtliche_grundlagen_und_voraussetzungen.
56. Council of Europe, *Trafficking in Organs in Europe*; and R. Teutsch, *Tod auf der Warteliste* (2005), http://www.wdr.de/themen/gesundheit/koerper/organspende/index.jhtml?rubrikenstyle=gesundheit.
57. World Health Organization, *Organ Trafficking and Transplantation Pose New Challenges*.
58. H. L. Schreiber and A. Haverich, "Richtlinien fur die Warteliste und fur die Organvermittlung," *Deutsches Arzteblatt* 97 (2000): 309–19.
59. Foster, "Trafficking in Human Organs," 144; and Vermot-Mangold, "Der Organhandel nutzt extreme Armut aus," 22.
60. Council of Europe, *Replies to Questionnaire for Member States on Organ Trafficking*, 22ff.
61. Council of Europe, *Recommendation 1611*, 1; N. Scheper-Hughes, *The Global Traffic in Human Organs: A Report Presented to the House Subcommittee on International Operations and Human Rights, United States Congress on June 27, 2001* (2001), http://www.publicanthropology.org /Timespast/Scheper-Hughes.htm, 1.
62. Scheper-Hughes, *The Global Traffic in Human Organs*, 5.
63. Ibid., 10.
64. Vermot-Mangold, "Der Organhandel nutzt extreme Armut aus," 22.
65. Council of Europe, *Trafficking in Organs in Europe*, sec. II, no. 15.

66. Vermot-Mangold, "Der Organhandel nutzt extreme Armut aus," 22.
67. Foster, "Trafficking in Human Organs," 148.
68. Council of Europe, *Recommendation 1611*, no. 1.
69. World Health Organization, *Organ Trafficking and Transplantation Pose New Challenges.*
70. Tomiuc, "Analysis."
71. Vermot-Mangold, "Der Organhandel nutzt extreme Armut aus," 20.
72. Council of Europe, *Trafficking in Organs in Europe*, sec. II, no. 11; and World Health Organization, *Organ Trafficking and Transplantation Pose New Challenges.*
73. Vermot-Mangold, "Der Organhandel nutzt extreme Armut aus," 22.
74. Foster, "Trafficking in Human Organs," 145f.
75. Council of Europe, *Trafficking in Organs in Europe*, sec. II, no. 12.
76. Ibid., sec. II, no. 11.
77. Vermot-Mangold, "Der Organhandel nutzt extreme Armut aus," 21ff.
78. Ibid., 21; and Council of Europe, *Recommendation 1611*, no. 1.
79. Vermot-Mangold, "Der Organhandel nutzt extreme Armut aus," 22; and Schroth, "Das Organhandelaverbot—Legimitat und Inhalt einer paternalistischen Strafrechtanorm," 889f.
80. Council of Europe, *Convention on Human Rights and Biomedicine* (1996), http://conventions.coe.int/treaty/en/treaties/html/164.htm.
81. Center for Genetics and Society, *Human genetics in the public interest. Council of Europe* (n.d.), http://www.genetics-and-society.org/policies/international/council.html; MEACTIONUK, *The 1996 Strasbourg Convention* (n.d.), http://www.meactionuk.org.uk/strasbourg.html; and Ruhr-Universität Bochum, *Memberstates That Signed the Convention* (n.d.), http://www.ruhr-uni-bochum.de/zme/Europarat.htm#liste.
82. Council of Europe, *Additional Protocol to the Convention on Human Rights.*
83. Council of Europe, *Replies to Questionnaire for Member States on Organ Trafficking*, 7ff., 22ff.
84. Ibid., 22ff.
85. Council of Europe, *Recommendation 1611*, no. 5ff.
86. S. Vasel 2005, *op. cit.*, p. 1.
87. Zentrale Ethikkommission, *Zentrale Kommission zur Wahrung ethischer Grundsatze in der Medizin und ihren Grenzgebiete* (n.d.), http://www.zentrale-ethikkommission.de.
88. L. C. Nickel, A. Schmidt-Preisigke, and H. Sengler, *Transplantationsgesetz. Kommentar mit einer umfassenden Einfuhrung* (Stuttgart: Kohlhammer, 2001), 6ff.
89. Ibid.
90. Transplantation-Information, *Multiorganentnahme—Was kann entnommen warden* (n.d.), http://www.transplantation-information.de/organspende_organspender/ multiorganentnahme _multiorganexplantation.html.
91. M. J. Cherry, "The Body for Charity, Profit and Holiness: Commerce in Human Body Parts," *Christian Bioethics* 6 (2000): 127–38.
92. Schroth, "Das Organhandelaverbot—Legimitat und Inhalt einer paternalistischen Strafrechtanorm," 873f.
93. Ibid., 873f.
94. Foster, "Trafficking in Human Organs," 145.

A Business and Economic Perspective

A Free Market for Human Organs. This research paper draws attention to the shortage of human organs, which, as surgical methods improve, can frequently be used to save the lives of the living after their owners are deprived of their use by death. The researchers propose the legalization of the sale of body parts as a legitimate free market activity, and argue that in such conditions the price of human body parts would fall to a sufficiently low level to discourage the theft of human organs that the present laws are intended to prevent.

Karanatka's Unabating Kidney Trade. This research paper discusses the results of an investigation by India's national magazine *Frontline* into the kidney trade. The investigation turned up explosive data that revealed the scale and dynamics of it in the area of Karnataka, India. The acquisition of kidneys by questionable and, in some cases, clearly illegal means, resulted by exploiting the poverty of potential donors by creating a sophisticated network that drew a clientele from near and far. This was done in spite of the presence of laws to the contrary and the existence of organizations supposedly trying to prevent the illegal kidney trade.

To Solve a Deadly Shortage: Economic Incentives for Human Organ Donation. The researchers have proposed there should be a governmentally regulated, posthumous organ market, with economic incentives for the donors, in order to increase the supply of transplantable organs. They review the available transplant technology; provide a short history of the donation and sale of organs, tissues, and cells; discuss the various legislative approaches that have been made to increase the supply of organs; and also analyze the problems with the open market approach. They conclude with a proposal for a regulated posthumous organ market.

A Free Market for Kidneys: Options, Futures, Forward, and Spot. The researchers conclude there is a significant body of literature explaining how a free market for kidneys would eliminate both the economic and medical shortage of kidneys, and would also supply a sufficient number of kidneys for those who need one in the future and thereby remove the entire backlog of 40,000+ patients waiting for a kidney transplant in the United States. This research paper attempts to fathom the financial market processes that would evolve were a free market for kidneys to be permitted.

A Free Market for Human Organs[*]

4

MEGAN CLAY, MA
Loyola University New Orleans, Louisiana

WALTER BLOCK, PhD
Loyola University New Orleans, Louisiana

Contents

Postscript	53
Discussion Questions	55
Endnotes	56
References	57

Every year thousands of men, women, and children[1] needlessly suffer and die because of a law, a simple legislative enactment that could easily be changed.[2] One may think that something like this could only happen in a Third World country, or believe that a responsible government would change the law that in effect if not by intention kills innocent people every day. Unfortunately, this is now happening in the United States.

It is currently illegal to buy or sell human organs. While roughly 80,000 people need organ transplants every year, only about 20,000 people receive them annually.[3] These 20,000 body parts come from people who donate their organs as a gift to humanity. They receive no remuneration for their acts of generosity. Because people do not have an economic incentive to donate their organs, many people take them to the grave where they will be of no use to anyone. The number of donated organs falls far short of meeting the demand for them. Consequently, people die tragically and needlessly waiting for transplants.

Figure 4.1 illustrates this situation. If a market clearing price were but allowed, supply and demand would intersect at point B, under which circumstance there would be no shortage of transplantable organs. However, at the governmentally mandated price of zero, demand at point D is in excess of A; hence, the shortage is brought about by unwise state policy.

---

[*] First published in *The Journal of Social, Political and Economic Studies* 27 (2) 227–236, 2002.

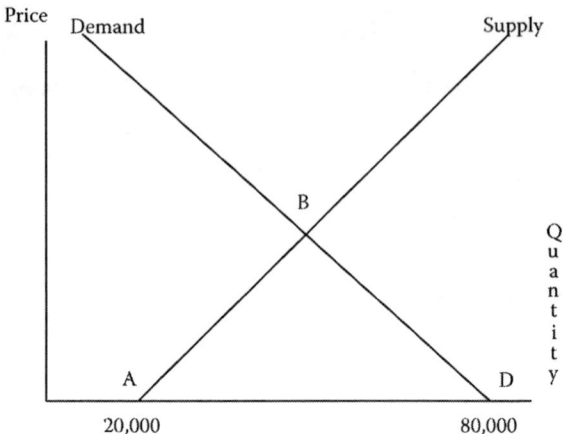

Figure 4.1

This shortage has created numerous other problems. Doctors and medical professionals must choose who receives an organ and who will die waiting for one. They often base this decision on age, sex, health status, and a calculation of postoperational life expectancy. For example a 60-year-old male, who would be expected to live 5 years after the operation, will be placed lower on the transplant list than a 10-year-old girl, who can be expected to live a full and normal life if she receives this operation.

At first glance this seems like a very equitable way of distributing the donated organs. But let us take a closer look. This practice requires fallible human beings to place more value on one life than another. The 60-year-old man did nothing of his own volition to be placed lower on the list. The 10-year-old girl did nothing to deserve the priority placement. This is hardly equitable. Rather, the current system enables medical bureaucrats to play God. Anyone who would take this role upon himself by that very fact establishes that he is not fit to do so.

The shortage has also created a black market for transplantable organs. There have been cases where body parts have been stolen from living people. Because it is illegal to buy and sell organs, their price is artificially high. This, in turn, encourages some people to engage in the mutilation of others for financial gain and others to enter into the black market. People are willing to pay these exorbitant costs to save their own life or that of a loved one.

Under the present system, one can sign up to be a donor at the local department of motor vehicles while applying for or renewing a driver's license or state identification card. This process involves only one question: "Would you like to be an organ donor?" A mark to that effect is placed on the back of the donor's driver's license or state identification card. However, when the donor dies a medical professional must still seek the consent of the next of kin. This is difficult for the family member who is forced to make a decision during a time of emotional distress.

For example, a 10-year-old boy dies in a car accident. The doctor breaks the news to the boy's mother and, because of the time constraints on transplantation, asks in virtually the same breath if she will sign a consent form so that he can transplant the boy's kidneys to a dying young girl. What would you say? To ask this question is almost to answer it.

A mother, who under normal circumstances would be comforted in knowing that her son's organs will be used to save a life after he can no longer use them, all too often refuses to sign the form because she cannot bear the thought of someone cutting open her recently deceased son to take his organs.

These deaths and excruciating moral dilemmas could be avoided by interpreting the signing of these donor cards as legally binding. Then, no permission would have to be garnered from suffering family members at a time of great tragedy, when it is most likely not to be given. The problem would still remain that all too few people sign these donor cards in the first place, many less than the total needs of would-be recipients. This problem can be addressed by allowing donors and their heirs to be financially compensated for their healthy organs after they die. The financial incentive will motivate more people to donate their organs, in one fell swoop eliminating the shortage of organs.

When signing up for the organ donation plan, the donor will be tested, and all of the pertinent medical information regarding the future transplantation will be recorded and sent to the organization that matches donors with donees. The donor and their next of kin will sign consent forms and receive a contract that states the amount the donor's family will receive if the organs are transplanted after their death.

Upon the donor's demise, if their organs are eligible for transplant, their name along with a list of their viable organs will be sent to organizations that have already compiled a list of people in need. The organs are then shipped for transplantation, and the relatives of the deceased will receive a check for the agreed-upon amount. Families will have more money to pay the final expenses of their loved ones. The organ donation organization bills the recipient or their insurance company.

Some may argue that a market for organs would make them too expensive. But transplantations are already very expensive procedures. Further, allowing profit motivations to come to bear would actually lower prices; this is because a greater supply of anything, organs specifically included, tends to drive prices in a downward direction. Poor people receive organ transplants under the current system because insurance, either private or public (Medicare or Medicaid), pays for all medical expenses. Why should we assume they would not or could not pay for the organ itself? This new system will reduce the waiting period for organs, which will decrease the overall period of time spent in the hospital, diminishing the overall cost of treating the patient.

Others say it is "wrong" to buy and sell kidneys or other such body parts because it would be immoral for someone to make a profit from the commercialization of such items.[4] Their argument is that this violates "human flourishing."[5] Tell that to the person on a kidney dialysis machine who is reduced to the position of looking forward, ghoul-like, to holidays such as Memorial Day or the July 4 weekend, since this is when motor vehicle accidents peak, and hence when these body parts are more available. The only "human flourishing" that occurs from this inhumane system is that these personal tragedies serve as the focus for memorable movies and television dramas.

If this vitally important institution is turned over to the marketplace, that will solve all of the problems the current system faces. Through this self-regulating mechanism, organs will be bought and sold freely. Everyone in need of an organ transplant will receive one. It will alleviate suffering and the financial burdens now plaguing families during a very emotionally trying time. Changing this law will improve the lives of everyone involved.

There is another objection that has been leveled against this life-saving idea of applying the strictures of free enterprise to organ donation: that a free market in organs would exacerbate their theft; that is to say, legalization of this market would lead to murder, in that pretty much the only way to steal an organ is to commit bodily harm to or murder the present possessor of it, or to withhold medical assistance from a seriously ill unwilling donor. The purpose of the present law, under which it is illegal to charge for these items, is to prevent atrocities of this kind. But if such organs were readily available, the profit that could be made by such actions would presumably be sufficiently small to render them profitless. After all, no one can earn a profit from seizing products with zero value.

But theft of organs already happens under the present system. In the black market, people are presently stealing organs. In contrast, in the proposed free enterprise system the original owner of the organ (or his estate) will receive the profit from the sale. Owners of body parts are more justified in benefiting from them than thieves.

In the event, however, that the very opposite is the case, legalization of markets in body parts will reduce robbery (and thus murder), not enhance it. We may indeed posit that the more money there is to be made from a product, the greater the danger of nefarious activity, other things being equal. But this mitigates in favor of free enterprise, not against it. To see this, consider Figure 4.2.

A Free Market for Human Organs

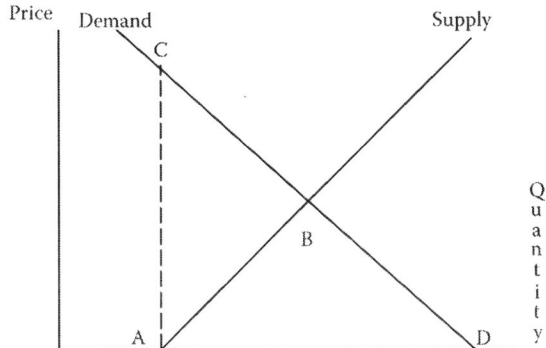

Figure 4.2

At present, society is at point A, where the supply curve intersects the Quantity axis. An amount A of bodily parts is forthcoming at the price zero. The market price would be B, if markets were but allowed to operate, because, at equilibrium, this is the point at which supply and demand would tend to be equated. The superficially correct point of this objection to free markets is that the price at B would serve as the gain to be made from pilfering an organ.

However, when price is kept down to zero (point A) by legislative fiat, that is not the end of the matter. Alternative costs, one of the determinants of prices, do not disappear. Instead, they arise, phantom like, in the form of black market prices. To wit, under the prohibition of purchases and sales, the illegal price will rise to C. This is the point at which the supply of organs intersects the demand curve. But note that at this point the profits to be made from theft, the distance between A and C, is in excess of the vertical distance from the Q axis to B. Thus, if a price of B can serve as an impetus for robbery, and it can, then so much more is this true of a price of C, since the latter is greater than the former. Far from creating body "snatching," then, the free enterprise system reduces the economic incentive for such dastardly activity.

We conclude that the case for repealing all laws that interfere with a free market in bodily organs is a strong one. That it will save numerous lives is a foregone conclusion. That present violations of this law are "victimless crimes," and ought to be legalized, is also suggested by our analysis.

Postscript

This is a highly charged issue. We do well, then, to risk repetitiveness and consider once again some reservations that many people will have to our "modest proposal." Here, in the words of a referee for the journal in which this chapter was originally published, is a report on one such set of objections:

> The prime objection to compensating relatives or other heirs for body parts, quite apart from the issue of murder by gangs (more likely in third world countries than inside the USA) is the concern that many relatives/heirs would be likely to hasten the death of the elderly and sick by deliberate lack of care, in order to sell the body parts after a "natural" death. Financial rewards for supplying body parts is regarded by a substantial and perhaps overwhelming proportion of the medical profession and general public, as highly inappropriate. Another difficulty is that no matter how low the price of used bodily organs falls, there are plenty of poor persons who would be eager to benefit from the sale of such parts, to their great detriment.

These objections stem from an almost visceral or instinctive revulsion at the idea of allowing prices, property rights, markets, and all the other accoutrements of modern economies to apply to so tender a product as parts of human beings. To bring the human body into the cash nexus is almost to deprecate its value; it is to treat something almost holy as one would a bushel of wheat or a slab of iron.

Nothing, however, could be further from the truth. To allow economic incentives to apply to so important and scarce a resource[6] is to do no more than bring rationality to it, of the same sort as we as a society rely upon to obtain food, clothing, shelter, and other products necessary to life. If parts of the human being are so important that nothing but the economic system of the former Soviet Union is "pure" enough to apply to them, then this should hold true for other crucial items, such as the aforementioned food, clothing, and shelter. But to implement any such plan would be to place ourselves in the very condition out from under which the USSR has so mightily struggled, at the cost of millions of precious lives.

If "murder by gangs" is the reason we should not allow "capitalist acts between consenting adults" (Nozick 1974, 163) with regard to human organs, then we must prohibit private property of all other things as well, for people kill for those as well. For example, houses, cars, jewelry, money, and so on—all of them would have to be socialized. The only problem here is that people can commit murder for such items whether they are owned in common or individually. No, there is no way to banish murder completely. But laws against this behavior work tolerably well with regard to every other item under the sun, and there is no reason this could not be also applied to human body parts. That is, here is an answer to the objection that we cannot legalize markets in organs because people will kill for them: let us have more police, plenty of scrutiny for these contracts, and so on. If there is any specific fear that more murders might be committed in this market than in others (e.g., drugs), then still more police should be assigned to this arena; no organ transplant contract could be consummated without documents attesting to the fact that the deal was completely voluntary and crime free, and the like.

Nor can we acquiesce in the "concern that many relatives or heirs would be likely to hasten the death of the elderly and sick by deliberate lack of care, in order to sell the body parts after a 'natural' death." First of all, no recipient really wants the body parts of an older person; they will wear out all too soon. But this is a minor difficulty, easily supplanted by the alternative fear that parents would withhold care from babies and children, whose organs would be in far greater demand, the better to kill them and reap the financial reward. However, this objection also fails. Certainly, any young person who dies an otherwise inexplicable death (e.g., other, say, than by automobile accident) would be subjected to an autopsy. If the youngster's body were then utilized for body parts, the scrutiny would be vastly intensified. Surely, laws against murder, already on the books, would put paid to all such schemes.

But the gravest objection to all such horror scenarios is that the supposed monetary incentives that give rise to them are already in existence. And not only that, but also the financial reasons for killing young people for their organs are greater at present than they would be under legalization (which all due safeguards) of this market. This point has been made in this chapter (see the text discussion regarding Figure 4.2) but bears repeating. One, we assume that the inducement to commit such monstrous crimes is positively correlated with the amount of money to be garnered in this heinous fashion. Two, we note that there is a greater price, at present, now, for black market organs under present institutional arrangements, than there would be under legalization (again, see the text discussion regarding Figure 4.2). Third, we conclude that the temptation to brutalize children (or anyone else for that matter), if it exists in the face of laws and public sentiment to the contrary, would be reduced if we legalized markets of this sort, Q.E.D.

Discussion Questions

1. What is the basis upon which doctors and medical personnel make a decision regarding the choice as to who will be given priority in receiving an organ?
2. How do the authors address the problem of the next of kin refusing to give permission for organs to be harvested from a deceased loved one, even though the decedent has signed a donor card?
3. What do the authors have to say regarding financial compensation being provided to family members for donating healthy organs after the death of a family member?

4. Why do individuals on dialysis machines in the United States look forward to such holidays as Memorial Day or the July 4 weekend?
5. What argument was made by the authors for repealing all laws that interfere with the free market in bodily organs?

Endnotes

1. According to Barnett and Saliba (forthcoming, 2), "Almost three thousand Americans die prematurely every year because they cannot get kidney transplants and more than forty thousand others suffer while waiting for kidney transplants." Two points must be made about this statistic. First, it involves only those in need of this particular body part; thus, the number underestimates the true problem. Second, roughly this number of people perished in the tragic events of September 9, 2001. George W. Bush is moving heaven and earth in order to render less likely a reoccurrence of the World Trade Center murders. Yet, with a mere stroke of the pen, our government could save far more lives; all they need do is end the legislative enactments that prohibit markets from this sector of the economy.
2. See on this Adams et al. (1999), Anderson and Barnett (1999), Barnett et al. (1992, 1993, 2001), Barnett and Kaserman (1995), Barnett (1988), Barnett and Saliba (forthcoming), Blair and Kaserman (1991), Block (1988), Block et al. (1999–2000), Kaserman and Barnett (1991), Rottenberg (1971), Schmidt and Vining (1986), and Vining and Schmidt (1988).
3. In 2001, 24,076 people received transplants in the United States (see Table 4.1); the waiting list consisted of 79,641 people (see Table 4.2).
4. See on this Radin (1987) and Kronman (1983). For rejoinders, see Block (1999, 2001, forthcoming).
5. Radin (1987, 1849).

Table 4.1 Number of Transplants Performed in 2001

Type of Transplant	Number
Kidney alone transplants (5,949 were living donors)	14,152
Liver transplants	5,177
Pancreas alone transplants	468
Kidney-pancreas transplants	884
Intestine transplants	112
Heart transplants	2,202
Heart-lung transplants	27
Lung transplants	1,054
Total	**24,076**

Source: Retrieved from http://www.unos.org/Frame_default.asp?Category=Newsdata.

Table 4.2 Estimated Number of Patients Listed on the National Transplant Waiting List by Organ and Overall as of May 31, 2002

Organ	Number of Patients
Kidney	52,226
Liver	17,487
Pancreas	1,318
Kidney-pancreas	2,526
Intestine	193
Heart	4,146
Heart-lung	210
Lung	3,777
Overall	**79,641**

Source: Retrieved from http://www.unos.org/Frame_default.asp?Category=Newsdata.

6. This word is not used to denigrate the importance of the human person. The very opposite is the case. Thousands of people are now going to the grave before their time, or being consigned to lives of great discomfort (e.g., being strapped to a kidney dialysis machine for hours every day) all because market allocation is being disallowed. In striving to ameliorate this sad condition, we are acting in accord with the importance of the human person, not against it.

References

Adams, A. F., A. H. Barnett, and D. L. Kaserman. "Markets of Organs: The Question of Supply." *Contemporary Economics Policy* 17 (April 1999): 147–55.

Anderson, W. L., and A. H. Barnett. "Waiting for Transplants." *The Free Market* 17, no. 4 (1999): 1–2.

Barnett, A. H., T. R. Beard, and D. L. Kaserman. "The Medical Community's Opposition to Organ Markets: Ethics or Economics." *Review of Industrial Organization* 8 (1993): 669–78.

Barnett, A. H., R. D. Blair, and D. L. Kaserman. "Improving Organ Donations: Compensation Versus Markets." *Inquiry* 29 (Fall 1992): 372–78.

Barnett, A. H., and D. L. Kaserman. "The Rush to Transplant and Organ Shortages." *Economic Inquiry* 33 (July 1995): 506–15.

Barnett, W., II. "The Market in Used Human Body Parts." *The Free Market* 6, no. 11 (1988): 5.

Barnett, W., II, and M. Saliba. "Free Market for Kidneys: Options, Futures, Forward, and Spot." *Managerial Finance*: Forthcoming.

Barnett, W., II, M. Saliba, and D. Walker. "A Free Market in Kidneys: Efficient and Equitable." *The Independent Review* 5, no. 3 (2001): 373–85.

Blair, R. D., and D. L. Kaserman. "The Economics and Ethics of Alternative Cadaveric Organ Procurement Policies." *Yale Journal on Regulation* 8 (1991): 403–52.

Block, W. "The Case for a Free Market in Body Parts." *The Free Market* 6, no. 3 (1988): 3.

Block, W. "Market Inalienability Once Again: Reply to Radin." *Thomas Jefferson Law Journal* 22, no. 1 (Fall 1999): 37–88.

Block, W. "Alienability, Inalienability, Paternalism and the Law: Reply to Kronman." *American Journal of Criminal Law* 28, no. 3 (Summer 2001): 351–71.

Block, W. "Toward a Libertarian Theory of Inalienability: A Critique of Rothbard, Barnett, Gordon, Smith, Kinsella and Epstein." *Journal of Libertarian Studies*: Forthcoming.

Block, W., R. Whitehead, C. Johnson, M. Davidson, A. White, and S. Chandler. "Human Organ Transplantation: Economic and Legal Issues." *Quinnipiac College School of Law Health Journal* 3 (1999–2000): 87–110.

Kaserman, D. L., and A. H. Barnett. "An Economic Analysis of Transplant Organs: A Comment and Extension." *Atlantic Economic Journal* 19 (June 1991): 57–63.

Kronman, A. T. "Paternalism and the Law of Contracts." *Yale Law Journal* 92 (1983): 763.

Nozick, R. *Anarchy, State and Utopia*. New York: Basic Books, 1974.

Radin, M. J. "Market-Inalienability." *Harvard Law Review* 100, no. 8 (June 1987): 1849–937.

Rottenberg, S. "The Production and Exchange of Used Body Parts." *Towards Liberty* 2 (1971): 322–33.

Schwindt, R., and A. R. Vining. "Proposal for a Future Delivery Market for Transplant Organs." *Journal of Health Policy and Law* 11 (Fall 1986): 483–500.

Vining, A. R., and R. Schwindt. "Have a Heart: Increasing the Supply of Transplant Organs for Infants and Children." *Journal of Policy Analysis and Management* 7, no. 4 (1988): 706–10.

Karnataka's Unabating Kidney Trade[*]

5

VIDYA RAM, MS
Bangalore, India

Contents

Analysis and Features of the Commercial Racket in Kidneys	60
Failure of Regulatory Bodies	61
A New Investigative Track	63
The Transplantation of Human Organs Act of 1994	64
The Development of a Sophisticated Network	65
Recommendations to Help Improve the Functioning of Regulatory Bodies	66
The Role of the Medical Profession	67
The Economies of the Organ Trade	68
Discussion Questions	70

Vijaykumar, aged 47, from Jalahalli in Bangladore was suffering from irreversible kidney failure; in medical parlance, he had end-stage renal disease (ESRD). In July 1998 he received a kidney from 33-year-old Shan Basha from Sahidapet in Vellore, Tamil Nadu. Shan Basha claimed that he was donating his kidney out of "compassion" for the recipient. Vijaykumar is one of 1,012 patients in Karnataka who, between January 1996 and March 2002, were officially cleared to receive kidneys from unrelated live "donors." The approval for all these donations came from the Karnataka Authorisation Committee, a body set up under the Transplantation of Human Organs Act of 1994 to ensure that no buying and selling of human organs take place.

Thanks to a recent police investigation that blew open the lid on a thriving trade in kidneys, hard evidence of a type not previously available for any state is now at hand. It consists of particulars of the recipients, donors, motives (claimed for the donation), hospitals, and doctors involved in virtually all cases of unrelated live kidney transplants in Karnataka over the past 5 years. A *Frontline* investigation gained access to a large sample—288 cases in one data set and 274 cases in another—of these particulars. The data in hand strongly suggest that far from being a demonstration of altruism, virtually every one of these cases of donation of a kidney on grounds of emotional

---

[*] Previously published in *Frontline* 19(7), 2002. Available at: http://www.frontlineonnet.com

"affection or attachment" or "compassion" is an exploitative and illegal financial transaction between a poor donor and a relatively well-to-do patient.

Analysis and Features of the Commercial Racket in Kidneys

An analysis of the sampled particulars highlights the following features of the commercial racket in kidneys in Karnataka:

- While most donors and recipients are from Bangalore, they also come from other parts of the state and from other states, indicating the formation of a nationwide network of agents.
- While there are areas of donor concentration, such as the Mandya district, these have become less marked over the years, suggesting that agents are learning to spread their net to prevent detection.
- Addresses of donors are frequently falsified in the records.
- A certain number of patients come from abroad and, in contrast to the period before the 1994 Act came into force, tend to bring with them donors from their own countries.
- Transplants in Karnataka are predominantly an exchange between men.
- Donors from a particular hospital tend to submit the same reason en bloc for the donation.
- Close to a fourth of 274 cases of unrelated live donors who went before the Authorisation Committee were shown to be in dependant relationships to the recipients or their families—as housemaids, watchmen, factory workers, and so on.

The evidence from the Karnataka data is that the racket has become increasingly sophisticated and networked over time. That the kidney trade is exploitative of the poor and the needy is highlighted by the large number of cases where donors are shown, in the second set of official records, to be employees or unrelated dependants of the recipients. Evidently, the committee had programmed itself to believe the fiction that the donations even in these 65 cases (scrutinized by *Frontline*) were not exploitative and did not involve any commercial consideration.

This large-scale and flagrant violation of the law was sanctioned by the very institutional mechanism set up to prevent it. It is clear that the act, by allowing unrelated donors to "donate" their kidneys after gaining the sanction of the Authorisation Committee, facilitates and provides legal cover to the buying and selling of kidneys. If the trade in Karnataka was inhibited for a brief period by the enactment of the legal prohibition, it has resourcefully adjusted itself to the new institutional mechanism and taken full advantage of the provisions for nonenforcement built into the act. As a result, unrelated live transplants clearly involving financial transactions are on the increase in Karnataka, and little is being done about it.

"Underlying the trade is the attitude that the poor can be bought by the rich," Dr. H. Sudarshan, the highly regarded chairman of the Karnataka Task Force on Health and Family Welfare and a winner of the Right Livelihood Award, Stockholm (which is sometimes described as the "alternative Nobel Prize"), told *Frontline*. "Vested interests are promoting unrelated [live] transplants. Large sums of money are shared by doctors and hospitals that perform such transplants. I believe it is the Authorisation Committee that has a special responsibility to prevent this and I would put more blame on them for not implementing the Act effectively."

Failure of Regulatory Bodies

The failure of the Appropriate Authority and Authorisation Committee, the two regulatory bodies set up under the 1994 Act, to discharge their statutory responsibilities is not a new story. Their insensitivity to the legal prohibition on the buying and selling of human organs, on pain of stiff punishment, is evident in their response to the recent unearthing of a massive and widespread trade in kidneys by the Mandya police (see Parvathi Menon, "Kidneys Still for Sale," *Frontline*, 15 February 2002). The police investigation established, *prima facie*, systematic violations of the act in Karnataka over a 4-year period. This unprecedented investigation has not, however, galvanized either of these bodies into follow-up action. The Authorisation Committee continues to give its approval to unrelated live transplants.

The Mandya story broke in mid-January 2002, and the Authorisation Committee held its first meeting for the year on February 16. From that date to March 2, 2002, ten applications for live unrelated transplants came before the committee for approval. Of these applications, eight were cleared. One case was rejected as the recipient failed to submit a medical certificate stating that he had ESRD, and another application was pending.

According to official data available to *Frontline*, the Karnataka Authorisation Committee has the dubious distinction of approving 1,012 out of a total of 1,017 applications that went before it between January 1996 and February 2002.

True, the committee was expanded and reconstituted in March 2001, and although it now boasts a police representative nominated by the Bangalore City commissioner of police, it has been business as usual since the Mandya story broke; there is no evidence that the seven-member committee has seriously reconsidered or improved its method of scrutinizing each case in a way that can expose a financial transaction. This became clear in conversations that *Frontline* had with some of the committee members.

In fact, when judging the merits of an application, the committee members appear to be more preoccupied with trying to convince themselves of the strength of the "emotional bondage" between the donor and the recipient than simply trying to apply common sense to judge whether money could be changing hands. "We take half an hour to grill the patient and the donor to see if there is really an emotional bond between them," Dr. G. V. Nagaraj, director of the Directorate of Health and Family Welfare Services and a member of the Committee, told *Frontline*. "It is so difficult to establish mala fide. You see the pathetic condition of the patient ... for example when a man becomes sick and he leaves behind a young wife." He seemed to shudder at the memory.

Dr. Nagaraj and another member of the Authorisation Committee (who did not wish to be named) mentioned the case of a 16-year-old girl who appeared before them as a donor. The committee rejected the case on account of her age and because a financial deal was obviously involved. Yet it did not file a complaint on this blatant violation of the act or indeed on the other four "rejected" cases over a 6-year period. *Frontline*'s repeated requests for an interview with the chairman of the Authorisation Committee, H. S. Kempana, who is secretary in the State's Law Department, were turned down by his office. His sole comment to *Frontline* was that he was answerable only to the High Court of Karnataka.

Karnataka's Appropriate Authority too appeared disinclined to strike while the iron was hot. Its response to the Mandya revelations made this clear. Under the 1994 act, the tasks of this authority are to grant registrations to hospitals to conduct transplants, to suspend such registrations if necessary, to enforce the required standards in hospitals through periodic inspections, and, most important of all, to investigate any complaint or breach of any provision of the act. The state's Appropriate Authority was reconstituted from five to seven members in December 2001. It is significant that the name of Dr. Philip Thomas of St. John's Medical College Hospital, an active campaigner against the kidney trade and an enthusiast for a cadaver-based transplant program, was quietly dropped in the reconstitution.

The first meeting of the reconstituted authority was held on January 29, 2002. At the meeting, a decision was taken to authorize Amar Kumar Panday, the zealous superintendent of police (S.P.) in the Mandya subdivision, to file a complaint in the jurisdictional court under Section 22 of the act. According to G. V. Krishna Rau, commissioner of the Health and Family Welfare Services and chairman of the Appropriate Authority, the scope of the brief given to the S.P. was wide. He was authorized to file complaints before the appropriate courts "in respect of all contraventions of the provisions of the Organ Transplant Act, 1994."

This development, with its promise of getting to the bottom of a trade that involved or affected a web of special interests—agents, hospitals, nephrologists and transplant surgeons, the official medical establishment, bureaucrats, and influential relatives of recipients and of the doctors involved in unrelated live kidney transplants—proved too good to last. According to informed sources, pressure was put on the state government. Soon enough, the case was taken out of the hands of the S.P. of Mandya and entrusted to the Corps of Detectives, where it now pretty much languishes.

The Appropriate Authority has not sorted out the jurisdictional confusion that persists over the status of the case. Rau told *Frontline* in early March that the authority proposed instead to issue a general directive "within the next 10 days" to all district police superintendents, authorizing them to pursue independent investigations into violations of the act. "In this general directive," he explained, "we will be specific about what constitutes an offence under the Act and what the police should be looking for. They will not have to wait for our formal authorisation each time."

Admitting that the Appropriate Authority had "not done much regulation since the initial registration of hospitals," Rau said it would now start to inspect each hospital before the renewal of its license. Despite the fact that 19 kidney agents were picked up by the police from outside and within the premises of prominent hospitals in Bangalore, the authority is not planning any action against the hospitals. Rau explained this stand by asserting that if the authority received concrete evidence about the role of hospitals in the trade, it would take action. "We should not be going soft on institutions," he assured *Frontline*. "We have enough reasons to suspect that things are not as they should be and we will request the police to keep a watch on hospitals." It appears that, for obvious reasons, the authority responsible for having violations of the 1994 Act investigated and prosecuted has chosen not to use the opportunity provided by the Mandya police exposé to get to the bottom of the large-scale buying and selling of kidneys.

A New Investigative Track

A promising new investigative track into the racket has been opened by a complaint filed by Alladi Jayasri, a reporter of *The Hindu*, before the Lokayukta, an ombudsman-like authority set up under a 1994 state act to inquire into allegations of corruption, maladministration, nepotism, and abuses of power. (India's first Lokayukta to inquire into allegations of corruption against public servants, including the chief minister, was established in Karnataka in 1984. The present Lokayukta is Justice N. Venkatachala, a former Indian Supreme Court judge.) Jayasri's complaint was registered before the Lokayukta on January 29, 2002. "Both the Appropriate Authority and the Authorisation Committee have been made party to the complaint by Alladi Jayasri," Dr. Sudarshan, who is also the Lokayukta's vigilance director for medical services, told *Frontline*. "It is an important development, and we are certainly going to pursue the complaint."

In her complaint, Jayasri has asked that action be initiated against the two bodies for "having failed to prevent, time and again, scams and scandals in organ (mainly kidney) trading, in gross violation of the Act." She has held the Appropriate Authority accountable for failing to perform the functions as notified under Chapter IV, Section 13 of the act. These are "(1) to suspend or cancel registration of transplant centers violating the law, (2) to enforce standards for hospitals, (3) to investigate any complaint of breach of the provisions of the act, and (4) to inspect hospitals periodically for examination of the quality of transplantation and follow-up medical care to persons who have undergone transplants and persons from whom organs are removed. Needless to say, the last two have been followed more in the breach, leading to repeated eruptions of scandals like the one in Mandya District on January 15th."

The role of the Authorisation Committee is squarely addressed here. As for the Authorisation Committee, the complaint notes, "it has failed to uphold the law, ethics and moral rectitude in allowing itself to be persuaded to issue clearances for hundreds of unrelated transplants, becoming a pawn in the hands of unscrupulous elements, and helping the organ trade thrive in Bangalore and other parts of the State." Jayasri has asked the Lokayukta to "accord priority" to an issue "that has had far-reaching, debilitating effects on society." Dr. Sudarshan believes that this complaint provides an excellent opportunity to expose and strike at the trade. Once the Lokayukta uncovers the complicity of different parties in the organ trade, the pressure to take action against them under the Transplantation of Human Organs Act can be stepped up.

The Transplantation of Human Organs Act of 1994

The Transplantation of Human Organs Act of 1994 is meant to "provide for the regulation of removal, storage and transplantation of human organs for therapeutic purposes and for the prevention of commercial dealing in human organs." It illegalizes the trade in kidneys and makes kidney-for-cash transactions a criminal offense, punishable with a term of imprisonment ranging from 2 to 7 years and a Rs. 10,000 to Rs. 20,000 fine. The act defines persons who can donate kidneys as "near relatives," specifically spouses, mothers, fathers, sisters, and brothers. The act also recognizes the concept of brain-stem death and makes provisions for the development of a cadaver-based organ transplantation program that can meet the demands of gravely ill patients and eliminate cash-for-organ transactions.

The progressive aims of the act are, however, defeated by two major built-in flaws. First, trade in kidneys or other human organs, or any other violation of the act, is a noncognizable offense. In other words, the police cannot launch independent investigations into such violations. Under Section 22 of the act, a court can take cognizance of offenses committed under the act only on a complaint made by the Appropriate Authority or an officer authorized by it, or by an individual who has given prior notice of not less than 60 days to the Appropriate Authority.

Despite the suspiciously large number of unrelated live kidney transplants that have taken place in Karnataka since the act came into force, despite periodic media reports, and despite the forthright views expressed by some doctors who oppose the buying and selling of kidneys from the high ground of professional and general ethics, the Appropriate Authority is yet to make a single complaint on its own to the police. The January 2002 investigation launched by the Mandya police was technically on a case of forgery after they obtained evidence that a residence certificate of a donor from Mandya, submitted to the Authorisation Committee, was forged. This led to the arrest of 19 suspected agents who were picked up from the premises of several prominent hospitals in Bangalore, including Lakeside Hospital and M.S. Ramaiah Hospital.

The act's fatal flaw lies in Section 9(3). This clause has made the act virtually unenforceable. It permits unrelated donors, for reasons of "affection and attachment towards the recipient or for any other special reasons," to donate their kidneys to ESRD patients provided they can convince the State Authorisation Committee that they are "donating" and not selling their organs. If the committee is persuaded that money has not changed hands, it can allow such a donation. The willingness of the committee to be persuaded that the unrelated live kidney donations are being made on account of "affection and attachment" or for some other "special reasons" is a key factor working in favor of the kidney trade. Neither the extreme implausibility of employees or unrelated dependants donating kidneys without money changing hands nor highly suspicious factors such as recipients and donors living far apart without ostensible connections have stood in the way of the committee approving transplants.

The Development of a Sophisticated Network

Over the years, a sophisticated network has been built by agents who, operating in various places including hospital corridors, put kidney patients from all parts of the country in touch with poor donors. The Authorisation Committee interrogates the donor and recipient separately and asks them a standard set of questions about their relationship—how long they have known each other, a description of the area the other lives in, and so on. Agents coach donors and recipients to face what has become a standard and predictable format of interrogation. The donor must submit a ration card, a residence certificate from the police, an affidavit stating the donor's willingness to donate the kidney, and basic hospital documents. The Mandya police investigations reveal that up to 80 percent of the verification documents from the police could be forged.

Frontline has scrutinized data covering almost half of the more than 1,000 cases that went up before the Authorisation Committee since its establishment in 1996. The data clearly establish that the committee bears much of the responsibility for the farce that has been made of the Transplantation of Human Organs Act of 1994. The committee considers a mere four to five cases a week. It spends around half an hour on each case. A committee member told *Frontline* that though members were aware that money had changed hands between the donor and recipient, they could do little besides accept the sworn testimony. "It is difficult to tell when a financial transaction takes place. Often the donor will say that he has worked for the patient for many years, that the patient has helped his family, and that he is deeply attached to the patient," admitted a member. The Authorisation Committee member was unable to explain why the committee does not look into cases in more depth or conduct random checks on donors' addresses when only four or five cases are considered every week.

Nor has the Appropriate Authority performed the role entrusted to it. "The only task that the Appropriate Authority has performed properly was the initial registration of hospitals performing kidney transplants," Dr. Philip Thomas, a former member of the Appropriate Authority, told *Frontline*. Since then the authority has neither conducted random checks on hospitals nor investigated any allegations of organ trading and hospital complicity that have been reported in the media from time to time. The authority's failure to carry out its mandated duties has resulted in other abuses of the law. Dr. Thomas told *Frontline* that the rules of the act forbid a doctor from performing kidney transplants in more than one hospital. A hospital gets around this rule by appointing an "expert," who is then free to call for assistance, invariably from a "friend" who performs transplant operations at another hospital. The Appropriate Authority can easily crack down on this practice, but it does not.

Recommendations to Help Improve the Functioning of Regulatory Bodies

As early as July 2001, the overt trafficking in kidneys was brought to the attention of members of the two regulatory bodies by Dr. Sudarshan, chairman of

Karnataka's Health Task Force. He made several recommendations to help the bodies improve their functioning. One recommendation was that both bodies should be reconstituted with the inclusion of a member of a concerned nongovernmental organization (NGO). Another was that the Appropriate Authority should meet at least once every 2 months.

Dr. Sudarshan also listed a set of criteria that hospitals must meet for their licenses to be renewed by the Appropriate Authority. Hospitals doing transplants must (1) have an ethics committee, (2) submit the detailed clinical documents and indications for the transplant, (3) submit the details of blood groups and cross-matching reports of all relatives of the patients, (4) ensure that all recipients of kidneys are residents of Karnataka for a minimum of 5 years, (5) perform medical check-ups on donors and recipients every 6 months and bear full responsibility for this, (6) notify the Appropriate Authority if a transplanted organ is rejected or if a patient dies, and (7) notify the Appropriate Authority if the donor has any "disability complications" or if the donor dies.

Another key recommendation of the chairman of the Health Task Force is that the Authorisation Committee should ensure that the donor and the recipient have lived in close association for a period of at least one year for the donor to form an "emotional attachment" to the recipient.

"Close association" should also be verified by a police authority, whose rank is not lower than that of a superintendent of police or an additional superintendent of police. The donor should produce his or her ration card and/or identity card as proof of residence. He or she should also produce a certificate from a psychologist or a psychologist worker. The psychologist must ensure that the donor is aware of the risks involved in donating a kidney and must verify the authenticity of the donor's "emotional attachment" to the recipient.

Only two of Dr. Sudarshan's recommendations were adopted. The Appropriate Authority and Authorisation Committee have been reconstituted, and the Authorisation Committee now requires donors to submit their ration cards.

The Role of the Medical Profession

The medical profession plays more than a passive role in the illegal trade. First, several doctors who spoke to *Frontline* in confidence referred to a doctor–broker nexus, even if there are nephrologists and transplant surgeons who take a conscientious professional stand against the trade in kidneys.

Second, several doctors with a vested interest in unrelated live transplants seem to play a subtle role by spreading medical disinformation. A kidney recipient in Bangalore told *Frontline* that his doctor had assured him that he would die if he did not have a transplant. Such advice is, of course, medically unfounded. Dialysis is a safe, reliable, and viable option for kidney patients, particularly for those living in cities with access to good-quality medical care. In fact, in many European countries only 30 percent of kidney patients opt for a transplant.

Third, many doctors involved in unrelated live transplants do not inform potential donors of the risks involved in donating their kidneys and the changes that would be required in their lifestyle post donation. A comprehensive study of kidney vendors in Iran provides ample proof of the negative effects, particularly in developing countries.

Finally, it is well established that many doctors encourage patients to opt for live unrelated transplants over cadaver transplants on the ground that the rejection rate is much lower when the kidney is from a live, even if unrelated, donor. As a generalization, this is self-serving propaganda.

The Economics of the Organ Trade

The economics of the organ trade is a new field of study in India and abroad. How does the market fix the price of a kidney? It clearly depends on whose kidney; the type of kidney and blood group of the donor; the condition, desperation, and purchasing power of recipients who are buyers; the conditions in which the vendors of kidneys live; the availability of medical capabilities and infrastructure in the field of kidney transplantation; the willingness of hospitals and doctors to shut their eyes to the illegality of what goes on; and the system's toleration of organ commerce, whatever the law might say.

What is clear is that an increasingly networked, broker-enabled kidney trade has emerged in India, with centers of transplant specialization such as Bangalore drawing a clientele from near and far. There is sporadic, mostly anecdotal, information on what precisely live vendors of kidneys get after brokers take their commission. Media reports suggest that the price of a kidney in South India ranges from Rs. 40,000 to Rs. 60,000 and that a poor or needy vendor gets anything between Rs. 25,000 and Rs. 40,000 after the broker deducts his or her commission from the purchase price. Various kinds of sharp practices, which deny vendors the full sums promised, have been reported.

Case particulars available for several hundred applications for unrelated live donations of kidneys in Karnataka suggest that not all the recipients are rich or well off and that, in fact, a considerable number of recipients belong to the middle class. For a patient, the cost of a kidney transplant operation could be anything from Rs. 150,000 to Rs. 300,000 or higher; the cost varies from hospital to hospital.

A few survey-based studies of the economics of the kidney trade in South India have been done, or are in the works. Their findings should be of great interest in India and abroad.

Is the Transplantation of Human Organs Act unenforceable? Before the central legislation came into force in Karnataka and other states doing large numbers of kidney transplants, notably Tamil Nadu and Maharashtra, it was not illegal to pay for a kidney. Large numbers of ESRD patients from various parts of India and even foreign countries flocked to Bangalore, Mumbai, and Chennai for transplants. A network of doctors and agents helped them procure kidneys from poor donors (see *Frontline*, 26 December 1997).

It was also not uncommon to see advertisements for kidney donors in newspapers. After Karnataka adopted the Transplantation of Human Organs Act in 1995, the number of unrelated live kidney transplants dropped dramatically, suggesting that the act was succeeding in its purpose. *Frontline*'s 1997 investigation revealed that while 354 unrelated live transplants were performed in 14 authorized hospitals in 1994, the number fell to 149 in 1995. But the trend was too good to last. Vested interests soon found a way to manipulate the act, aided by apathetic and negligent regulatory bodies. The graph of unrelated live kidney transplants soon began to rise. In 1996 the number was 160, and in the first 10 months of 1997 it was 165. Since then the figures have run off the charts, with the Authorisation Committee clearing 192 applications (with no rejections) in 1999, 222 applications (with no rejections) in 2000, and 169 applications in 2001.

In the light of the act's failure, many opponents of the kidney trade believe that the 1994 legislation is unenforceable. They argue that Section 9(3), which allows unrelated persons to donate their kidneys "by reason of affection or attachment towards the recipient or for any other such reason," will always provide cover for the trade. Dr. M.K. Mani, chief nephrologist at the Apollo Hospitals in Chennai and a distinguished campaigner against the trade in kidneys, has an article on this subject titled "Making an Ass of the Law." It was published in *The National Medical Journal of India* (Vol. 10, No. 5, 1997). The article highlights the fact that the unrelated live donor program, which is exploitative of the poor and hampers the growth of a cadaver-based transplant program, flourishes "with a seal of approval from the Authorisation Committee" and that a law meant to prohibit trade in human organs "now provides protection for those very commercial dealings." It is clear that as long as the loophole exists, agents will continue to find ways of linking poor donors to ESRD patients; and that for the buying and selling of kidneys to stop, Section 9(3) must be scrapped.

The Karnataka experience demonstrates that 7 years after the adoption of the Transplantation of Human Organs Act of 1994, the kidney trade continues to thrive, stronger than ever before.

Discussion Questions

1. What were the features of the commercial racket in the sale of kidneys in Karnataka?
2. What evidence was presented to support the conclusion that the appropriate authorities are failing to adequately enforce the provisions of the Transportation of Human Organs Act of 1994?
3. What dubious distinction was given to the Karnataka Authorisation Committee regarding the approval of kidney transplants?
4. What was supposed to be accomplished by passage of the Transplantation of Human Organs Act of 1994?
5. What is the fatal flaw of the Transplantation of Human Organs Act of 1994?
6. Dr. Sudarshan, chairman of the Karnataka Health Task Force, made several recommendations to help the authorizing bodies improve their functioning. What were these recommendations?
7. What criteria was set forth by Dr. Sudarshan in order for hospitals to get their licenses renewed by the appropriate authorities?
8. What is Section 9(3) of the Transplantation of Human Organs Act of 1994?
9. What has been the experience in Karnataka since the adoption of the Transplantation of Human Organs Act of 1994?

To Solve a Deadly Shortage
Economic Incentives for Human Organ Donation

CURTIS E. HARRIS, MS, MD, JD
University of Oklahoma School of Medicine, Norman, Oklahoma

STEPHEN P. ALCORN, JD
District Attorney's Office, Oklahoma County, Oklahoma

Contents

A Brief Overview of Transplant Technology	72
What Is an Organ?	73
Donation and Sale of Regenerative Organs and Self Replenishing Tissues and Cells: Problems and Answers	74
Blood	74
Reproductive Tissue	75
Tissue	76
Nonregenerative Tissues: The Legislative Approach	77
Uniform Anatomical Gift Act (1968)	77
NOTA (1984)	78
UAGA (1987)	78
Proposed Legislation: UAGA H.R. 2418 (1999)	79
Understanding the Issues	80
Presumed Consent	80
Nationalization of Cadavers	81
Pure Altruism	82
The Open Market Approach	84
Real and Imagined Problems	84
Living Donor Organ Market	85
Market Theory as Applied	85
Objections to a Living Donor Market	86
The Early Attempts to Establish Open Market Reimbursement	86
A Proposal for a Regulated Posthumous Organ Market	87

* First published in *Issues in Law & Medicine* 16 (2), 213-233, 2001.

Conclusion	88
Discussion Questions	89
Endnotes	89

Currently 68,000 Americans are waiting for an organ donation, with a name added to the list every 16 minutes. Twelve Americans die every day because a needed vital organ is not available. The congressional answer has been the Uniform Anatomical Gift Act, which was designed to promote public awareness and health care provider education, and to prohibit the sale of most human organs.[1]

Where gaps in the law prohibiting the sale of human tissue have been left or allowed, a thriving market exists, meeting the needs of Americans for blood, tissue, and human reproductive cells. However, vital organs are prohibited from sale.

Proposals have been made over the years to adopt free market principles to the open sale of organs, allowing vital organs to be bought and sold for whatever prices the market could sustain. The potential for abuse in a system such as this is real and has always prevented the serious consideration of such an open market.

This chapter proposes a governmentally regulated, posthumous organ market in which licensed brokerage houses operate under the oversight of the Food and Drug Administration. Though regulated, flexibility will be necessary to allow the laws of supply and demand to control most aspects of the market. Through this combination of regulation and a free market, needless loss of life can be prevented and equity in organ distribution maintained.

A Brief Overview of Transplant Technology

Doctors in the Soviet Union conducted the first kidney transplant in 1936, using a cadaver. The first successful live kidney transplant was accomplished in the United States in 1956. The first successful heart transplant was accomplished in South Africa in 1967.[2] These early procedures were scientific advances but provided limited medical benefit to the patients. Transplants were always hindered by the recipients' rejection caused by antigenic differences remaining after tissue typing and donor–recipient matching.

The 1980 introduction of Cyclosporin-A was a major breakthrough in allograft transplants because it controlled the recipient's immune response.[3] The benefit can be seen by noting the increase of one-year transplant survivals during the 10 years following the introduction of Cyclosporin, which increases ranged from 25 to 50 percent, depending on the tissue type.[4]

Immunosuppressants, such as Cyclosporin-A and more recent drugs, do have a drawback: they suppress all immune responses, leaving the organ recipient vulnerable to certain types of infection. Presently, intensive suppression is only necessary in the first few weeks following a transplant operation. Thereafter, smaller doses may be used, but immunosuppression is necessary for the remainder of the recipient's life.[5]

Sources of tissue other than human tissue have been proposed. Transplantation of animal organs (xenotransplantation) and biomechanical organ replacements have received much attention in the popular media recently, though xenotransplantation is not new. Prior to the development of the kidney dialysis machine in the 1960s, there were numerous primate-to-human kidney transplants. Success of these early transplants was, at best, limited. Scientists observed hyperacute rejection in almost every case. In the early 1990s, scientists again looked at xenogenic transplants, this time the focus was on the liver. But to date the most successful transplant has only lived 70 days before rejecting the new organ.[6]

In 1999 German scientists reported completed pig-to-human kidney transplants, with survival lengths up to 70 days. These recent successes have seemed to indicate potential future success in combating hyperacute rejection, but there is still much difficulty with delayed rejection.[7]

Xenogenic kidney transplantation will likely be the first tissue type to enter clinical trial because organ dysfunction or rejection can be safely remedied through currently available dialysis techniques. But even with this capability, there currently are no clinical trials, and scientists are struggling with the problems of cross-species disease, public acceptance, and ethical concerns.[8]

Bioengineers have had limited—yet encouraging—success in manufacturing organs. A typical example is a mechanical kidney developed at the University of Michigan. As with a dialysis machine, the mechanical kidney filters the blood of toxic matter, but this device goes further. The mechanical kidney incorporates live kidney cells, which pass sugar and salts back into the blood. Currently, the machine is desktop size and has been tried on dogs.[9]

Both xenotransplants and mechanical devices show possibility, but even their most ardent proponents say that clinical use is 20 years away. Neither solution holds much promise as an answer to the current shortage of human organs. Human tissue sources, though scarce, remain the best available answer to organ failures.

What Is an Organ?

An organ is a part of the body having a special function as part of an integrated living system.[10] Organs may be divided into two categories, *vital* and *nonvital*. Vital organs are those which cannot be removed without loss of function necessary to support life. Examples are heart, lungs, liver, pancreas, stomach, and kidneys. One of two paired vital organs can be considered nonvital if the other is functioning properly, such as a kidney.[11]

For the purpose of this chapter, it is important to identify regenerative organs as well as human tissue and cells capable of self replenishment including skin, blood, hair, sperm, and oocytes.[12] Human blood is the best example of a commonly donated regenerative organ. Blood continues to replenish, allowing a person to give blood and leaving the donor in no significantly worse condition than before the donation.[13]

Donation and Sale of Regenerative Organs and Self Replenishing Tissues and Cells: Problems and Answers

Blood

Self replenishment of blood led to transfusions as early as the beginning of the nineteenth century. But the procedure was frequently unsuccessful in the early days of transfusions, which resulted in the procedure being outlawed in many countries. The world wars drove the need for blood and brought scientific advancements that started to raise the success rate of transfusions to acceptable levels.[14]

The 1960s saw advancements in blood component therapy, which allowed the storage of greater quantities of blood. The ability to store blood components, in turn, allowed the growth of organizations such as the American Red Cross and many community blood banks.

Altruistic donation fell short of demand, and, though controversial, the blood market was eventually commercialized. Richard Titmuss has summarized the objections of many to the sale of blood.

> [I]t represses the expression of altruism; it erodes the sense of community; it sanctions the making of profits in hospitals and clinical laboratories; it legalizes hostility between doctor and patient; it subjects critical areas of medicine to the laws of the marketplace; it places social costs upon those least able to bear them—the poor, the sick and the inept; it increases the danger of unethical behavior in various sectors of medical science and practice; and it results in situations in which proportionately more and more blood is supplied by the poor, the unskilled, the unemployed. Negroes and other low income groups and categories of exploited human population of high blood yielders so that blood is redistributed from the poor to the rich.[15]

Fears over the safety of paid donor blood proved justified as commercial blood banks distributed infected blood, decimating the hemophiliac population of the United States. In 1982 in high-risk areas, such as San Francisco, as much as 3 percent of donated blood was infected by human immunodeficiency virus (HIV).[16]

This problem was quickly minimized in 1985 by the addition of an HIV-screening test. Screening in the past 20 years has become remarkably effective. Currently nine tests for infectious diseases are conducted on each unit of donated blood.[17] Between 1985 and 1997 there were only 38 documented cases of AIDS caused from blood that had been properly screened for HIV. With a national average of three infections a year, there is a one in 4 million chance of receiving HIV-infected blood.[18]

The question no longer concerns a donor being infected before donating blood. Rather, the question has become, has the blood been infected long enough to test positive in screening tests? Most infectious diseases will show positive during the screening process if the donor has been infected for at least 2 months. Closing this 2-month window is now the focus of scientists and medical doctors. One such approach is nucleic acid amplification (NAT). NAT is a research initiative in selected blood banks such as the Oklahoma Blood Institute (OBI) in Oklahoma City. NAT allows for direct testing of the genetic material of viruses such as hepatitis and HIV. Organizations like OBI no longer have to wait for the body's immune response to the antigen but can identify the virus immediately, closing the 2-month window.[19]

Irrespective of whether the blood came from a paid donor or from a volunteer, technology has created a safe blood supply. Two of the safest and most respected blood banks in the country are commercial operations: Hema Care in Sherman Oaks, California, and the University of Iowa's DeGowin Blood Center. Both of these institutions utilize the same screening tests as discussed in this section, but all donors are screened twice in an attempt to catch viruses hidden during the initial screen. This step adds cost to their product, but it ensures the highest possible level of safety available with current technology.

As will be discussed in this chapter, there is reason to believe that as the risks have been generally minimized in blood donation, these challenges can be controlled equally well for organ donation.

Reproductive Tissue

A second category of regenerative organs and self-replenishing cells is reproductive cells. The sale of sperm has been widespread for years and is not prohibited by federal law. Some state statutes ban the sale of body parts specifically, except sexual cells, while others apply a legal exception that allows donors of oocytes ("eggs") and sperm to be compensated for their "time and inconvenience."[20]

The legal exception allowing compensation for time and inconvenience (as opposed to sale) is more prevalent in the practice of oocyte donation. There are over 200 private oocyte donation agencies in the United States, many of these with databases of over 300 women willing to donate. The women are paid an average $5,000–8,000 per donation. Agencies routinely refuse to admit that the oocytes are being purchased, claiming instead that the money is merely compensation for the women's time and inconvenience.[21]

Of note, recent case law suggests that this legal exception may not be necessary in all circumstances. In 1992 in *Davis v. Davis*, the Tennessee Supreme Court heard a divorce case to determine the disposition of a couple's frozen embryos.[22] The court determined that the embryo deserves respect greater than that accorded to human tissue, but not the same degree of respect afforded a fully developed human. The court ruled the divorcing spouses each had decisional authority over the frozen embryos *as property*. This authority included the right to destroy, donate, or use the embryos.[23]

The following year, a California Court of Appeal addressed the issue of a property interest in sperm during probate of an estate. Following the *Davis* lead, the court did confer a special status to sperm because of its potential to create life, but recognized that the donor's estate had a *property* interest in the nature of ownership, even after his death. The court ruled that, just like any other piece of property, the deceased could dispose of his sperm in accordance with the wishes he set forth in his will.[24] Taken together, these two cases strongly suggest that, absent statutory prohibitions, reproductive tissues are subject to direct sale by the donor without invoking the legal exception of time and inconvenience.[25]

Tissue

Tissue constitutes a third subcategory of regenerative organs and tissue. A tissue is a group or collection of similar cells and intercellular substance that acts together in the performance of a particular function.[26] These tissues include skin, bone, nerve, fascia, tendon, heart valve, dura mater, bone marrow,[27] and dedicated stem cell lines.[28] Because of the ethical problems surrounding stem cell research, organ system tissue transplants and tissue research may be the most contentious transplant issue in the United States today.[29]

In 1998, after years of study, embryonic stem cells were isolated. Stem cell research has shown promise in the laboratory for a range of disease treatments, including rheumatoid arthritis, diabetes, Alzheimer's disease, Parkinson's disease, and repair of spinal cord injury. Because stem cells are primitive, underdeveloped cells, they have the potential to be used for the production of in vitro replacement organs. But the most promising short-term uses are in immunology and the treatment of immunological disorders. Stem cells can be induced to differentiate into both T and B lymphocytes,[30] which are the immune system's primary weapons against pathogens and cancer.[31]

The central controversy arises from the source of the stem cells. Embryonic stem cells are harvested from human embryos, obtained from stillborn or aborted fetuses. Because the major source of stem cells is from abortions and because of the real potential that the sale of such tissue could encourage abortion, many states have banned the use of fetal tissue in medical research. Presently, such laws in Utah, Louisiana, Illinois, and Arizona have been declared unconstitutional.[32] The U.S. District Court for Arizona declared the statute "vague," in that it did not differentiate between experimental and standard practice.[33]

Nonregenerative Tissues: The Legislative Approach

Uniform Anatomical Gift Act (1968)

By 1968, 42 states had adopted some form of organ donation statute. The law for regenerative and nonregenerative tissues varied from state to state, but most were at least loosely based on the common law. But the laws were confusing and sometimes inconsistent. The issue of interstate transactions was not addressed.[34] In order to improve donor organ availability and simplify the law, the National Conference of Commissioners on Uniform State Laws drafted the Uniform Anatomical Gift Act (UAGA) of 1968. The UAGA was designed to address and answer 12 questions:

1. Who may, during his lifetime, make legally effective gifts of his body or a part thereof?
2. What is the right of the next of kin, either to set aside the decedent's expressed wishes, or themselves to make the anatomical gifts from the dead body?
3. Who may legally become donees of the anatomical gift?
4. For what purposes may such gifts be made?
5. How may gifts be made, such as by will, by writing, by a card carried on the person, or by the telegraphic or recorded telephonic communication?
6. How may a gift be revoked by the donor during his lifetime?
7. What are the rights of the decedent's estate in the body after removal of the donated parts?
8. What protection from legal liability should be afforded to surgeons and others involved in carrying out anatomical gifts?
9. Should such protection be afforded regardless of the state in which the document of gift is executed?

10. What should the effect of an anatomical gift be in case of conflict with laws concerning autopsies?
11. Should time of death be defined by law in any way?
12. Should the interest in preserving life by the physician in charge of the patient preclude him or her from participating in the transplant procedures by which the donated tissue or organ is transferred from the now deceased patient to a new host?[35]

But the complexity of the statute and the rapid advancement of transplant research discouraged federal enforcement of its provisions.

NOTA (1984)

While the 1968 UAGA was influential in standardizing state statutes, it had only moderate effect on the availability of organs. In an attempt to address the national shortage of organ donors and regional disparities in availability, Congress passed the National Organ Transplant Act (NOTA) of 1984. NOTA enabled the Secretary of Health and Human Services (HHS) to establish a nationwide Organ Procurement and Transplantation Network (OPTN), the main objective of which was to coordinate the allocation of organs among regional organ procurement organizations. NOTA was an effort to make organ donation both more efficient and effective. It did not attempt to regulate the then-operational national organ donation system, except in one provision: NOTA prohibited the purchase and sale of human organs.[36] The single most important effect of NOTA was the establishment of a section within the Department of Health and Human Services (HHS) for monitoring organ donation on a nationwide level.[37]

UAGA (1987)

In 1987 the continued shortage of organs once again prompted congressional action. Congress amended the 1968 Uniform Anatomical Gift Act to require all public and private hospitals to inquire into the donor status of every patient at the time of admission. If the patient was not a donor, a hospital designee was to discuss the option of organ donation with the patient and to record the patient's response in the medical record.[38]

In emergency situations or in the case of incapacitation, law enforcement officers and other emergency responders and hospitals are required to make a reasonable search for documents indicating the patient's donation wishes. If no such documentation is found, medical personnel are required to discuss the option of donation with the patient's family. In contrast to some states' statutory provisions, the donor's prior intent supersedes the family's wishes.

The failure of a caregiver to comply does not result in any criminal or civil liability, but may result in administrative sanctions.[39]

Consistent with NOTA, the amendment included a prohibition against the sale or purchase of human organs. While the 1968 UAGA was quickly adopted by all states, the 1987 amendment has been adopted by less than half of the states.

Proposed Legislation: UAGA H.R. 2418 (1999)

In July 1999, Representative Michael Bilirakis (R-FL) sponsored H.R. 2418, the Organ Procurement and Transplantation Network Amendments of 1999.[40] H.R. 2418 has a unique emphasis on living donors. Recognizing advances in medical technology, the bill attempts to encourage living donors by allowing payment of travel and subsistence expenses incurred in the course of an organ donation or a living donation.[41]

> The Secretary may make awards of grants or contracts to States, transplant centers, qualified organ procurement organizations ... for the purpose of (1) providing for the payment of travel and subsistence expenses incurred by individuals toward making living donations of their organs, and (2) in addition, providing for the payment of such incidental non-medical expenses that are so incurred as the Secretary determines by regulation to be appropriate.[42]

Of note, the 1987 Amendment to the Uniform Anatomical Gift Act prohibition against providing "valuable consideration" in exchange for an organ specifically does not prohibit reimbursement of a live donor.[43] The reimbursement language in H.R. 2418 is strong and clear, authorizing the secretary of HHS to determine what is "appropriate." Though far from a general reversal of a prohibition on the sale of organs, H.R. 2418 does signal a willingness to acknowledge the role that limited financial compensation can play in organ donations.[44]

On April 4, 2000, H.R. 2418 was passed on a vote of 275 to 147.[45] But once again Congress failed to address adequately the availability of organs, and debate focused on distribution and the role of the United Network for Organ Sharing (UNOS).[46] The House bill then went to the Senate for consideration, where support was less assured. Sen. Bill Frist, a heart surgeon, tried to negotiate a compromise with Sen. Edward Kennedy, which was intended to settle the contentious issue of regional versus national distribution.[47] Unfortunately, since the Uniform Anatomical Gift Act of 1968 was passed, little has changed to improve organ donation. Many Americans still die each year because they do not have a transplant organ available.

In many ways, UAGA (1968), NOTA (1984), and UAGA (1987) have actually hindered effective programs to encourage recruitment of organ donors. The statutes appear to forbid any valuable consideration for the donation of organs, closing the door to innovative approaches such as estate tax relief, payment of expenses associated with donation such as lost wages, travel expenses, coverage of other existing medical bills, and funeral expenses. These federal statutes have also made it difficult for medical institutions to make transplants profitable or at least cost-effective. Without this profit incentive, many medical centers invest their limited resources into other areas of service. Though passed with good intentions, UAGA and NOTA have actually interfered with the recruitment of donors and have hindered medical progress.

Understanding the Issues

Presumed Consent

Most European countries have adopted a "presumed consent" system of organ procurement: that is, in the absence of written instructions to the contrary, it is presumed the decedent has agreed to the donation of organs at the time of death. This idea has grown in popularity and has been adopted by several South American countries, including Argentina, Brazil, and Chile.[48]

France was the first country to adopt presumed consent. The 1976 law states, in part,

> Organs may be removed for therapeutic or scientific purposes from the cadavers of persons who have not, during their lifetime, indicated their refusal to permit such a procedure. However, where the cadaver is that of a minor or of an incompetent person, organs may be removed for transplantation purposes only with the authorization of the person's legal representative.[49]

Further, a physician must check the patient's medical record for a written refusal to donate, and if one is not found make a "reasonable effort" to ascertain if such a refusal exists in writing apart from the patient's medical records, usually by consulting the patient's immediate family. This later provision has caused the French system to operate more as a voluntary donation system controlled by the family than as a truly presumed consent system. French physicians inquire as to the wishes of the next of kin more than 90 percent of the time. Twelve years after adoption, this form of modified presumed consent has had little impact. France still fails to meet its need for organs. In 1998, 4,075 patients were waiting for a kidney, 523 for a heart, 163 for lungs, and 189 patients for a liver.[50]

Belgium allows physicians to harvest organs without family consent. As in France, most Belgium doctors continue to consult with family members and will not normally act contrary to family wishes.[51] But the change in the law in Belgium did improve organ availability; after three years of presumed consent, organ procurement increased 183 percent. Despite these modest improvements, available organs are still fewer than needed. In 1988 Belgium transplanted 342 kidneys, leaving 803 patients waiting; and 96 hearts were transplanted, with 34 patients waiting.[52]

Austria has come closest of any nation to achieving a true presumed consent system. The law is similar in almost all respects to that of France and Belgium, but differs in one key aspect; the Austrian doctor is under no obligation to look beyond the patient's medical records to find a refusal to donate. The result of this difference has led to much better success in procuring organs. Austria procures kidneys at twice the rate of the United States and most European countries. Despite this impressive statistic, the system is not a complete success.

If Austria's high rates of procurement were due only to its presumed consent law, one would expect it to outpace other countries in all categories of organs covered by the law. This, however, is not the case. As compared to France and Belgium, Austria's harvest rates are only slightly higher concerning livers, and are actually lower concerning hearts. Although many proponents and opponents of presumed consent may agree that the Austrian system has increased organ harvest, it still runs a shortage of organs. In 1988, Austria had 270 kidney transplants with 1,116 patients waiting, 46 heart transplants with 15 patients waiting, 32 liver transplants with 10 patients waiting, three lung transplants with eight patients waiting, and eight pancreas transplants with 12 patients waiting.[53]

There are advantages of presumed consent. France, Belgium, and Austria all procure organs at a higher rate than does the United States, and of the systems currently used, it appears to be the most effective. As practiced, presumed consent has flaws. In countries where physicians involve the family, presumed consent fails because physicians are reluctant to inflict further grief by asking for consent to a procedure the families may not understand. Further, there is a lingering fear of social abuse: "the poor, uneducated, and the legally disenfranchised might bear a disadvantageous burden, and only the more advantaged groups would exercise autonomy, since only the more advantaged groups would be aware of their right to opt-out."[54] Finally, presumed consent may discourage altruism, not only in the area of organ donation but also in other aspects of life, such as the donation of time and money to organizations that rely on generosity.

Nationalization of Cadavers

Though limited to only a few countries, the harvesting of organs as a national resource, without the consent of the donor or family (nationalization of cadavers) is practiced. The most infamous form of nationalization involves state control over the bodies of executed prisoners.

Currently, both China and Serbia are reported to remove organs from executed prisoners. What distinguishes nationalization of cadavers from presumed voluntary consent is the inability of the donor or family to "opt out" of the donation.

Chinese law allows the removal of an executed prisoner's organs in three situations: (1) if the prisoner's body is not claimed, (2) if the prisoner has consented, or (3) if the prisoner's family has consented. There is evidence, however, that indicates China does not feel bound to follow these laws. Executions appear to have been scheduled around transplant needs, and some executions are done in a manner to keep the donor alive until the organ can be removed.[55]

It has been estimated that China performs 2,000–3,000 organ removals from executed prisoners a year. The procedure was outlined in a Chinese government document:

> The use of corpses or organs of executed criminals must be kept strictly secret, and attention must be paid to avoiding negative repercussions. [The removal of organs] should normally be carried out within the utilizing unit. Where it is genuinely necessary, then with the permission of the people's court that is carrying out the death sentence, a surgical vehicle from the health department may be permitted to drive onto the execution grounds to remove the organs, but it is not permitted to use a vehicle bearing health department insignia or to wear white clothing. Guards must remain around the execution grounds while the operation for organ removal is going on.[56]

It is very unlikely that the United States will follow China's lead. Such a practice is both a perversion of any existing organ donor method and a probable violation of the Eighth Amendment.[57] Further, the number of prisoners executed in the United States falls far short of the numbers necessary to make any meaningful difference in the shortage of vital organs.[58]

Pure Altruism

In America, the nationalization of cadavers has never been seriously considered,[59] and presumed consent is disfavored. Personal autonomy is strongly embedded in our laws and values, and any law that even appears to interfere with autonomy will face stiff opposition. Personal physical autonomy has been held to be a constitutional right in such cases as *Roe v. Wade*,[60] *Planned Parenthood v. Casey*,[61] and *Cruzan v. Director, Missouri Department of Health*,[62] and any law proposing presumed consent would surely be challenged under these precedents.

The United States has always relied upon altruism for organ procurement. While this system leaves the decision to the individual and preserves personal autonomy, it does so at the expense of effective organ procurement. Though Congress and the states continue to tinker with various forms of both awareness and encouragement, few programs have proven to be effective. A noteworthy exception has been Pennsylvania's Organ Donation Trust Fund, established by statute in 1994.[63] The trust fund authorizes the state to pay up to $3,000 to the donor's hospital or funeral home to cover donor-associated expenses. Even though no payments have yet been made, the program has been remarkably successful: 3 million Pennsylvanians have signed up to donate organs, and citizens have donated nearly $1 million to the trust fund. This is a remarkable achievement, and if even a small percentage of registered donors actually follow through with an organ donation, it will make a real difference. This success can be compared with Virginia, which had only approximately 180,000 potential donors registered with the Department of Motor Vehicles in 1998.[64]

The federal government has yet to take any bold or innovative steps to increase organ donation, and what has been done thus far has arguably been worse than doing nothing. Time and effort has been spent in disputes over distribution of existing organs rather than finding new organ donors. The altruistic system in the United States has fallen short, failing badly to close the gap between organ donation and organ need. The various versions of the Anatomical Gift Act have produced no real change in the number of available organs.

Between 1989 and 1992 the demand for organs increased 66 percent, while donations during that same period increased 33 percent. During those years, 10,000 people died while waiting for an organ transplant.[65]

The number of transplant operations continues to rise every year. In 1998, 20,861 transplants were performed, but the need for transplants continues to outpace supply. As of March 2000, 68,371 were on the waiting list to receive an organ.

With great fanfare, the HHS announced that in 1998 organ donation increased 5.6 percent, the first substantial increase in 3 years. Yet HHS admits demand increased that year by almost 14 percent. To meet this demand, HHS proposed a new campaign designed to increase donation 20 percent over 2 years. If adopted, the program would focus on three areas HHS has determined to be key: public awareness, health care provider education, and legislative initiatives.[66]

Even assuming that this program succeeds in achieving its 20 percent goal, there will still be 41,993 people on the waiting list in need of an organ. The inadequacy of the HHS plan is even more apparent if demand continues to rise at a 14 percent rate: 53,751 people will be without a vital organ by the end of the year 2000. Currently, as mentioned at the beginning of this chapter, a new name is added to the national waiting list every 16 minutes.[67]

By any calculation, the need for organs has become critical. The government continues to propose solutions that have previously failed to provide an answer. While HHS continues to insist that altruism will work, 12 Americans are dying every day.[68] It is time for a fundamental change in the system.

The Open Market Approach

Real and Imagined Problems

Objections to an open market approach to organ procurement generally fall into four basic categories: fear and urban myth, concern over unhealthy organs, objections to the trade in human flesh, and the overall availability of organs.[69]

Much of the fear and urban myth is encouraged by the entertainment industry. Popular shows such as *Walker, Texas Ranger* and *Law and Order* portray organ-snatching criminals. *Coma*, the popular book and movie written by Robin Cook, tells the story of a criminal gang that abducts young people to provide organs for wealthy individuals. Books, movies, and television tap into our fear, and distort both facts and the capabilities of science and physiology.

Fanciful entertainment has made a population fearful to even consider an open organ market. Urban myths invariably include stories told by someone who knew someone whose friend had been on a business trip and remembers blacking out in a bar after only a drink or two. The unfortunate business traveler awoke in a tub of ice with staples in his back and a kidney removed.[70]

History has also fueled the fear of an organ market. English medical schools during the nineteenth century purchased cadavers at 11 times the average worker's weekly salary. By the 1820s, "resurrectionists" were snatching bodies from cemeteries throughout the country. The practice eventually led to the actions of the notorious Burke and Hare, who lured derelicts into their Edinburgh apartment with the promise of a fine local malt only to murder and then sell them to a medical school. Today Scottish tour guides still relish the squirms and gasps of tourists when they recount the story in front of the infamous apartment.[71]

A similar reaction occurred in the United States when reports of an eBay auction of a kidney were widely published. On September 2, 1999, a healthy man auctioned his kidney on the World Wide Web. Bidding started at $25,000 and had reached $5,750,100 by the time website administrators halted the process. Though assumed by most to be a joke, it received general public condemnation.[72]

Poorly grounded public opinion aside, there are several valid and thoughtful concerns regarding the open organ market. One concern is that the market will be flooded with unhealthy organs. It is assumed that poor, malnourished individuals will sell their organs out of desperation, or that drug abusers and alcoholics will sell organs to get money to continue their habits.

Issues of equity and human dignity are also of concern. Will the poor in Third World countries be lured by exaggerated fees and promises? Will governments begin to look at prisoners as an economic resource, as China has? It is immoral to economically entice the poor to submit to dangerous procedures so that the wealthy can continue physically punishing lifestyles?[73] Is the human body really a commodity, and, if so, what does this say to our strong opposition to slavery and the economic exploitation of children and women worldwide? Finally, if a market system exists, will anyone voluntarily donate? This could mean that only the wealthy would have a chance to receive a costly organ.[74]

Living Donor Organ Market

Organ markets have been proposed using both live and posthumous donors. In a living market system, individuals would be allowed to sell nonvital organs, such as a kidney, part of a liver, and possibly a lung. This right of sale would place nonvital organs in a similar category as is currently held by blood, sperm, oocytes, and body tissue—all of which are legally sold.

A live donor market is not an entirely foreign concept to Americans. Last year 4,017 living donors gave kidneys to relatives, friends, or acquaintances. These donations accounted for almost 31 percent of all kidneys transplanted. Between January and September 1999, 100 live donors gave part of their livers.[75]

There are even two cases reported in 1999 in which individuals made an undirected donation of a kidney. This allowed the medical centers involved to accurately choose the appropriate candidate for the organ, even though the patient was a stranger to the donor.[76]

Proponents of a live donor market are convinced that even more donors would step forward if given a certain kind of nudge: an economic incentive.

Market Theory as Applied

One need look no further than oocyte donation to see an example of market theory applied to organ procurement.[77] First, it is important to realize oocyte donation is complex and clearly invasive. Oocyte extraction starts with a 3-week treatment of a hormone called Lupron. This drug completely halts ovulation for a month. The donor then injects Pergonal and Metrodin (follicle stimulating hormones) into her buttocks every morning for 8 days. This forces ovarian hyperfunction, causing engorgement of the ovaries and rapid oocyte development. After the eighth day, the donor receives a final shot of a hormone, human chronic gonadotropin. Exactly 36 hours later, she is put under general sedation. An ultrasound probe is inserted into the donor's vagina, and a needle is then inserted into each ovary, extracting 12 oocytes, one at a time.[78] Therefore, in both complexity and risk, oocyte donation parallels organ donation in several regards.

Recently an advertisement seeking oocyte donors appeared in an Ivy League newspaper. In the first week, 200 women responded; and in the second, 100.[79] Though oocyte donation was first done in 1984, it is predicted that 5,000 women will donate this year. What drives these young women to become donors despite the obvious risk and discomfort? Money. They receive between $4,000 to $35,000 per donation. Proponents of a living donor organ market feel that they can be equally successful.

Objections to a Living Donor Market

Exploitation of the poor is the most frequent objection to a living donor organ market. The concern is that some people may see the sale of their organs as the only solution to their economic hardship.[80]

Opponents of an organ market point to the current trend of oocyte donation: most are from students at private colleges who are receiving little financial help from family. These women see donation as their only way to cope with the rising costs of a quality education. Thus, a logical question arises: do we want to live in a United States, where, in order to receive a quality education, one must sell a body part, an oocyte ... or a kidney?

A worldwide black market is also a concern. In 1989 the World Health Organization passed a resolution condemning the sale of human organs for transplant purposes based on documented abuses in poor nations. The 1980s saw a growing black market for organ sales in the Middle East. In 1991 a 35-year-old Egyptian man sold his kidney because he was poor and had no prospect of work. He simply decided to sell what he had left to sell—his body.[81]

Finally, the real example of China's sale of organs from executed prisoners and the fear that the practice may become more common is enough to give anyone pause. A system that protects against abuses but encourages donors must be found.

The Early Attempts to Establish Open Market Reimbursement

A free market in organs was a serious reality in 1983, when a Virginia man, H. Barry Jacobs, founded International Kidney Exchange Ltd. His company proposed to act as a broker, representing those in need of an organ and finding those willing to sell. Jacobs offered to pay up to $10,000 for a healthy kidney, and the purchaser would pay for the cost of the kidney, all related expenses, and a brokerage fee of $2,000–5,000 per kidney.

Jacobs intended not only to recruit sellers in the United States, but also to look to Third World sources. Acknowledging that informed consent from illiterates would be difficult, he planned to videotape consent.

Six months after Jacobs announced his intentions, the State of Virginia banned the sale of organs. Shortly thereafter, the U.S. Congress took similar steps. The Jacobs experiment in a completely free market with no government control or guidance was disturbing. It was the extreme in organ procurement, and the very situation that critics of an organ market system feared.

But a market in organs need not, in fact should not, be entirely free or open. There are few if any areas of the American economy that do not have some government regulation or control, especially if the market is significant. If the market in organs were a controlled market, akin to the radio and television industry, it is likely that organ shortages could be addressed without the objections and fears mentioned earlier.[82] Direct and indirect financial encouragement can be structured to avoid abuses, and to reserve altruism as a central motive.

A Proposal for a Regulated Posthumous Organ Market

In light of the problems and concerns noted above, we propose the following plan to partially regulate a market in organs and expand the rights of donors. First, we believe that a posthumous market would be the most widely supported of the market systems, chiefly because it addresses the major concerns raised by opponents of a living donor market. To function well, this system must establish a statutory right to dispose of one's organs; and it must allow a contractual agreement for monies to be paid to the donor's estate upon death and the retrieval of fit organs. Further, the contract should be based on performance and not on a promise, allowing the donor, but not the family, to revoke the contract at any time.

Payment would only be made for those organs that were fit. A medical center would not have to pay for a liver that was, subsequent to the contract, destroyed by alcohol or incident to the donor's death.

Inasmuch as the donor would never himself receive the money, it would decrease the likelihood of organ sales encouraged by drug abuse or situational depression. This approach would also reduce, though not eliminate, the likelihood of the potential abuse of the poor and other vulnerable groups since the sale of organs would be effective only upon the death of the donor.

The decedent's relatives would be prohibited from selling his organs without the prior consent of the decedent, and this consent could only take the form of a valid contract—thus allowing for control of one's body even after death.

Other safeguards should be added to this system. Prior to entering into this contract, the donor would be required to undergo a screening process that would include a mental health assessment. This screening would ideally ascertain any hidden motives as to donation or mental instability at the time of the decision, and establish informed consent.

No minor would be allowed to contract, nor would parents be allowed to enter their child into a contract. This would alleviate fears of children being conceived solely for the purpose of growing organs.

As in insurance policies, an organ market would have "slayer provisions" as well as suicide clauses. If a third-party beneficiary murdered the donor, he would not be allowed to be unjustly enriched by this criminal act. Nor would a contract be valid in the case of suicide, thus eliminating the concern of contracting for the betterment of his family's immediate needs.

Intriguing contractual arrangements could be driven by the market. There may be a "healthy lifestyle" bonus. Runners may receive a higher contracting price than those with a sedentary lifestyle. Nonsmokers and people at their ideal height and weight may receive a financial bonus. These items and benefits could be driven by supply and demand of the market.

A completely free market would invite the kind of abuse that so far has doomed any serious consideration of an organ market. In this area, governmental regulation would be not only beneficial but also crucial. The U.S. Food and Drug Administration (FDA) would be a logical candidate to oversee an organ market. Through the FDA, the government can address the concerns of a trade in organs while allowing the country to benefit from an increased supply.

The FDA could issue a limited number of licenses to private companies that would serve as brokerage houses. The cost of governmental oversight would be subsidized by licensing fees. These fees could also be used to develop altruistic donation programs as well as transplant opportunities for the under and uninsured.[83] The FDA could choose to impose a flat per organ donation rate but would need to provide for market driven price fluctuations.

Conclusion

Currently 68,371 Americans are on waiting lists to receive an organ. Twelve will die each day because there is no transplant organ available. Altruistic donations of organs have increased, but donations lag far behind the increase in demand. A creative solution to the shortage of donated organs should include the controlled posthumous free market sale of organs. It is time we learn from the successes of the plasma and reproductive cell markets and implement a well-conceived, governmentally regulated posthumous organ market.

Discussion Questions

1. What was the major proposal set forth in this chapter to address the issue of the shortage of organs?
2. What are the important dates of transplant technology?
3. What benefit was derived by the introduction of Cyclosporin-A in kidney transplants?
4. What is xenotransplantation?
5. What are some of the difficulties associated with primate-to-human transplant?
6. What is an organ?
7. What are examples of regenerative organs as well as human tissue and cells?
8. What are some of the early objectives cited by Richard Titmuss to commercialize the sale of blood?
9. What are the odds today of receiving HIV-infected blood through blood donations?
10. What is an oocyte donor paid on average for her donation?
11. In 1998, embryonic stem cells were isolated and have shown promise in treating which diseases?
12. The Uniform Anatomical Gift Act of 1968 answered which 12 questions?
13. What are the major provisions of the National Organ Transplant Act (NOTA) of 1984?
14. What amendment was made by Congress in 1987 to the 1968 Uniformed Anatomical Gift Act?

Endnotes

1. See generally *Ellis v. Patterson*, 859 F.2d 52 (8th Cir. 1988); and *Todd v. Sorrell*, 841 F.2d 87 (4th Cir. 1988).
2. David E. Jefferies, "The Body as Commodity: The Use of Markets to Cure the Organ Deficit" (note), *Ind. J. Global Legal Stud* 5 (1998): 621, 623.
3. The rejection problem is not present in transplants between identical twins (syngenic graft), but is present in all grafts between genetically dissimilar members of the same species (allograft). Robert Berkow et al., eds., *The Merck Manual of Diagnosis and Therapy* (Rahway, N.J.: Merck Research Laboratories,1992), 347, 352–53.
4. Berkow, *The Merck Manual of Diagnosis and Therapy*, 347.
5. Ibid., 352.

6. Franklin Hoke, "As Cross-Species Transplantation Move Ahead, Some Scientists Call for Caution, Restraint," *The Scientist* 9, no.16 (August 21, 1995): 1.
7. M. Storck and D. Abendroth, "Human Xenogenic Kidney Transplantation from the Clinical Viewpoint," *Zentralbi, Chir* 124 (1999): 616 (in German).
8. See *Ellis v. Patterson* and *Todd v. Sorrell.*
9. Josie Glausiusz, "Spare Parts: Bioengineers Foresee a Time When You Can Grow Your Own Organs," *Discover*, August 1999, http://www.britanica.com/bcom/magazine/article/print/0.5746.00.html.
10. Clayton L. Thomas et al., eds., *Tabor's Cyclopedic Medical Dictionary* (Philadelphia: Davis, 1993), 1368.
11. Gloria J. Banks, "Legal and Ethical Safeguards: Protection of Society's Most Vulnerable Participants in a Commercialized Organ Transplantation System," *Am. J. L. & Med.* 21 (1995): 45, 53.
12. Realizing that oocytes, though finite in number, are normally produced in greater quantities than a woman would use over the course of her lifetime.
13. Banks, "Legal and Ethical Safeguards," 46.
14. Ibid., 48.
15. Ibid., 40–50.
16. Ronald O. Gilcher, M.D., president and CEO, medical director, Sylvan N. Goldman Center, Oklahoma Blood Institute, personal interview, March 21, 2000.
17. Hepatitis B Surface Antigen (HbsAg), Antibodies to the Hepatitis B Core (Anti-HBc), Antibodies to the Hepatitis C Virus (Anti-HCV), Antibodies to the Human Immunodeficiency Virus, Types 1 and 2 (Anti-HIV-1, -2), HIV-1 p24 Antigen, and Antibodies to Human T-lymphotrophic Virus. Types I and II (Anti-HTLV-I, -II), and Syphilis.
18. Gilcher, personal interview.
19. NAT technology can be expected to remain in the forefront of blood donation research for the next 15 years. NAT is capable of identifying any pathogen but it is only a screening technique. The next step will be pathogen inactivation. Pathogen inactivation will kill all pathogens in the blood rendering it completely safe and the screening process will be used as quality control. See ibid.
20. Banks, "Legal and Ethical Safeguards," 50. The term *replenishing* is used as an acknowledgment that the testes are producing additional sperm and not the cell itself. See also note 12.
21. See generally Rebecca Mead, "Eggs for Sale," *The New Yorker*, August 9, 1999, 56.
22. A human pre-embryo exists when the oocyte is still in the ovium stage, either before the ovum has been fertilized or during the period of time prior to the second week of development. See Thomas, *Tabor's Cyclopedic Medical Dictionary*, 1358.
23. *Davis v. Davis*, 842 S.W. 2d 588 (Tenn. 1992).
24. *Hecht v. Superior Ct.*, 16 Cal. App. 4th 836 (1993).
25. California courts have looked at property rights of certain cell lines in *Moore v. Regents of University of California*. John Moore had hairy cell leukemia, and sought treatment at the UCLA Medical Center. After extensive research, Mr. Moore's physicians recognized that there was a great deal of economic potential in the commercial use of certain cell line derived from his splenic tissue. The regents and physicians patented the cells and sold the patent for over

$440,000 and stock options. Mr. Moore asserted a property right to his cells, even after they had been removed. The Court of Appeals held that Mr. Moore had an unrestricted right to the use, enjoyment, and disposition of his cells, and, thus, property law did apply. The California Supreme Court reversed the outcome of the lower courts on the grounds that Mr. Moore had relinquished possession of his cells and lost any property right. The court also held that under California law, an individual who donated any body part could not receive valuable consideration. It is important to note that the court's holding was not broad. The court did note that there may be a circumstance in which one would have property rights to his cells after removal from his body, but such facts were not present in Mr. Moore's case. Taken together, these cases show that there can be a property right in a person's cells, tissues, and organs. Being the owner of property confers rights and dominions over the object. The owner has the right to possess and enjoy the property, to dispose of the property, and to transfer his right of ownership in that property to another. In transferring this right, the property owner has the authority to demand compensation. Common law has long recognized that everyone is the manager and master of his or her own affairs and property (*Rerum suarum quilibet est moderator et arbiter*). *Moore v. Regents of the University of California*, 793 P. 2d 479 (1990).

26. The primary tissues are epithelial, connective, skeletal, muscular, glandular, and nervous. Thomas et al., *Tabor's Cyclopedic Medical Dictionary*, 2000.
27. Banks, "Legal and Ethical Safeguards," 47.
28. A stem cell is a self-renewing cell that divides to give rise to a cell with an identical development potential and/or one with a more restricted development potential. James Darnell et al., eds., *Molecular Cell Biology*, 3rd ed. (New York: Scientific American Books, 1995), 215.
29. The most fundamental and extraordinary of the stem cells are found in the early stage embryo. These embryonic stem (ES) cells, unlike the more differentiated adult stem cells or other cell types, retain the special ability to develop into nearly any cell type. Embryonic germ cells, which originate from the primordial reproductive cells of the developing fetus, have properties similar to ES cells. See National Bioethics Advisory Committee, *Ethical Issues In Human Stem Cell Research: Executive Summary* (Washington, DC: National Bioethics Advisory Committee, 1999), 1–2.
30. The immune system is divided into two primary effector cell subtypes. B-lymphocytes produce antibodies, while T lymphocytes provide important regulatory as well as cytotoxic functions. Both cell types develop from hemotopoietic stem cells through tightly regulated processes of differentiation. Thus transplantation of such stem cells should theoretically allow the repopulation of immune systems destroyed by immunosuppressive drugs and treatment or by pathogens such as HIV. Melissa J. DeBoer, Oklahoma Medical Research Foundation, personal interview, April 5, 2000.
31. "Chemotherapy, Stem Cell Transplant Helps Rheumatoid Arthritis," *Annuals of Internal Med.* 131 (1999): 507.
32. *Forbes v. Woods*, 71 E. Supp. 2d 1015 (D. Ariz. 1999); *Margret S. v. Edwards*, 794 F. 2d 994 (5th Cir. 1986); *Lifchez v. Hartigan*, 735 F. Supp.. 1361 (N.D., Ill., 1990); and *Jane L. v. Bangerter*, 61 F. 3d 1493 (10th Cir. 1995).

33. Following a 4-year funding ban on embryonic research, the U.S. Congress is once again debating funding. Congress is caught between patients' rights groups and pro-life groups. In the end, Congress may not make the decision based on what is best scientifically but, rather, on which group they can least afford to alienate. See *Forbes v. Woods*, 71 E. Supp. 2d 1015 (D. Ariz. 1999), discussed in Associated Press Wire Service "Judge Rules on Tissue Research Ban," October 6, 1999.
34. Monique Gorsline and Rachelle L. K. Johnson, "The United States System of Organ Donation, The International Solution, and The Cadaveric Organ Donation Act: 'And The Winner Is...,'" *J. Corp. L.* 20, no. 5 (1995): 13–14.
35. Lisa E. Douglass, "Organ Donation, Procurement and Transplantation: The Process, The Problems, The Law," *UMKC Law Review* 65 (1996): 201, 206.
36. Ibid., 208.
37. Ibid.
38. Ibid., 210.
39. Gorsline and Johnson, "The United States System of Organ Donation," 18.
40. H.R. 2418, 106th Cong. 1 (November 1, 1999).
41. Ibid., 24.
42. Ibid.
43. 42 U.S.C. sec 274e (1987) (Prohibition of Organ Purchase).
44. It is worth noting that the current version of the bill being considered removed wording from the originally offered amendment, striking the enumeration of what constitutes a "valuable consideration" and replacing it with a broadly worded statement: a valuable consideration does not include a benefit, the exchange of which is expressly contemplated by organ distribution policies, demonstration projects, or programs duly established or sanctioned by the board of directors of the Organ Procurement and Transportation Network. H.R. 2418, S. 1, 106th Congress 4© (July 1, 1999).
45. Rep. Michael Bilirakis, *Bill Summary and Status*, 106th Congress, April. 5, 2000, http://Thomas.loc.gov/cgi-bin/bdquery/z?d106:HR02418:@@@X.
46. The United Network for Organ Sharing is a Richmond, Virginia–based private organization contracted by the federal government to run the national transplant distribution system.
47. Juliet Eilperin, "House Acts to Reject Rules on Transplants," *Washington Post*, April 5, 2000, A02.
48. Jefferies, "The Body as Commodity," 634.
49. Ibid., 636.
50. Ibid., 636–37.
51. Ibid., 637.
52. Ibid.
53. Ibid., 639.
54. Ibid., 641.
55. Ibid., 643.
56. Ibid.
57. U.S. Constitution, Eighth Amendment, "Excessive bail shall not be required, not excessive fines imposed, nor cruel and unusual punishments inflicted" (emphasis added).

58. Since 1990, 350 people have been executed in the United States; Amnesty International, *Rights for All: The Death Penalty in the USA*, May 1999, http://www.amnestyusa.org/rightsforall/dp/index.html.
59. In 1998 Missouri State Representative Chuck Graham sponsored a bill in the state legislature that would have allowed inmates on Missouri's death row to gain clemency by donating a kidney. The bill though debated, was defeated in the States House Criminal Law Committee. Kim Bell, "House Committee Appears Unlikely to Pass Bill on Death Row Organ Donors," *St. Louis Post Dispatch*, March 26, 1998, at B4, B4.
60. *Roe v. Wade*, 410 U.S. 113 (1973).
61. *Planned Parenthood v. Casey*, 505 U.S. 833 (1992).
62. *Cruzan v. Director, Missouri Department of Health*, 497 U.S. 261 (1990).
63. 20 Pa. Const. Stat section 8622 (1994).
64. In 1999 the Virginia DMV launched a new initiative through which DMV employees would ask registering drivers if they wished to be organ donors instead of merely providing the block to check on the form. In the first 3 months, the program saw a fourfold increase in drivers agreeing to be organ donors. Editorial, "The Virginia DMV's Noble New Cause," *Roanoke Times & World News*, May 20, 1999, A20.
65. Douglass, "Organ Donation, Procurement and Transplantation," 202.
66. U.S. Department of Health and Human Services, Press Release, *Organ Donations Increase in 1998 Following National Initiative and New Regulations*, April 16, 1999, http://www.hhs.gov/news/press/1999pres/99ou16b.html.
67. Robert D. Gibbons, "Waiting for Organ Transplantation," *Science* 287, no. 237 (2000).
68. Douglass, "Organ Donation, Procurement and Transplantation," 202. Though 4,380 lives may seem statistically insignificant when compared to other causes of death such as motor vehicle accidents, which claim 41,826 lives a year, one must never forget that, behind statistics of mortality are grieving families. Twelve families each day grieve over a preventable loss. See Joyce A. Marlo et al., "Births and Deaths: Preliminary Data for 1998," *Nat'l Vital Statistics Rep.*, October 5, 1999, 5–7, at 5.
69. Douglass, "Organ Donation, Procurement and Transplantation," 228.
70. The Department of Health and Human Services (HHS) has an "Urban Myth" website. The businessman story and others are debunked on the website. U.S. Department of Health and Human Services, "Organ and Tissue Donations—Myths," July 20, 1999, http://www.organdonor.gov/myth.html.
71. Jefferies, "The Body as Commodity," 1, nn. 2, 3.
72. Amy Harmon, "Illegal Kidney Auction Pops Up on Ebay's Site," *New York Times*, September 3, 1999.
73. Lloyd R. Cohen, "Increasing the Supply of Transplant Organs: The Virtues of a Futures Market," *Geo. Wash. Law Rev.* 58, no. 1 (1989): 1–51.
74. Ibid., 24.
75. Denise Grady, "The New Organ Donors are Living Strangers," *New York Times*, September 20, 1990, http://www.nytimes.com/library/national/science/092099hthdonor-volunteer.html.

76. Not all medical centers are comfortable with undirected donations; one of the two donors had to contact a number of facilities before being accepted by the University of Minnesota. Johns Hopkins and Minnesota have accepted undesignated gifts but have required the donors to go through a lengthy screening process including a psychological exam. Grady, "The New Organ Donors are Living Strangers."
77. This is not to suggest that oocyte donation is without its critics, or that the practice itself is moral. Many feel it is a sad commentary on the United States that bright Ivy League college students find it necessary to sell parts of their bodies to afford a top-level education. This article addresses the oocyte market only as a measure of comparison.
78. Mead, "Eggs for Sale," 60.
79. Ibid., 65.
80. Gorsline and Johnson, "The United States System of Organ Donation," 37.
81. Banks, "Legal and Ethical Safeguards," 73.
82. See Gorsline and Johnson, "The United States System of Organ Donation," 31–44.
83. This is not to say that a constitutional right to receive an organ would exist. In this respect, the organ market would operate no differently than the current medical system. The Courts of Appeal in both the Fourth and Eighth Circuits have held that states are not required to fund organ transplants under Medicaid even if a transplant offers the patient's only chance for survival. See *Ellis v. Patterson*, 859 F.2d 52 (8th Cir. 1988); and *Todd v. Sorrell*, 841 F.2d 87 (4th Cir. 1998).

7 A Free Market for Kidneys
Options, Futures, Forward, and Spot*

WILLIAM BARNETT II, PhD
Department of Economics, Loyola University, New Orleans, Louisiana

MICHAEL SALIBA, PhD
Department of Economics, Loyola University, New Orleans, Louisiana

Contents

Introduction	95
Kidney Demand and Supply	96
The Market for Kidneys	98
Financing Transactions: Options, Futures, and Forward Markets	101
Spot Markets	102
Kidney Prices	105
Summary and Conclusions	106
Appendix	107
Discussion Questions	110
Acknowledgments	110
Endnotes	110
References	111

Introduction

Almost 3,000 Americans die prematurely every year because they cannot get kidney transplants, and more than 40,000 others suffer while waiting for such medical procedures. Moreover, even if the entire backlog of 40,000 patients waiting for a kidney transplant could be eliminated, some 22,000 new patients join the list each year (Scientific Registry of Transplant Recipients 2000; United Network for Organ Sharing 2002). This health care problem is not due to lack of medical knowledge and technology or inadequate supplies

---

* First published in *Managerial Finance* 30 (2), 38–56, 2004.

of medical personnel and relevant equipment. Rather, the problem is the result of a shortage of transplantable kidneys.

The sale and purchase of such body parts is prohibited by the National Organ Transplant Act of 1984 (U.S. Congress 1984). Were this law to be repealed or amended, buyers would bid the price above the current mandated zero initial price and sellers would respond by increasing the quantity supplied. Consequently, the economic shortage would be eliminated (Adams et al. 1999; Anderson and Barnett 1999, Barnett et al. 1992; Barney and Reynolds 1989; Blair and Kaserman 1991; Block 1988; Block et al. 1999–2000; Carlstrom and Rollow 1997; Hansmann 1989; Kaserman and Barnett 1991; McKenzie and Tullock 1989; Rottenberg 1971; Vining and Schwindt 1986).

However, in addition to an economic shortage there is a situation that we refer to as a *medical shortage*, defined as a situation in which, regardless of whether an economic shortage exists, someone who needs a kidney transplant cannot get one because no transplantable kidney is available.

Virtually all expenses not included in private insurance plans are currently covered by Medicare, Medicaid, or both (see Medicare, *Your Medicare Handbook, 1995* and *Medicare Coverage of Kidney Dialysis and Kidney Transplant Services 1995*). That, combined with the fact that during any analytically relevant period of time, only a tiny fraction of the more than 285 million Americans requires a kidney transplant, results in the demand curves for transplants and hence for the requisite kidneys being truncated at a price greater than the opportunity cost of providing the marginal transplant and its requisite kidney. That is, the demand for transplants and hence for these human organs can be satiated, thereby eliminating the medical shortage of kidneys (Barnett et al. 2001).

This chapter is an attempt to fathom the financial and market processes that would evolve were a free market in kidneys to be permitted. What types of institutions would develop? How would transactions be facilitated? What would happen to the price of kidneys in the short term and over the longer term? We attempt to provide some insights into these issues and how such a market would function.

Kidney Demand and Supply

The demand for kidneys unlike the demand for most goods is truncated. That is, it is satiated at a positive price; the quantity demanded does not increase if the price falls below the satiation price. On this point, see Figures 7.1 and 7.2. Prior to the paper by Barnett et al. (2001), the demand curve for kidneys was shown as a typical demand curve, originating at a finite, positive price on the vertical axis and declining continuously, until the price reached zero, at which the quantity demanded is positive and finite. However, as these

A Free Market for Kidneys

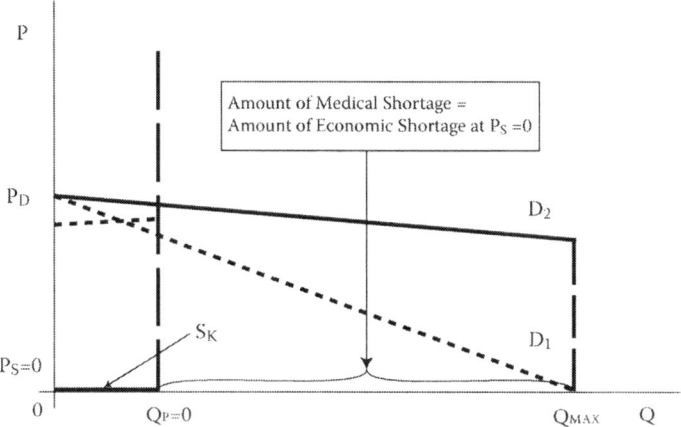

Figure 7.1 Regulated market for kidneys.

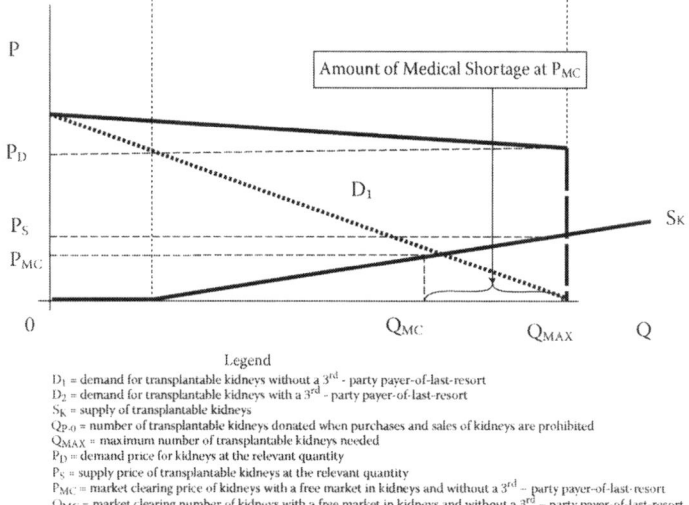

Figure 7.2 Unregulated market for kidneys.

authors point out, as long as the government remains as the payer of last resort, the demand curve is actually truncated at a price greater than zero because the maximum quantity of kidneys demanded is equal to the number of people on the waiting list, and no more. That is, the demand curve does not decline until the price reaches zero, but is curtailed at a positive price. Moreover, they also demonstrate that the demand price exceeds the expected supply price at that quantity, defined as the maximum number of kidneys needed. Thus both the economic and the medical shortage will be eliminated when price controls are ended. If an individual has two functioning kidneys, there is no value placed on a third transplantable kidney from another person. Thus the demand for these organs is approximately equal to the number of people on the waiting list for a kidney.

Because only one kidney is required to lead a healthy life, their potential supply during a particular time period is enormous relative to the demand: one from each member of the (living) population with two working kidneys, plus twice the number of brain deaths that occur during that time period. Because there is a relatively insignificant number of brain deaths, the potential supply is approximately as large as the population.

Since there is a very large, pent-up demand consequent on the long standing shortage of kidneys, if a free market were suddenly permitted the price would likely be relatively high, initially. This fact, coupled with the relatively price inelastic short-term supply curve, would imply a relatively high price. As an example, Dennis Prince describes the posting of an offer of a kidney for sale on eBay. He notes that the price of this kidney rose from $25,000 to nearly $6 million during the week while this item was listed (Prince 1999).

Because the demand for kidneys is typically nonrecurring, over time it would decrease as the pent-up demand declined. Moreover, as advances in medical technology lead to reduced risk as well as less pain and suffering for sellers, the number of living people willing to offer a kidney at a given price will rise over time, thus increasing the supply.

Therefore, the truncated demand curve will shift to the left over time until the pent-up demand is met. After that, shifts could occur in either direction depending on what changes occur in the value individuals place on a transplantable kidney, but such changes in demand are not likely to vary significantly from year to year. Consequently, as the pent-up demand is fulfilled the number of kidneys required to satisfying the maximum demand would decrease rapidly. This would tend to lower price. And the expected increase in supply would lower price even further over time. The lists of people waiting for kidneys would be rapidly eliminated.

The Market for Kidneys

Each individual has an antigen typing. For purposes of transplanting, there are six markers that are considered in determining whether a particular kidney will function properly in another person's body. The only mandatory characteristics that the two individuals must share is blood type. However, the more markers that match between the supplier and the recipient, the less likely the recipient's body is to reject the transplanted kidney and the less rejection medication the recipient must take after the transplant operation. (From a telephone interview with Bruce Pinsonat at Louisiana Organ Procurement Agency. Metairie, La., May 6, 2002)

A Free Market for Kidneys

There are two sources from which the potential supply would come: cadaveric and living. Kidneys may be salvaged from a cadaver if the individual suffers brain death, provided the vital organs are in good shape and can be kept that way until surgically removed and transplanted. There are four possibilities regarding the harvesting of cadaveric kidneys.

1. The individual may have received payment while living for one or both kidneys to be harvested upon his death.
2. The individual may have arranged while living that after death, a payment would be made to his estate, to one or more particular individuals, and/or to one or more charities or other organizations.
3. A dying person's family or legal heirs could make the arrangement if the dying person is comatose or otherwise unable to make a decision, with payment going to any of the parties mentioned in (2).
4. The individual's family or the person designated with power of attorney may choose to offer one or both kidneys upon the individual's death.

Relative to the number of people needing a kidney, the entire cadaveric supply is currently far from sufficient to meet the demand. Individuals are encouraged to donate their kidneys upon death, but relatively few do due to lack of sufficient incentives, and, of those who do, even fewer are useful for transplant due to the brain death criteria.

Currently, when an individual becomes brain dead and has not previously agreed to donate his kidneys upon death, the family is sometimes approached by one of the organ donation agencies for permission to recover one or more body parts. Unfortunately, it is very difficult for an individual's loved ones to make the choice to donate while they are grieving over the death, and, as a result, many usable organs are not recovered. Under a free market where money is paid for kidneys, whether family members or others would be able to sell the individual's kidneys is unclear. Since the supplier would not be the person receiving payment for the kidneys, the question would arise as to whether the individual would have approved of the sale, and if so, why was this not arranged prior to death, given that a market in kidneys existed.

While the number of cadaveric kidneys that would be available under a free market is difficult to predict, both the supply of and demand for them are likely to be very small. This is the result of the fact that relatively few people experience brain death while their bodily organs are still viable. According to the Center for Organ Recovery and Education, between 10,000 and 12,000 Americans die each year who would be potential suppliers of one or more cadaveric bodily organs. Of these, only 5,200, or 50 percent, actually donate

(Center for Organ Recovery and Education, http://www.pitt.edu/htk/wasted.htm). Kidney(s) from such individuals would have to be harvested for use within a relatively short period of time after the death, beyond which this organ is no longer usable, and it would have to be properly transported and stored until a patient whose need matched one of the available kidneys is located.

In a free market, the demand for kidneys to be harvested upon an individual's death is also likely to be very small. The price paid to the (living) seller would be the present value of the kidney(s) to be received upon the death of the seller. Because it is very difficult to predict (1) when and how an individual will die and (2) in what condition his body organs will be upon death, the present value might well be very small, resulting in relatively few such kidneys demanded. In contrast, given the very large potential supply from living individuals, a person who could benefit physically from a transplant can be matched more precisely with a certain living potential supplier before the kidney is removed, thus reducing both the risks and costs mentioned above.

Thus the major source of supply is likely to be kidneys from living persons. Since only one functioning kidney is necessary to lead a healthy life, the potential supply from living individuals is enormous relative to the demand. The survival rate for people in the United States with only one functioning kidney is the same as for those with two (Organ Selling, 2). To the extent that this fact becomes widely known, many individuals should be willing to sell one of their kidneys. Assuming a waiting list of 50,000 against a potential supply of 150 million, only .03 percent of the population would have to become kidney suppliers to eliminate the pent-up demand.[1] Beyond the transition phase, a much smaller percentage of the population would have to supply these items in order to meet the demand and avoid a shortage and resulting waiting lists.

The ability to more closely match the supplier and the demander given the very small demand and the large potential supply from living individuals will further decrease the attractiveness of cadaveric kidneys. This will further depress the (present value) price both of those kidneys contracted for prior to death and those purchased after death, assuming the latter is permitted by law.

There will be a very small recurring demand for a kidney by those who either have received a transplant or have supplied one. It is possible that a patient might require another transplant in the event of malfunction of the original one; but as medical technology improves, the failure rate and therefore the incidence of individuals requiring a second organ should fall. In the event that the remaining kidney of an individual who was a living supplier fails, there will be a sufficient quantity available for replacement. This reduces the risk that a living supplier faces as a result of offering a kidney for sale in the market. The fact that it would be much more likely that an individual who sold one of his kidneys could acquire a replacement if the remaining one were to malfunction would encourage many people to give up one of these organs while living. Currently, given the severe shortage of kidneys, it is not surprising that living individuals are reluctant to donate one of their own.

Financing Transactions: Options, Futures, and Forward Markets

Although options, forward, or future markets for kidneys might be a possibility, it is not likely that any of them would emerge. Certain characteristics are necessary for such markets to exist.[2] Burns (1979, 33–34) states,

> The efficiency of markets for future transactions relates to the ease of effecting transactions and to the quality of the information that they provide. Like the efficiency of spot markets, the efficiency of forward and futures markets is a function of the liquidity of the assets traded, the orderliness of market conditions, and the quality of the markets' organization. The concept of efficiency of markets for future transactions contains, however, an additional aspect which derives from their multidimensional nature.
>
> In effect, there are two (2) elements—the observed and unobserved—of forward and futures markets. The observed element consists of prices (or price quotations), volume of transactions, and open interest in these markets; the unobserved element relates to expectations about spot prices (and, more broadly, spot markets) in the future. The additional aspect of these markets' efficiency consists of the quality of information that the observed element—reported daily in the *Wall Street Journal* for most futures markets—conveys about the unobserved element, particularly about expected future spot prices.

First, due to the relatively small demand (beyond the transition phase required to clear the waiting list), the kidney market would be thin. Second, even if the supplier fully intends to deliver at some point in the future if the holder of an option decides to exercise it or upon arrival of the delivery date in the case of a futures contract, the supplier may renege and it is unlikely in the extreme that the courts would enforce the contract. It is difficult to imagine a situation in which a person is forced to undergo surgery to have one of his kidneys removed for sale to another individual because of an earlier agreement to that effect. The people most likely to be judgment proof are also likely to be a substantial percentage of the sellers of kidneys, making this segment unattractive for options and futures markets due to reneging and the lack of court enforcement to remove a body part against one's will.

A forward market is more likely than an options or futures market. Individuals could sell the future rights to one or both of their kidneys for money to be received at the time of such sale. Organ brokers or financial intermediaries could make one payment, buying the rights to one or both organs for a lifetime, or annual payments of lesser amounts, in effect leasing the rights for a year. Such yearly payments would have the advantage that people would have to stay in contact with the broker, and the amount of such annual payment could even be made contingent upon the physical condition of the seller. If, after death, the deceased's relatives object to the kidney(s) being removed, they could be offered the option of making repayment, with interest, to the brokerage firm, subject to the firm's consent. Or, the financial intermediary might insist that the contract be honored. However, there are problems that may limit the size of this type of market. Reneging could be a major problem, which would be handled by putting up good faith money or a margin, but this could be a predicament for the poor and it could potentially be a difficulty for all if the courts refused to enforce such contracts by requiring the seller to have one of his kidneys removed. However, it is much more likely that the judicial system will enforce these contracts post mortem rather than against the living.

Spot Markets

What is likely to emerge is a spot market in kidneys. Those living individuals who desire to sell one of their kidneys, assuming the price and other relevant factors are satisfactory, would make this known through a listing with one or more brokers.[3] Whether potential sellers of these body parts would be listed with only one broker, or with multiple financial intermediaries, would depend on the expense of the test that establishes the antigen type and individual markers for a particular person's kidney. If this expense is relatively low, potential sellers might be willing to incur these expenses themselves and to provide the results to multiple brokers, much as do those who take college entrance exams such as the ACT and SAT. Students pay to take the exam(s) and then indicate to which colleges and universities they wish their scores to be sent. To insure accuracy, colleges and universities require that the results be sent to them directly from the testing source. The same type of situation would likely pertain in the case of kidney testing. In this case, the potential seller would be listed with multiple brokers, in which case the search for a kidney prior to a transplant would be limited—probably to only one broker due to the overlap in listings.[4]

However, if this disbursement is large, potential sellers are less likely to be willing to incur these expenses, given the low probability of actually being able to sell a kidney coupled with the relatively modest expected price they would receive. In such case, the broker would likely gather preliminary information from a potential seller, primarily in the form of past medical history.

Assuming this initial investigation revealed no cause for concern regarding the viability of the person's kidney for transplant purposes, the broker would then incur the expense of the antigen testing.[5] In such case, potential sellers are likely to be listed with only one broker, and prior to a transplant, the search for a usable kidney would include inquiries into the offerings of each of the relatively few members of this industry. The fees the brokers would charge to the buyers would cover the expense of antigen testing.

It is most unlikely that the brokers would charge a listing fee to potential sellers directly. It should be noted that because of the truncated demand curve, it is virtually certain that there would exist a gap between the demand and supply prices at the actual quantity of kidneys exchanged. This difference would equal the amount of rent per kidney exchanged that would depend upon bargaining. Everyone in the transplant industry (doctors, hospitals, nurses, brokers, insurance companies, etc.) would attempt to capture as much of this benefit as possible for themselves. There is no way of knowing how this would play out. Those groups that were able to do so, say doctors, insurance companies and brokers, would try to price discriminate at both ends (i.e., both in terms of the prices paid and charged for kidneys). And, in all likelihood any group that thought they could hide their own price discrimination (engage in covert price discrimination), while other(s) could not (overt price discrimination), would seek regulation outlawing covert price discrimination. That is, although inframarginal rents are present in virtually all markets, the normal competitive forces of supply and demand tend to compete away, in relatively short order, any rents at the margin. However, because of the truncated demand curve, this particular market is different. There would be rents at the margin that would remain, and not be competed away. As a result, either there would be collusion on the part of some market participants to acquire the rents and then divide them among themselves, or the competition would take place in the political arena, in which case the rents would be converted to wasteful expenditures, in other words, payments designed to get politicians and/or bureaucrats to provide an edge over others in the industry.

Physicians with a patient who could benefit from a kidney transplant would search the files of one or more brokers until one or more organs with a satisfactory price-to-antigen test result ratio were located. Although the only marker that must match between the supplier and recipient of a kidney is blood type, the closer the match, the more likely the kidney is to function properly and the fewer antirejection drugs the patient must take following the transplant. Thus, the better the match, the higher the price that the purchaser (patient, insurance company, and/or government)[6] would be willing to pay to reduce the chances of rejection and/or expenditures on postoperative medication.

Given the widespread governmental regulation of the medical industry, ostensibly for the benefit of the customers, it is very likely that governments would regulate brokers in the "pre-owned" kidney industry. Undoubtedly, they would be required to be licensed. This might be justified in some sense if it prevented, or at least reduced, instances of kidney theft, by requiring licensed brokers to maintain proper records as to the source and destination of each kidney that came into their possession. Licensed brokers would be the only entities from which a transplant patient could legally acquire an organ (excepting cases of altruistic gifts between live donors and recipients).[7] It is most unlikely that any money would be paid to the kidney owner until this item was actually removed.

How would the actual financing work? Whether the patient, hospital, doctor, or transplantee's insurance company (or other third party) would be the one to pay the seller directly might vary from case to case. The ultimate payer could be any one of these. For example, take the case of a hospital buying blood for a patient. The hospital rebills (with a markup) the patient or the party responsible for this product. However, this need not be the case, and transplant doctors might well prefer to buy the kidney themselves and include the price thereof (including a markup, of course) in their bill. No doubt the markups mentioned above would include as much rent as possible. On the other hand, the insurance companies might try to purchase the kidneys directly, capturing as much of the rents as they could. There is no way of knowing how it would turn out, save that if the rents would be high as is likely, the issue would be resolved either through currently illegal forms of collusion or through "rent seeking"[8] in the political process.

A second purpose of licensing would be to reduce the likelihood of error or fraud by brokers concerning the antigen profile of the kidney and other relevant factors (e.g., the medical history of the seller).[9] Further protection could be afforded through requirements that licensed brokers be obliged to carry insurance or be bonded to compensate the recipients of kidneys in cases of fraud and/or human error.[10]

The brokers who bring the suppliers and demanders of kidneys together would play an important part in reducing transactions costs. Their role would be to gather and store information about those who are willing to sell a kidney assuming the price and other conditions were acceptable.

It is possible that the brokers might instead constitute joint ventures with insurance companies. The providers of health insurance may become the principal purchasers of kidneys. These firms are already involved in the types of actuarial calculations and financial transactions that would be involved. Brokers similar to the organ procurement organizations that exist today, but who are prevented by law from offering monetary incentives to potential suppliers, might be alternatives to insurance firms. However, in this case it is very likely that the joint venture would buy the kidney, and thus be, de facto, if not de jure, a reseller.[11]

In either case, if insurance companies became resellers or brokers, compensation for kidneys purchased for resale could be made in cash and/or in the form of reduced health insurance premiums. That is, in exchange for giving up a kidney now or in the future, including upon death, the insurance company would reduce the individual's health insurance premiums.

The amount by which insurance premiums would be reduced for cadaveric kidneys as opposed to those emanating from living individuals likely would be tiny, because only a small percentage of people would actually yield usable organs upon death. Thus, this might not be the most efficient means of procurement, but it might be attractive to some, especially those who were not covered by group health insurance plans.

Kidney Prices

Just as we cannot know ex ante what the market clearing price of any good would be, it is impossible to have this information with regard to kidneys. The heterogeneity of such body parts, moreover, suggests that there would be a range of prices, the upper and lower limits of which would depend on the supply and demand for different types of these organs.

The price paid to the supplier of a kidney (i.e., the original owner) would include payment for (1) the kidney itself, (2) the pain and suffering endured by the supplier as a result of the surgical removal, (3) the risk that something would happen in the process of removal to cause additional harm to the supplier, (4) the risk of failure of the remaining kidney, and (5) the possibility that should this latter occur, there would not be a suitable replacement forthcoming from the market.

The minimum price for which the kidney would be sold in the market by a broker would be the sum of (1) the price paid to the original owner; (2) the expense associated with extracting and after-extraction care, including any testing ordered by the broker or others prior to extraction; (3) transfer expenses; (4) overhead expenses; and (5) brokers' fees.

The buyer of the kidney from the original owner would in all probability pay for all aftercare, no matter how much is required. The less aftercare expenses required, the more the buyer would be willing to pay for the kidney itself.

Transfer expenses include the act-of-sale transfer of title, transportation, and tracking. Although the temptation to acquire a kidney illegally by theft from an unwilling "donor" is not likely to arise if there were a free market in these items,[12] evil people might do just that and then sell such ill-gotten material to unsuspecting buyers. A tracking system would eliminate this possibility as a source of concern, but the attendant expenses would have to be borne by the ultimate purchasers of kidneys as part of the price paid.

The broker would incur expenses associated with acquiring and maintaining a database of information regarding the supply and demand of kidneys. These overhead expenses would include labor, capital, supplies, maintenance, and so on and would tend to be recovered in the broker's fees.

The price for a kidney transplant would thus include (1) the price of the kidney, (2) the fees charged for the transplant process, and (3) the expected mandatory aftercare expenses. Since insurance companies and the government will be the major third-party payers, kidney transplant prices would be governed by what these financiers are willing to pay, much like the case for other medical procedures in which either or both of them are involved.

Summary and Conclusions

If the National Organ Transplant Act of 1984 were repealed or amended to permit the sale and purchase of kidneys, and assuming that the government remains as the financer of last resort, both the economic and medical shortages of kidneys would be eliminated in short order. Market processes and financial institutions would evolve to facilitate these exchanges.

It is likely that a type of spot market would emerge and most unlikely that options, futures, or forward markets would develop. The main reasons for this are (1) the thin market; and (2) the possibility that a seller might renege and the courts not require specific performance of the contract. A third reason is the heterogeneous nature of kidneys.

The spot market would be comprised of buyers—most likely the third-party payers (insurance companies and the government) and/or doctors and/or hospitals, sellers, and brokers who would not take possession of kidneys offered for sale, but rather facilitate the transactions. A list of those individuals willing to sell a kidney and the specific characteristics of each would be maintained by the brokers, similar to the lists of real estate for sale which are maintained by intermediaries in that field. Patients (through their doctors or third-party payers) would consult such lists in their effort to locate a suitable kidney for transplant, much as potential purchasers of real estate consult brokers.

These middlemen would be licensed (or privately certified) both for tracking purposes to deter the illegal harvesting and sale of kidneys and to protect the patient against both fraud and human error. Given our present political-economic culture, in any system actually likely to be implemented, only licensed brokers would be able legally to offer kidneys for sale and these brokers would likely be required to carry insurance and be bondable. They

A Free Market for Kidneys

might form joint ventures with insurance companies in similar manner to the organ procurement agencies that exist today.

It is impossible to know ex ante what the range of prices for kidneys would be, just as it is impossible to know ex ante the market-clearing price of any good. What is certain is that the range of market-clearing prices would adjust to eliminate any shortage or surplus of kidneys.[13] Moreover, because of the increased supply that would be elicited by the free market process, prices would presumably be far less than current shadow prices. As in any market, the price would include the amount paid to the original owner of a kidney; broker expenses including tests, extraction, and postextraction care; transfer and overhead expenses; and normal profits. These elements become a part of the overall price of the kidney transplant, which is controlled by what individual patients, insurance companies, and the government are willing to pay for the procedure.

Appendix

Working (1997, 277) lists four (4) requisites for the success of a futures market:[14]

1. The contract terms and commission charges must be such as to attract appreciable use of the futures contract for merchandising purposes.
2. There must exist a possibility of attracting enough speculation to provide at least a reasonable fluid market.
3. Handlers of the commodity must have reason to make substantial use of the futures contracts as temporary substitutes for merchandising contracts they will make later [fn23]
4. There must exist adequate public recognition of the economic usefulness of the futures market.

fn23. This is 'hedging' according to a definition that I [Working] once proposed ('Hedging Reconsidered,' *Journal of Farm Economics*, Nov. 1953, 35, p. 560); but that definition has not won enough acceptance to allow using the term here with confidence that it will carry the intended meaning.

Hieronymous (1971, 18) provides a list of common characteristics of traded commodities from the FTC:

(1) homogeneity such that commercial units are interchangeable, (2) durability, or minimum degree of perishability, and (3) an adequate supply of the actual commodity flowing to or through the terminal market where the futures market is established. They added that a large volume of trade is obviously not a prerequisite, but is essential to the highest efficiency of a futures market.

He also provides a longer list from Baer and Saxon (1948, ch. 6) that includes the following:

1. Units must be homogeneous. It is a condition precedent for all futures trading that units of commodity be interchangeable. The trader does not buy or sell a contract for a specific or identified grade or specific lot but buys or sells according to established grades and descriptions. The commodity need not be tangible but must be describable.
2. The commodity must be susceptible of standardization and grades. Differences make it impossible for every unit of a commodity to be regarded commercially as the equivalent of every other. If standards can be established so that by inspection and classification the commodity may be divided into a definite number of well defined, uniform grades the units of each grade become homogeneous, the commodity is suitable for futures trading.
3. Supply and demand must be large. The authors use alligator pears as an example of a commodity for which a satisfactory futures market could not be maintained. Both the supply and demand are small, consequently speculators with large financial resources might gain control so that it would cease to be a natural and free market and become merely a battleground for contending speculative factions.
4. The supply must flow naturally to market. Not only must a supply of a commodity be large, but also its flow to world markets must also be substantially free and unhampered by artificial restraint, whether by government or private agencies. They cite several examples of commodities whose supply has been substantially affected by individual government actions and marketing agreements.
5. Supply and demand must be uncertain. If supply and demand are both certain, prices are capable of ready adjustment without the intervention of any organized market machinery. When supply and demand are large, and both uncertain and subject to wide fluctuations from season to season or year to year, a condition exists where the forces of supply and demand on free markets is constantly changing. This interplay of uncertain economic forces produces the constant fluctuations in price that must exist in any successful futures market.
6. The commodity should not be too perishable because the futures contract may call for a delivery of units of the commodity many months into the future. Consequently, the commodity must be capable of being stored at all times and for considerable periods to meet requirements of the market in times of scarcity. A commodity subject to rapid deterioration does not meet this requirement.

The same authors discussed commodities not adaptable to futures trading. Here they list (1) perishable commodities as fresh fruits and vegetables, (2) manufactured goods whose supply can be controlled and whose styles change, and goods where the supply is under "monopoly" control, citing sulphur with the supply controlled by two major producers.

In looking over the list of commodities traded, it is clear that the lists of requirements do not explain why some commodities are traded and others are not nor why the volume of trading ranges so greatly by commodities and over time. Some common characteristics can be identified. First, they are all bulk commodities that can be described and the separate lots of which are more or less interchangeable. Second, none of the commodities has been processed or manufactured to the point of being a product identified with the processes of a particular firm; in general they are bulk commodities but are not, in a strict sense, raw materials. Third, prices are variable and relatively competitively determined.

There are characteristics that are not common to all of the commodities. Most notable is the high degree of perishability of some. Cattle, hogs, iced broilers, and fresh eggs are the most notable examples. For some of the commodities, for example corn, there are many suppliers and many users so that there is no important control of either the supply or use of side by a few firms; the conditions of atomistic competition [are] fairly met. But for others, there is a relatively high degree of concentration as in the case of broilers and soybean oil where a few firms control a high proportion of the supply. Some of the commodities flow through a marketing system of country points, subterminals, and terminal markets to and through a distribution system. But for others the flow of actual product is highly decentralized as in the case of fats and oils, potatoes, and livestock. A centralized market is not a prerequisite to futures trading. Several of the commodities, grains in particular, have supply, demand, and price structures that are much affected by various kinds of governmental programs.

From these considerations it appears to be a mistake to impose a very rigorous set of prerequisite characteristics for eligibility for futures trading. It seems that if a commodity is describable, interchangeable with other similarly described lots, and has a variable price, it may be traded on an organized futures market. Perhaps the appropriate question is not why some commodities are traded but rather why so many others are not.

According to Gray (1978, 239):

The first prerequisite to the success of a futures market is hedging use. There must be reason for commercial buyers and sellers of the commodity to want to substitute futures contracts temporarily for merchandising contracts. The reason may be financing of inventories, forward pricing, or obtaining shopping convenience. Typically, some combination of these reasons will already have given rise to some kind of time contracts. In order to appeal to hedgers, the contract, delivery terms, months, and locations must all conform closely to commercial movement. Secondly, the market must attract speculation, chiefly to offset the tendency for short hedging to exceed long hedging. When these two conditions are met, a market can grow to its optimal level and continue over long periods to provide balanced price estimates, as have the larger markets shown earlier in the diagram.

Based on the foregoing, kidneys do not seem to be a type of good that is conducive to a futures market.

Discussion Questions

1. What does the author suggest is the principal reason for the backlog of patients waiting for transplants?
2. What conclusion does the author reach regarding kidney demand and supply?
3. What are the four possibilities regarding the harvesting of cadaveric kidneys?
4. What are the major sources of kidneys?
5. Why are living individuals so reluctant to donate one kidney?
6. The author has suggested that although options, forward, or futures market for kidneys might be a possibility, it is not likely that any of them will emerge but that certain characteristics are necessary for such markets to exist. What are these characteristics?
7. What does the author believe is likely to emerge in the spot market in kidneys?
8. What factors would affect the price of a kidney sold by the original owner?

Acknowledgments

The authors of the present chapter thank two referees for helpful suggestions and criticisms of an earlier draft.

Endnotes

1. There might be implications for the welfare system based on commodifiable kidneys and other body organs. At present, recipients are not qualified to receive welfare payments if they own cars, homes, and so on. They are required to first sell them and live off the avails, before they are eligible for this program. Will body parts be added to this list under a regime of free contracts in this field?
2. See the appendix for three authors' lists of these requisite characteristics.
3. Because of the nature of the good and the process for physically transplanting the kidney, it is most unlikely that the middleman would take either ownership or possession of the organ; rather, they would act as brokers, matching buyers with sellers for a fee.
4. Given the limited size of the market, it is most likely that there would be only a very few brokerage firms in the industry. In that case, potential sellers of kidneys would probably list their availability and test results with every broker, making multiple searching unnecessary for the buyers' agents (i.e. their doctors or insurance companies). It is possible that a multiple-listing service, as prevails in real estate markets, would arise.
5. This might not apply to those sellers whose kidneys are not likely to be in "high" demand (e.g., in the United States those with type AB blood).
6. Although the incentives of these three would presumably not be identical.

7. It should be noted that a system of certification provided by a private competitive market would be a more efficient means to achieve the same end. See Friedman (1962, ch. 9).
8. In other words, "booty seeking" or "theft."
9. Again, this purpose also could be more efficiently served by a system of competitive private certification. See Friedman (1962, ch. 9).
10. There is no reason to think that absent government regulation brokers would not have recourse to insurance and bonding; in fact, it is virtually certain that they would.
11. Is there a danger that patients might feel that a multipurpose firm, one that treats sick patients and also harvests organs from dead ones to provide to those who need transplants, might stint in the care of the former due to this conflict of interest? If so, and/or to the degree that this is a legitimate fear, then firms that are involved in both these markets would tend to be shunned by the former in their role as paying customers.
12. So as otherwise-inexpensive, illegal drugs fetch very high prices in the necessarily black markets in which they trade precisely because they are illegal, so also do stolen kidneys sell for relatively high prices in their black markets. And just as legalization of drugs would call forth increased production with reduced risk and, therefore, greater supplies at lower prices, such that the illegal trade in drugs would cease to exist, legalized sales of kidneys would have similar effects, including the elimination of theft of kidneys for sale in the black market. That is, the black market demand for stolen kidneys would be nonexistent because people could acquire legal kidneys less expensively and without the risk of criminal penalties.
13. Because the demand curve is truncated at the maximum quantity (Qmax) of kidneys demanded, there exists no true market-clearing price. At the demand price for Qmax a surplus exists that would tend to drive the price down to the supply price at Qmax; however, at Qmax the demand price exceeds the supply price, which would tend to force the price up. The market price might oscillate irregularly between the demand and supply prices. Or the demand price might be reduced by the third-party payers and or the supply price might be driven up because of increased costs associated with attempts by sellers to capture the rents. If either or both of these actions prevailed, eventually, the market might reach a situation where the supply curve intersected the demand curve at the point of truncation. In that case, there would be no more rents to be sought after and the market would clear. However, given that the demands and underlying supply conditions would be in a constant state of flux, such a situation is not likely to long prevail.
14. On this subject, see Working (1977, sec. 4, ch. 2., esp. 277–99).

References

Adams, A. F., A. H. Barnett, and D. L. Kaserman. "Markets of Organs: The Question of Supply." *Contemporary Economics Policy* 17 (April 1999): 147–55.

Anderson, W. L., and A. H. Barnett. "Waiting for Transplants." *The Free Market* 17, no. 4 (1999): 1–2.

Baer, J. B., and O. G. Saxon. *Commodity Exchanges and Futures Trading.* New York: Harper and Brothers, 1948.
Bakken, H. *Futures Trading in Livestock: Origins and Concepts.* Chicago: Chicago Mercantile Exchange, 1970.
Barnett, A. H., T. R. Beard, and D. L. Kaserman. "The Medical Community's Opposition to Organ Markets: Ethics or Economics." *Review of Industrial Organization* 8 (1993): 669–78.
Barnett, A. H., R. D. Blair, and D. L. Kaserman. "Improving Organ Donations: Compensation Versus Markets." *Inquiry* 29 (Fall 1992): 372–78.
Barnett, A. H., and D. L. Kaserman. "The Rush to Transplant and Organ Shortages." *Economic Inquiry* 33 (July 1995): 506–15.
Barnett, W., II. "The Market in Used Human Body Parts." *The Free Market* 6, no. 11 (1988): 5.
Barnett, W., II, M. Saliba, and D. Walker. "A Free Market in Kidneys: Efficient and Equitable." *The Independent Review* 5, no. 3 (2001): 373–85.
Barney, D., Jr., and L. Reynolds. "An Economic Analysis of Transplant Organs." *Atlantic Economic Journal* 17 (September 1989): 12–20.
Blair, R. D., and D. L. Kaserman. "The Economics and Ethics of Alternative Cadaveric Organ Procurement Policies." *Yale Journal on Regulation* 8 (1991): 403–52.
Block, W. "The Case for a Free Market in Body Parts." *The Free Market* 6, no. 3 (1988): 3.
Block, W., R. Whitehead, C. Johnson, M. Davidson, A. White, and S. Chandler. "Human Organ Transplantation: Economic and Legal Issues." *Quinnipiac College School of Law Health Journal* 3 (1999–2000): 87–110.
Burns, J. M. *A Treatise on Markets: Spot, Futures, and Options.* Washington, DC: American Enterprise Institute for Public Policy Research, 1979.
Caplan, A. L. *If I Were a Rich Man Could I Buy a Pancreas? And Other Essays on the Ethics of Health Care.* Bloomington: Indiana University Press, 1992.
Carlstrom, C. T., and C. D. Rollow. "The Rationing of Transplantable Organs: A Troubled Lineup." *Cato Journal* 17 (Fall 1997): 163–77.
DeJong, W., J. Drachman, S. L. Gortmaker, et al. "Options for Increasing Organ Donations: The Potential Role for Financial Incentives, Standardized Hospital Procedures, and Public Education to Promote Family Discussion." *The Milbank Quarterly* 73, no. 3 (1995): 463–79.
Friedman, M. *Capitalism and Freedom.* Chicago: University of Chicago Press, 1962.
The Grain Trade, vol. 5. Washington, DC: Federal Trade Commission, 1920.
Gray, R. W. "Why Does Futures Trading Succeed or Fail: An Analysis of Selected Commodities." In *Readings in Futures Markets, Book III: Views from the Trade,* ed. A. E. Peck, 235–48. Chicago: Board of Trade of the City of Chicago, 1978.
Hansmann, H. "The Economics and Ethics of Markets for Human Organs." *Journal of Health, Politics, and Policy and Law* (Spring 1989): 57–85.
Hieronymous, T. A. *Economics of Futures Trading: For Commercial and Personal Profit.* New York: Commodities Research Bureau, 1971.
Held, P., M. Pauly, R. Bovbjerg, J. Newmann, and O. Salvatierra. "Access to Kidney Transplants." *Archives of Internal Medicine* 148 (1988): 2594–600.
Jonasson, O. "Waiting in Line: Should Selected Patients Ever Be Moved Up?" *Transplantation Proceedings* 21, no. 3 (1989): 3390–94.
Kaserman, D. L., and A. H. Barnett. "An Economic Analysis of Transplant Organs: A Comment and Extension." *Atlantic Economic Journal* 19 (June 1991): 57–63.

Kifner, J. "Selecting Patients When Resources Are Limited: A Study of US Medical Directors of Kidney Dialysis and Transplantation Facilities." *American Journal of Public Health* 78, no. 2 (1988): 144–47.

Kjellstrand, C. "Age, Sex and Race Inequality in Renal Transplantation." *Archives of Internal Medicine* 148, no. 6 (1988): 1305–9.

McKenzie, R. B., and G. Tullock. *The Best of the New World of Economics*. Homewood, IL: Irwin, 1989.

Medicare. *Medicare Coverage of Kidney Dialysis and Kidney Transplant Services: A Supplement to Your Medicare Handbook*, Publication No. HCFA 594B. Washington, DC: Government Printing Office, 1995.

Medicare. *Your Medicare Handbook 1995*, Publication No. HCFA 10050. Washington, DC: Government Printing Office, 1995.

Organ Selling. http://www.pitt.edu/htk/our.htm.

Peck, A. E. *Readings in Futures Markets, Book III: Views from the Trade*. Chicago: Board of Trade of the City of Chicago, 1978.

Prince, Dennis. "Organ for Sale—Not Wurlitzer." September 3, 1999. http://www.auction-watch.com/awdaily/dailynews/1-090399.html.

Richards, J. R. "Nephrarious Goings On: Kidney Sales and Moral Arguments." *The Journal of Medicine and Philosophy* 21, no. 4 (August 1996): 375–416.

Rottenberg, S. "The Production and Exchange of Used Body Parts." *Towards Liberty* 2 (1971): 322–33.

Schwindt, R., and A. R. Vining. "Proposal for a Future Delivery Market for Transplant Organs." *Journal of Health Policy and Law* 11 (Fall 1986): 483–500.

Scientific Registry of Transplant Recipients. 2002. http://ustransplant.org/tables/K1200111-01.html.

Sells, R. A. "Resolving the Conflict in Traditional Ethics Which Arises from Our Demand for Organs." *Transplantation Proceedings* 25, no. 6 (December 1993): 2983–84.

United Network of Organ Sharing. May 22, 2002. http://www.unos.org.

U.S. Congress. "National Organ Transplant Act." In *Life from Death: The Organ and Tissue Donation and Transplantation Source Book, with Forms*, ed. P. G. Williams. Oak Park, IL: The P. Gaines Co., 1984.

Vining, A. R., and R. Schwindt. "Have a Heart: Increasing the Supply of Transplant Organs for Infants and Children." *Journal of Policy Analysis and Management* 7, no. 4 (1988): 706–10.

Working, H. "Economic Functions of Futures Markets." In *Futures Trading in Livestock: Origins and Concepts*, ed. H. Bakken. Chicago: Chicago Mercantile Exchange, 1970.

———. *Selected Writings of Holbrook Working*, comp. A. E. Peck. Chicago: Board of Trade of the City of Chicago, 1977.

A Medical, Ethical, and Philosophical Perspective

Medical Tourism: Organ Trafficking and Kidney Transplantation. This research paper has been written by a physician with years of experience as a nephrologist who has concluded that, despite the great success of kidney transplantation, there is a fair amount of frustration because of an inability to provide enough kidneys to address the need for a rapidly growing population of patients with end-stage renal disease (ESRD). In the United States, 65,000 patients are on the waiting list and 3,000 of them die yearly while on being on such a list. Because of this sad reality, organ sale from commercial living donors (CLDs) or vendors has now become evident. The author closely examines cultural barriers associated with kidney transplantation along with organ trafficking and transplant tourism, its extent, developing laws and international alliances, equitable reimbursement for donors as well as protections for them, promising medical practices that are emerging in this area, and the kinds of financial incentives that should be made available to promote kidney donation.

Body Values: The Case against Compensating for Transplant Organs. The researchers discuss a proposal to compensate families for the transplantable organs of deceased family members. They suggest that such a proposal assumes the body is dissociable from the self and can be treated as property. The researchers have also examined recent legislative proposals that would deal with this issue and discuss legislative proposals in Congress and recommendations adopted by the American Medical Association, the United Network for Organ Sharing, and the American Society of Transplant Surgeons.

Autonomy, Constraining Options, and Organ Sales. The researcher argues that although there continues to be a chronic shortage of transplant organs, the suggestion that we should try to alleviate it through allowing a current market in them continues to be morally condemned, usually on the grounds that such a market would undermine the autonomy of those who would participate in it as vendors. Against this objection, others have argued that such markets would *enhance* the autonomy of the vendors through providing them with more options, thus enabling them to exercise a greater degree of control over their bodies.

Markets and the Needy: Organ Sales or Aid? The researcher believes organ shortages have become more acute, and as a result the support for a market in organs has steadily increased. While many have argued for such a market, it is Gerald Dworkin who most persuasively defends its ethics. As Dworkin points out, there are two possibilities here—a futures market and a current market. The researcher follows Dworkin in focusing on a current market in the sale of organs from living donors, as this is generally considered to be the most difficult to justify. One of the most pressing concerns here is that such a market will exploit the poor.

Selling Bits and Pieces of Humans to Make Babies: *The Gift of the Magi Revisited.* Reproductive medicine, a sector of a health care system increasingly captured by the demands of the marketplace, is enmeshed in a drive to sell certain human bits and pieces, such as gametes, cells, fetal eggs, and fetal ovaries, for reproductive purposes. The ethical objections are raised by Kant and Radin to the sale of human organs. They believe this is incompatible with human dignity and worth. Moreover, they assert that such sales nullify the reproductive paradigm, irretrievably replacing it with a manufacturing paradigm. This represents a change in kind, not just of degree, in the way that we view our capacity to generate children, and it destroys our concept of reproduction as an essentially human activity. In the face of a struggle to retain those common ethical values at the foundation of reproductive medicine, this form of commodification of the human body should be viewed as ethically unacceptable.

Medical Tourism
Organ Trafficking and Kidney Transplantation

8

SNEZANA (ANA) MIJOVIC-DAS, MD, FASN
Department of Nephrology, Albany Medical College, Albany, New York

Contents

Introduction	117
Cultural Barriers to Kidney Transplantation	118
Organ Trafficking and Transplant Tourism	118
Why We *Should* Oppose Organ Trafficking	119
The Extent of Organ Trafficking	120
Consequences to the Vendors	121
What Are the Alternatives? The Amsterdam Forum and the Iranian Model	121
Developing an Organ Donation System	122
Promising Practices	122
Financial Incentives to Promote Donation	122
Developing Laws and International Alliances	123
Developing Sensitivity for Human Rights	123
Reimbursing the Donor and Other Protection Measures	124
Conclusion	124
Appendix A: Medical Tourism: Organ Trafficking and Kidney Transplantation	125
Pera Pop of Belgrade: A Case Study	125
Ana Mijovic-Das MD, Nephrology, AMC	
Discussion Questions	127
Endnotes	127
References	129

Introduction

Kidney transplantation is a medical miracle of the twentieth century. It has prolonged and improved the lives of hundreds and thousands of patients worldwide. Our better understanding of immune system as well as the availability of effective immunosuppressive therapy together with successful surgical procedures have made organ transplantation almost a routine medical procedure. It is the best way to treat patients with end-stage renal disease (ESRD) who otherwise will spend the rest of their lives on dialysis if organ transplantation is not available. Altruistic donation of organs and tissues, "the gift of life," has been the main principle of transplantation since its beginning.

Cultural Barriers to Kidney Transplantation

Despite the great success of kidney transplantation, there is a fair amount of frustration both in the transplant community and in the general public because of our inability to provide enough kidneys to address the needs of a rapidly growing population of patients with ESRD. The ongoing debate over the most effective response to organ shortage both in the United States and internationally is often faced with the conclusion that the current system intended to be based on altruism has failed and only the system of financial incentives continues to thrive. Very often in this debate, we tend to forget the important factors such as wide cultural differences in organ donation practice in various regions in the United States and outside of it.

Living related donations, living unrelated donations, deceased donations after brain death, extended criteria donations, or donations after cardiac death are all accepted concepts with wide inconsistency in practice because of cultural differences.

Both Japan[1] and Italy[2] have very long waiting lists. In Japan there is reluctance to accept brain death criteria, and only recently has it been permitted by law. In Italy, there is a reluctance to approach the family and less than 10 percent of transplants are from living donors.

In the United States, kidney transplantation from biologically unrelated living donors has become common and accounts for about 20 percent[3] of all living donor transplants, while in Europe such transplantation is not very common and most unrelated donation in Europe is from spouses, while in the United States spouses account for only 30 percent of unrelated donors.[4] For example, in Portugal unrelated living donation is illegal. Variations present even within the country are difficult to explain. In the United States, the rates of living and deceased donations vary from state to state, living unrelated donation is common in some centers and uncommon in others, and variations are present in extended criteria donations and in the use of kidneys from donors whose death was determined by cardiac criteria.

Organ Trafficking and Transplant Tourism

In the United States alone, despite efforts to increase the number of available kidneys for transplantation, 65,000 patients are on the waiting list for kidney transplantation. It has been estimated that a shortage of available kidneys is largely responsible for the deaths of at least 3,000 patients in the United States on the waiting list every year.[5] Because of this sad reality, organ sale from commercial living donors (CLDs) or vendors has now become evident. China, India, Pakistan, Egypt, Brazil, the Philippines, Moldavia, Romania, and Colombia are known to be "hot spots" for organ trafficking.[6]

Transplant tourism is defined as the purchase of a transplant organ abroad; this includes access to an organ while bypassing the laws, rules, or processes of any or all countries involved (United Network of Organ Sharing, or UNOS).[7]

Transplant tourism may be legal and appropriate when a recipient and donor pair travels from countries without transplant services to countries where organ transplantation is performed, or if a person travels across borders to donate or receive a transplant from a relative.

Why We *Should* Oppose Organ Trafficking

It is global injustice to use the poor segment of a population as a source for organ donation in exchange for payment ranging from $1,000 to $5,000, while the brokers take from wealthy recipients $100,000 to $200,000.[8]

One example of a kidney trade is the presence of "kidney colonies," such as one in Tamil Nadu in India where poverty is extremely high and kidneys serve as financial help. In this Indian state, over 5,000 people have donated their kidneys for financial survival. Based on a special survey, one or more occupants in 10 percent of the households have sold a kidney, although financial gain obtained by selling a kidney does not lead to long-term benefits.[9] It was reported that 6 years after donation, the percentage of paid donors below the poverty line increased from 51 to 71 percent, and more than 80 percent reported deterioration in health.

Physicians who do not take part in organ transplants now have responsibilities for the medical care of those recipients when they come back to their own countries after getting the kidney transplant from an unknown vendor. Very often, recipients come to the doctor's office with poor documentation about the operation and an unknown risk of donor-transmitted infections such as hepatitis, tuberculosis, or malignancy. Transplant tourists, when they return to their own countries, can present a public threat for transmissible infections such as avian flu, tuberculosis, schistosomiasis, acute hepatitis, and HIV. Transplant tourists have a more complex posttransplantation course with a higher incidence of acute rejection and severe, infectious complications, although kidney function for those who survived was quite acceptable.[10]

The clinical outcome of ten patients who underwent kidney transplantation outside the United States (all but one had a living donor) between

September 2002 and June 2006 was retrospectively reviewed at the University of Minnesota Medical Center. Kidney function and graft survival were generally good. Major problems were incomplete perioperative information communicated to the posttransplant center and a high incidence of posttransplant infections. The reports of several other studies present similar findings.

Health care providers should see the transplant tourists when they return to their countries, but those from the United States who receive kidneys outside the country are not eligible for government (Medicare and Medicaid) or pharmaceutical assistance. In Israel, the government prohibits the insurance reimbursement of transplant costs for Israelis who undergo a purchased organ transplant in countries where buying and selling organs are illegal.[11]

The Extent of Organ Trafficking

Countries that have facilitated organ trafficking such as Pakistan and the Philippines do not give precise data about the number of foreign patients who travel to these countries for transplants. However, newspapers in the Philippines from February 2007 reveal over 3,000 kidney sales to foreigners. The Cebu Province in the Philippines is calling for transplant tourists to increase the national commercial transplants.[12] At least 2,000 kidney transplants have been performed in Pakistan to transplant tourists according to data from Sindh Institute of Urology and Transplantation in that country.[13] It is estimated that Egypt performs at least 500 kidney transplants a year, and the majority of these transplants are performed with kidneys purchased from CLDs.[14] There are some reports that transplant tourists have received kidney transplantation from tsunami victims in Chennai, India.

At a recent World Health Organization (WHO) regional meeting that took place in Slovenia, the representative from Moldavia reported the requests of Israeli physicians to open transplantation practice in Moldavia. The request was denied, but no measures against insurance companies have been initiated to stop Israeli medical tourists from getting transplants in Moldavia. According to WHO statistics, at least 100 nationals from countries such as Saudi Arabia, Taiwan, Malaysia, and South Korea go abroad for commercial kidney transplants. At least 20 nationals from countries such as Australia, Japan, Oman, Morocco, India, Canada, and the United States travel as transplant tourists for trafficking organs.

Striking figures are coming from China: in 2006 there were 11,000 transplants, and among them 8,000 kidney transplants were obtained from executed prisoners (10 percent of the total number of annual organ transplants done in programs of organ trafficking). Of note is that most recently, China has accepted the Human Transplantation Act and in 2007 the number of transplants to foreign patients decreased by 50 percent. Nevertheless, the reduction of Chinese activity led to increase in the Philippine activity in organ trafficking.[15] According to U.S. data, 119 U.S. citizens from 55 transplant centers in 26 states received kidney transplants in 18 foreign countries after a median of 1.5 years spent on the U.S. waiting list.

Consequences to the Vendors

A Pakistani study of 239 vendors revealed that the majority of CLDs sold their kidneys in order to pay a debt (93 percent); 85 percent reported no economic improvement in their lives.[16] Egypt is another country where an extensive work-up of victims of organ trade was conducted, and a significant deterioration in health condition in 80 percent of cases of those who donated a kidney was reported. This is a reflection of poor donor screening as well as preexisting health conditions of CLDs. The majority of them reported that they have been working in labor-intensive jobs[17] and that a kidney sale does not solve the problem of their existence, and 81 percent of CLDs spent their money in 5 months post nephrectomy.

CLDs do not like to reveal their identity: 91 percent reported social isolation after their donation, 85 percent were unwilling to be known publicly as an organ vendor, and 94 percent regretted their donation.

The studies in Pakistan and Egypt are similar with findings in India, Iran, and the Philippines regarding the deterioration of health condition of CLDs, long-term financial disadvantages, social rejection, and regrets about their commercial donation.[18]

What Are the Alternatives? The Amsterdam Forum and the Iranian Model

As an international community, we need to fulfill the goals of the Amsterdam Forum, and provide ethical protocols for donor selection and obtain long-term care for live kidney donors.[19] A cash payment system targets the poor, privileges those who can pay, undermines altruistic donation, and has escaped government regulations. The "Iranian model" is based on compensated, government-regulated, living–unrelated donor renal transplant program. As a result, the number of kidney transplants increased, and in 1999 the transplant waiting list was completely eliminated.

Currently, Iran has no waiting list and more that 50 percent of patients with ESRD in the country are living with a functioning graft. Foreigners are neither permitted to get a kidney transplant from Iranian living donors nor permitted to volunteer as a kidney donors for Iranian patients. An argument against this model is that kidney donors are poor and illiterate, while most recipients are educated and rich. This model includes a lack of medical coverage for donors beyond one year following the transplantation.

Developing an Organ Donation System

Each country should establish a system of deceased organ donation to increase the donor pool. In that respect, the balance between culture and religion has to be addressed; the public should be educated on the benefits of organ donation, especially in Islamic and other countries where religion influences most people's beliefs. Can we learn from each other's experiences in transplantation? Can we recognize the national and cultural barriers and cross them successfully as we did with other barriers in transplantation?

Promising Practices

In Spain, national investment in transplantation as the best treatment of ESRD has led to the world's most effective organ donation program; transplantation rates are the highest in the world, and the waiting time for transplants is relatively short. In the United Kingdom, living donor transplantation, which was once uncommon, now accounts for more than 40 percent of all kidney donations with an increase of 24 percent during 2005–2006 alone. In the countries participating in Euro-Transplant, a program that involves a rapid placement of kidney from old donors to older recipients has been fairly successful in using kidneys that might have been discarded otherwise.

Performance of ABO incompatible transplantation, once regarded as a dangerous procedure, has been tried in Japan in response to a lack of deceased donor organs. Now it is routinely practiced with excellent results in some centers in the United States. Non-heart-beating donation, which was not accepted in many countries, has become a main source of deceased donors' kidneys in Japan and is now considered as a promising resource.

Financial Incentives to Promote Donation

A number of transplant experts state that providing financial incentives to donors as an alternative to altruistic organ donation needs careful reconsideration. The establishment of a "single-purchaser system," or selling of an organ by an individual to a state agency, was recommended. For example, in the United Kingdom, the National Health Service is to buy kidneys from donors, and no direct interaction between donors and recipients is allowed. This system has many problems, and there is no doubt that those who are poor will be selling their organs and will be disadvantaged by the state instead of by an individual person. It is likely that financial compensation will be different in different countries for donors, and it would further promote and encourage "transplant tourism."

In 1988, a compensated and regulated living–unrelated donor renal transplant program was adopted in Iran. The government pays for medical and surgical fees. After renal transplantation, the living unrelated donor receives an award, health insurance for one year, and a gift of about US$1,200. This is usually not enough, and recipients are to provide more gifts, or, if the recipient is poor, charitable organizations provide such gifts.[20] The Iranian model has significant ethical problems and cannot be accepted broadly. The donors are usually poor, and they stay poor after donating organs, which results in long-term dissatisfaction among many of them. At the same time, there is a lack of care for donors as health insurance provides care for one year only.[21]

Developing Laws and International Alliances

The alliance of International Society of Nephrology and other professional societies, with WHO to influence health authorities at the World Health Assembly, is needed to fight organ trafficking. Countries with poor regulations and law structures such as Pakistan, the Philippines, Egypt, and some others should ask governments to play a central role in establishing laws on transplants. Ministries of health should have an essential role in observing tightly the transplant practices in order to improve the global situation of organ trafficking and transplant tourism.

Developing Sensitivity for Human Rights

In 2004, the WHO asked its members to take action to protect the poorest and most vulnerable groups from transplant tourism and sale of tissues and organs. In the spring of 2008, the Transplantation Society and the International Society of Nephrology invited 150 representatives of scientific and medical bodies from around the world to attend the International Summit on Transplant Tourism and Organ Trafficking in Istanbul. The Istanbul Declaration on organ trafficking and transplant tourism, based on the principles of the Universal Declaration of Human Rights, was accepted. The Istanbul Declaration clearly states in Principle Six that "organ trafficking and transplant tourism violate the principles of equity, justice and respect for human dignity and should be prohibited." According to the WHO guiding principles, organs, tissues, and cells should be donated freely and without monetary reward. The sale of organ for transplantation by living persons or by the next of kin of deceased persons should be prohibited.

Reimbursing the Donor and Other Protection Measures

Prohibition of selling and buying organs, tissues, and cells does not prevent reimbursing the expenses that the donor has incurred in the process of donation, including loss of income, or the payments of other expenses related to recovering or processing the donation as stated in the Istanbul Declaration. Principle Six of the Istanbul Declaration says that "comprehensive reimbursement of documented cost of donating an organ does not constitute a payment for an organ, but is rather part of legitimate cost of treating the recipient." This reimbursement should be made by the party responsible for paying the cost of treating the transplant recipient such as a government health department or health insurance. Reimbursement for approved cost should be paid directly to those who are providing the service—the hospital providing the donor's medical care. Reimbursement of the donor's lost income and out-of-pocket expenses should be administered by the agency handling the transplant rather than paid directly from the recipient to the donor.

Pharmaceutical companies involved in transplantation as well as health insurance companies should give their support to the global mission to fight organ trafficking. The international transplant community should clearly convey the message that organ markets to exploit the poor and the vulnerable should not be present, and programs to assure donors' safety and obtain social benefits to address donors' needs must be developed. The legacy of transplantation is not to make poor victims of organ transplantation and medical tourism more desperate and impoverished, but rather it should be a celebration of the gift of health by one individual to another.

Conclusion

Despite great success of kidney transplantation there is a fair amount of frustration because of inability to provide enough kidneys to address the need for a rapidly growing population of patients with ESRD. In the USA 65,000 patients are on waiting lists and 3,000 die yearly while on waiting lists. The organ sale from CLDs has been has been widespread; 5–10 percent of nearly 70,000 kidneys transplants annually are obtained by organ trafficking. Transplant centers in "hot countries" have been well known to encourage the sale of organs to the tourist recipients from the client countries. Alternative programs must be developed to make more organs available and to provide good care of donors, their needs, and social benefits.

Engaging governments to make laws on transplantation and Ministries of Health to control transplant practices is essential to improve the global situation of organ trafficking/transplant tourism. The alliance of international professional organizations such as International Society of Nephrology and other societies, all working with WHO, in order to influence health authorities at World Health Assembly to fight the organ trafficking/medical tourism is a must. Selling and buying of organs should be prohibited and only be donated freely and without monetary reward. The entire international community should support the global fight against organ trafficking and illicit medical tourism. However, the prohibition of selling and buying organs should not affect reimbursement to donors for documented costs, including loss of income or expenses related to cost of recovering and medical expenses incurred for post discharge care.

Appendix A: Medical Tourism: Organ Trafficking and Kidney Transplantation

Pera Pop of Belgrade: A Case Study

Ana Mijovic-Das MD, Nephrology, AMC

I would like to share with you one very illustrative and pathetic story that I came across at the airport as I was traveling to Malta. While I was going through a weekly periodical at the airport, I came to know about a person, known as Pera Pop, who most recently gave in a popular magazine an *ad*, "I am Pera Pop. I am 30 years old and my Blood group is B +. I am selling a kidney to any interested party for 100 000 Euros (150 000 US dollars)."

He left his email address for a contact. The journalist who wrote the story, Borko Pavicevic (*Ilustrovana Politika*, April, 29, 2010), contacted Pera Pop and interviewed him.

Pera Pop told him that the world's economy crisis has affected him a lot. He lost his house, car, and job. He took a large amount of money from the bank and from private investors. He lost the business, and he was left with debts of about 100,000 euros. "I have heard that one can live without one kidney, and that is why I have decided to sell one to recover the financial loss," said Pera Pop to the journalist who talked to him. Pera Pop said that he had received about a hundred responses, but he decided to act on two of them, one coming from England and the other from Russia.

Several weeks after I read this story, I decided to contact the author of the text and hear whether he had heard about Pera Pop recently. The newspaper reporter contacted Pera Pop, and he refused to talk in a microphone, but he wanted to put on paper his experience and he wanted me to share his story with this audience. Pera Pop began his story first about losing several hundred pounds through the internet. As a matter of fact, a woman by the name of Dianah Brimm emailed him and, via dianahbrimm@yahoo.com, presented herself as a physician from London Renal Transplant Centre, a very famous European center for the transplantation of kidneys. She contacted him and offered 100,000 euros for his kidney.

At her request, he sent to her personal account several hundred pounds in order to procure a visa for his coming to England. After having done this, Pera Pop was supposed to get the papers necessary for obtaining a visa for entering the United Kingdom. According to the agreement, he was supposed to travel to London for transplantation, and just before the procedure he was supposed to have 100,000 euros deposited in his bank account. Dr. Dianah Brimm never called him back after he sent the requested amount of money. "I felt terrible," lamented Pera Pop, and he does so whenever he thinks of that time. "It looks like I was insane. Before I sent this money to England, I checked the list of doctors working in London Renal Transplant Centre and there was no name of Dr. Dianah Brimm.

"Unfortunately, instead of concluding that this is a lie, I, out of my poverty, wanted to believe that it might be the administrative mistake so her name was omitted, and I sent my money to England and I never got it back."

But this is not the worst that has happened to him, continued Pera Pop; next he told his story of the second offer, which came from Russia. "Once I realized that nothing would happen out of my trip to England, I had established contact and I got in touch with the man known as Alex Dergaus [livingdonors@yahoo.com]," continued Pera Pop.

He thought that with him he somehow had a better way of communication. Alex first requested from Pera Pop a copy of his passport together with documents regarding his blood type. After Pera did the first steps, Alex explained to him how the "mission" would take place. Pera would come on his own money to the place of designation of which he would be informed. He would be received by Dergaus's assistant, who would put him in a hotel while he would wait to come to the hospital where he would be tested for HIV/Hep C. Once when he was cleared with his results, Pera Pop with other donors from different parts of the world would travel to New Zealand, where transplantation would take place. Pera needed to buy his own ticket to come to the first destination, where initial evaluation would happen. He was also responsible for a plane ticket to go to New Zealand.

After he got the instructions, Pera Pop had started his preparations. Meanwhile via Skype he talked several times with Alex, who at the last moment told Pera Pop that the first place to come to was Moldova.

"I was very excited while I was leaving Belgrade Airport," he continued the story, "and could not believe even in the worst dream of mine what had happened to me. Once I landed in Moldova, I was received by one young man who immediately recognized me most likely because I sent to him the photograph of mine during our correspondence. He brought me to one old and dilapidated house, where I saw many people like me. I was given food and water, and I was told to get rest. I do not recall anything else and how I fell asleep. Now I know for sure that 'something' was in the food."

Pera woke up out of town in an open field. It took him some time to recall finding out what had happened after he felt a little clearer in his head. His pockets were without money, and the big scar at the lower part of his back confirmed to him that money was not the only thing that he lost. He lost his kidney as well.

Now, Pera Pop has one kidney instead of two. He has also an old debt that is even bigger because of interest. Besides, he has trauma that he never will be able to resolve, and his organ is "with people from Russia." Thus, he finished his sad story,

"I am Pera Pop, born in Belgrade, Serbia, 30 years old, blood type B+."

Discussion Questions

1. What conclusion does the author reach when comparing a system of altruism with one that provides financial incentives as it relates to organ donations?
2. What locations are known as "hot spots" for transplant tourism?
3. Why did the author conclude that the medical community should oppose organ trafficking?
4. What is an example of a "kidney colony"?
5. What are the kinds of infectious and other related problems that can be created by transplant tourists once they return to their countries?
6. What are the consequences to the vendors of kidney transplantation?
7. What are the elements of the Iranian model of kidney transplantation?
8. What are some of the most promising international practices as they relate to organ donations?
9. What is Principle Six in the Istanbul Declaration?

Endnotes

1. K. Tanabe, "Cultural Barriers to Kidney Transplantation: A New Frontier," Gabriel Danovitch, Forum by Lippincott Williams and Wilkins, 2007. Retrieved from http://www.eurotransplant.nl .
2. G. P. Segoloni, et al., "Living Donor Kidney Transplant in Italy: Is Underutilization Justified?" *Transplant Proc* 36 (April 2004): 473.
3. G. M. Danovitch, et al., "Current Status of Kidney and Pancreas Transplantation in the United States, 1994–2003," 5 *Am J Transplant* (2005): 904; and Tanabe, "Cultural Barriers to Kidney Transplantation."

4. Tanabe, "Cultural Barriers to Kidney Transplantation."
5. E. A. Friedman and A. L. Friedman, "Payment for Donor Kidneys: Pros and Cons," *Kidney International* 69 (2006): 960–62, cited from A. Lita, "Organ Trafficking: A Time for Action," *Kidney International* 74 (2008): 839–40. Retrieved from doi:10.1038/ki2008.389.
6. A. Lita, "Organ Trafficking Poses Global Challenges," *Humanist Network News* (12 September 2007), cited from Lita, "Organ Trafficking." Retrieved from http//humaniststudies.org/enews/?id=314&article=5.
7. "UNOS Board Further Addresses Transplant Tourism," June 26, 2007. Cited from D. A. Budiani-Saberi and F. L. Delmonico, "Organ Trafficking and Transplant Tourism: A Commentary on the Global Realities," *American Journal of Transplantation* 8 (2008): 925–29. Retrieved from http://unos.org/news/newsDetail.asp?id+891.
8. N. K. Clare, "Organ Trafficking and Transplantation Pose New Challenges," *Bulletin of the World Health Organ* 82, no. 9 (2004): 715, cited from Lita, "Organ Trafficking."
9. D. J. Rothman, et al., "The Bellagio Task Force Report on Transplantation, Bodily Integrity and the International Traffic of Organs," *Transplant Proc* 29 (1997): 2739–45, cited from Lita, "Organ Trafficking."
10. C. Y. Sun et al., "Commercial Cadaveric Transplant: An Ethical Rather than Medical Issue," *Clin Transplant* 20 (2006): 340. Retrieved from http://www.uptodate.com.
11. D. A. Budiani-Saberi and F. L Delmonico, "Organ Trafficking and Transplant Tourism: A Commentary on the Global Realities," *American Journal of Transplantation* 8 (2008): 925–29.
12. "RP Admits Rampant Traffic in Human Organs," cited in Budiani-Saberi and Delmonico, "Organ Trafficking and Transplant Tourism." Retrieved from http://www.manilatimes.net/national/2007/feb/07/yehey/top.stories/20070207top1.html.
13. "Delmonico Visit to Karachi," Pakistan, January 2007, cited in Budiani-Saberi and Delmonico, "Organ Trafficking and Transplant Tourism."
14. A. E. El-Agroudy et al., "Long Term Follow Up of Living Kidney Donors: A Longitudinal Study," *BJU International* 100 (2007): 1351–55, cited in Budiani-Saberi and Delmonico, "Organ Trafficking and Transplant Tourism."
15. Budiani-Saberi and Delmonico, "Organ Trafficking and Transplant Tourism."
16. A. Naqvi, "A Socio-Economic Survey of Kidney Vendors in Pakistan," *Transplant International* 20 (2007): 909–92, cited in Budiani-Saberi and Delmonico, "Organ Trafficking and Transplant Tourism."
17. D. Budiani, "Consequences of Living Kidney Donors in Egypt" (presentation at the Middle East Society on Organ Transplants, Kuwait, November 2006), cited in Budiani-Saberi and Delmonico, "Organ Trafficking and Transplant Tourism."
18. Madhav Goyal, et al., "Economic and Health Consequences of Selling a Kidney in India," *JAMA* 288 (2002): 1589–93, cited in Budiani–Saberi and Delmonico, "Organ Trafficking and Transplant Tourism."
19. Ibid.

20. "A Report of Amsterdam Forum on the Care of the Live Kidney Donor: Data and Medical Guidelines," *Transplantation* 7916, suppl. (2005): 553–66, cited in Budiani-Saberi and Delmonico, "Organ Trafficking and Transplant Tourism."
21. Ahad J. Ghods and Shekoufeh Savaj, "Iranian Model of Paid and Regulated Living: Unrelated Kidney Donation," *American Society of Nephrology* 1 (2006): 1136–45.

References

Alam, Awatif Ali. "Public Opinion on Organ Donation in Saudi Arabia." *Saudi Journal of Kidney Disease and Transplantation* 18, no. 1 (2007): 54–59.

Budiani-Saberi, D. A., and F. L. Delmonico. "Organ Trafficking and Transplant Tourism; A Commentary on the Global Realities." *American Journal of Transplantation* 8 (2008): 925–29.

Canales, M. T., B. L. Kasiske, and M. E. Rosenberg. "Transplant Tourism: Outcomes of United States Residents Who Undergo Kidney Transplantation Overseas." *Clinical Transplantation* 82, no. 12 (27 December 2006): 1658–61.

Costa, Alessandro Nanni, J. M. Castellvì, i Simón, Antonio G. Spagnolo, Nunziata Comoretto, Jean Laffitte, Håkan Gäbel, et al. "A Colloquium on the Congress A Gift for Life: Considerations on Organ Donation." *Transplantation* 88, no. 7S (15 October 2009): S108–S158.

Daar, Abdallah S. "The World Health Organization Resolution on Human Organ Transplantation: Will It Result in Action?" *Transplantation* 79, no. 6 (27 March 2006): 641–42.

Danovitch, Gabriel. "Cultural Barriers to Kidney Transplantation: A New Frontier." *Transplantation* 84, no. 4 (27 August 2007): 462–63.

"The Declaration of Istanbul on Organ Trafficking and Transplant Tourism." *Kidney International* 74 (2008): 854–59.

Delmonico, F. L. "The International Realities of Live Donor Kidney Transplantation." *Kidney International* 75 (2009): 1003–5.

Ghods, Ahad, and Shekoufeh Savaj. "Iranian Model of Paid and Regulated Living-Unrelated Kidney Donation." *Clinical Journal of American Society of Nephrology* 1, no. 6 (2006): 1136–45.

Horvat, L. D., S. Z. Shariff, and A. X. Garg. "Global Trends in the Rates of Living Kidney Donation." *Kidney International* 75 (2009): 1088–98.

Lorber, M. "High Volume Kidney Transplantation in a Developing Economy." *Transplantation* 81, no. 11 (15 June 2006): 1521–22.

Merion, R. M., A. D. Barnes, M. Lin, V. B. Ashby, V. McBride, E. Ortiz-Rios, J. C. Welch, et al. "Transplants in Foreign Countries among Patients Removal from the US Transplant Waiting List." *American Journal of Transplantation* 8, 4 part 2 (2008): 988–96.

Nöel, L. "The Data on Transplantation in Saudi Arabia Are Complex and Require Additional Framework for Interpretation." *Kidney International* 76 (2009): 914.

Pavicevic, Borko. "A Kidney for 100 Euros." *Ilustrovana Politika*, 29 April 2010.

Port, F. K., R. M. Merion, E. C. Roys, and R. A. Wolfe. "Trends in Organ Donation and Transplantation in the United States, 1997–2006." *American Journal of Transplantation* 8, part 2 (2008): 911–21.

Reed, A. I., R. M. Merion, J. P. Roberts, G. B. Klitmalm, M. M. Abecassis, K. M. Olthoff, and A. N. Langnas. "The Declaration of Istanbul: Review and Commentary by the American Society of Transplant Surgeons Ethics Committee and Executive Committee." *American Journal of Transplantation* 9, no. 11 (2009): 2466–69.

Rodriquez-Iturbe, B. "Organ Trafficking: A Time for Action." *Kidney International* 74, no. 7 (2008): 839–40.

Starzl, T. L. Terperman, D. Sutherland, H. Sollinger, J. Roberts, C. Miller, R. Merion, et al. "Transplant Tourism and Unregulated Black Market Trafficking of Organs." *American Journal of Transplantation* 9 (2009): 1484.

Sun, C-Y., C-C. Lee, C-T. Chang, C-C. Hung, and M-S. Wu. "Commercial Cadaveric Renal Transplant: An Ethical Rather Than Medical Issue." *Clinical Transplant* 20, no. 3 (2006): 340–45.

Sung, R. S., J. Galloway, J. E. Tuttle-Newhall, T. Mone, R. Laeng, C. E. Freise, and P. S. Rao. "Organ Donation and Utilization in the United States, 1997–2006." *American Journal of Transplantation* 8, part 2 (2008): 922–34.

Tilney, N. L. "A Statement from the Transplantation Society against Organ Trafficking and Commerce in Organs." *Transplantation* 85, no. 8 (27 April 2008): 1067.

Tilney, N. L., J. Murray, R. Thistlethwaite, D. Norman, F. Delmonico, D. Hanto, A. Leichtman, et al. "Promotion of Altruistic Donation." *Transplantation* 88, no. 6 (27 September 2009): 847.

Wigmore, Stephen, and John L. R. Forsythe. "Incentives to Promote Organ Donation." *Transplantation* 77, no. 1 (2004): 159–61.

Body Values
The Case against Compensating for Transplant Organs[*]

9

DONALD JORALEMON, PhD
*Anthropology Department, Smith College,
Northampton, Massachusetts*

PHIL COX, PhD
Philosophy Department, University of Massachusetts at Dartmouth

Contents

Commodification	133
Reason and Rescue	135
Science and Superstition	137
Discussion Questions	138
Endnotes	139

The issue of financial compensation for organ donation is back on center stage as a result of legislative proposals in U.S. Congress and recommendations adopted by the American Medical Association (AMA), the United Network for Organ Sharing (UNOS), and the American Society of Transplant Surgeons (ASTS). Recently introduced congressional bills relating to organ donation include two that would authorize tax credits for cadaveric donations.[1] Another bill, by some readings, would grant authority to the Secretary of Health and Human Services to override the prohibition against donor compensation in the National Organ Transplantation Act of 1984 so as to support pilot studies assessing the impact of moderate incentives (such as funeral benefits) on donor rates.[2]

The AMA's House of Delegates, at its annual meeting in June 2002, approved a recommendation from the organization's Council on Ethical and Judicial Affairs to encourage pilot studies of compensation for cadaveric donations.[3] The studies would have to include consultations with the population affected, their methods would have to pass scientific muster and be

---

[*] First published in *Hastings Center Report* 33 (1) 27–33, 2003.

approved by oversight bodies, and they could use only "incentives of moderate value and at the lowest level that can be reasonably expected to increase organ donation."[4] The studies would involve only cadaveric donations, not donations from live donors, and they would not sidestep the present organ allocation system (as governed by UNOS). UNOS and ASTS quickly responded to the AMA action with supporting resolutions.[5]

The AMA proposal is based on a utilitarian ethic that is especially clear in the following passage: "Whether or not [incentives] are ethical depends upon the balance of benefits and harms that result from them."[6] A number of opponents agreed with past AMA President Lonnie Bristow when she said, "Please do not be seduced by the idea that the ends justify the means."[7] Rex Greene, an oncologist and a delegate to the AMA's House of Delegates from California, made a similar point when he said, "I would state that, no matter what the outcomes of these studies, it does not answer ethical questions."[8] Despite this strong opposition and in the face of a negative recommendation from the Reference Committee on Amendments to Constitution and Bylaws, the proposal passed.

These are only the most recent episodes in a two-decade-long discussion about whether organs and money can ethically be mixed.[9] The combination of legislative proposals and aggressive support from medical societies indicates that proponents of incentives believe the time is right to move the discussion from the pages of bioethics journals to the public arena. In doing so, they seek to inoculate their proposals against attack by claiming the moral high ground (they ostensibly seek only to advance the interests of desperate patients on waiting lists) and by minimizing the scope of the actions proposed (they propose "incentives," not payments, and only "pilot studies," not policy changes).

This chapter responds to the most frequent criticisms of the present altruism-based system, and elaborates on the case for keeping the cash out of transplantation. The arguments canvassed here refer variously both to the cadaveric organ acquisition addressed by the AMA proposal and to the use of live donors—or vendors—which is known as *inter vivos* donation. Although the AMA proposal is only for cadaveric organ acquisition, a natural next step is to consider employing financial incentives for *inter vivos* donation.

The major alternative schemes proposed for organ acquisition range from fully voluntary to coercive, where "coercive" plans are those that attempt to encourage or force people to do something they would not otherwise be inclined to do. (See Figure 9.1.) Plans also vary in terms of what they posit about the relationship between physical bodies and the "self" or "person." Some treat the "person" as having a necessarily embodied existence. In these, "I" am not distinct from my physical being; the body is understood *as* the self. Others treat the body as property, as something distinct from the self that is

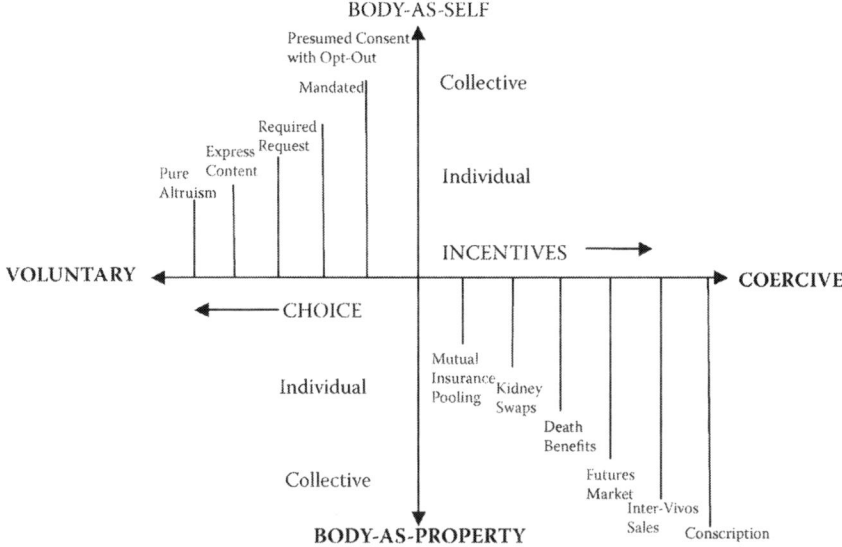

Figure 9.1 Body, Self, and Organ Acquisition.

"owned" by a disembodied (or at least anatomically localized) self. Both of these conceptions range from individualistic to collectivist understandings of identity. For example, the property conception can justify an individual's rights to dispose of his or her body parts ("I own my own body"), or it can be generalized to legitimate disposal by some collective entity ("The state owns my body"). Likewise, "embodiment" can be seen in purely individualistic terms or in reference to a shared identity with some larger social group.

Commodification

Proponents of incentives have repeatedly advanced several critiques of the current altruism-based approach to organ procurement. Three of these critiques seem to be especially significant: (1) that compensating for organs is no different from many other permissible forms of body commodification, (2) that it is hypocritical to prohibit an activity that you would wish to engage in were you in a similar situation, and (3) that it is unethical not to do everything possible to increase donations because so many die for the lack of an adequate supply of organs.

The worry about commodification is that the buying and selling of human organs would lead to an increasing objectification of the human body. Commerce in organs would encourage people to view individual human beings as saleable commodities and would to that extent compromise and denature human dignity, so the argument goes.[10] Other forms of this concern are voiced in discussions of surrogate motherhood, cloning, genetic testing and therapy, and some other topics in biotechnology and medical research.

Yet commercialization advocates have a ready rejoinder: Selling an organ is not different in kind from selling one's labor in other, often quite legal, ways—commercial surrogate motherhood, choosing to work a very risky job, and, in some jurisdictions, the sexual service industry. Physical risk, exploitation, and commodification are arguably a matter of degree rather than of kind, and one cannot consistently deny the "choice" of engaging in these other activities while exceptionalizing organ commerce.

However, admitting the similarities (or even ethical identities) between, say, the presumed exploitation of prostitution and the exploitation of organ selling should not be taken as an argument for legally, socially, or ethically embracing all kinds of exploitation. Working as a diamond miner in South Africa is demonstrably dangerous to life and limb; selling the right lobe of one's liver, or a lung, is also demonstrably dangerous.[11] Both force a devil's bargain on the economically desperate of trading life and limb for sustenance. Yet admitting the exploitative and hence ethically objectionable nature of highly dangerous working conditions is not an argument for *expanding* the range of dangerous occupations or risky labor–body exchanges. Rather, objecting to such kinds of exploitation or to the selling of one's labor or physical well-being should be taken as a reason for working to *reduce* the kinds of work or exchange that are so risky.

The concern about commodification takes on additional considerations in the context of cadaveric donation—the sort of donation that the AMA proposal addresses. Most commentators agree that as a matter of law and common morality, *inter vivos* donations should rely on noncoercive, voluntary organ acquisition plans that endorse what we refer to as the *body-as-self* view. When cadaveric donations are considered, however, commentators differ. Some still prefer voluntary, body-as-self organ acquisition, but some argue for using incentives to encourage donation, and they favor the body-as-property view of the organ.[12] The key point of contention, in courts of law as well as at the bedside of patients, is whether death immediately ends the body-as-self connection and opens the door to the application of property concerns and the logic of commodities—since the "person" is no longer there, who owns the material body, and how much may they profit from its disposition? Even scholars sensitive to the significance of body–self integrity seem prepared to accept that death means instant disembodiment of the person and transformation of the body to property, or at least a circumscription of the continuing right of the deceased to have his or her wishes honored in respect to the treatment of the corpse.[13]

We know from a massive ethnographic record that the cessation of biological functions is rarely seen as being commensurate with the separation of the self from the body.[14] The distinction made by social scientists between social and biological death captures the undeniable fact that a person's identity is commonly thought to remain with the body for some time after physical death has occurred. The cultural work achieved by mourning rituals is to complete the disconnection that biological death initiates. This is not, as Margaret Radin would have it, an example of fetishism—a superstitious belief that rational thought ought to banish.[15] Rather, it is a basic human recognition that our "self," our identity, exists in the space of social relations, and that the ongoing flow of social life necessitates a gradual disaggregation of the deceased from the ties to the living that constituted the social self.[16]

These observations help explain the moral intuition some feel that the commodification of cadavers is abhorrent. It is this intuition that causes medical staff to hesitate when called upon to request a donation, that explains the fear felt by kin that their loved one's body would be mutilated during organ removal, and that makes understandable the reservations felt around the world to declaring a person dead at brain death and permitting cadaveric organ transplantation. The claim that dead bodies "are no longer inextricably intertwined with a person," and are therefore only protected as property,[17] may capture the direction of recent legal interpretations, but it is badly out of sync with the real world and the way families actually respond to the death of relatives. It would be wise to assess plans for acquiring organs against a real-world standard, rather than by legal or philosophical reasoning alone.

Reason and Rescue

Inter vivos sales have also been promoted by what could be called the "reasoned ideal" argument. In response to anti-incentive critics, some ask, "But what would *you* do if your child's life depended on your selling one of your kidneys? How can you deny to others a choice that you yourself might make if you were in their circumstances?" This claim often invokes an example of a parent in the developing world who has already lost some of her children to malnutrition or preventable disease. The sale of a kidney can generate the equivalent of 10 years' wages for, say, an itinerant Indian worker (although the promised financial gain often fails to materialize, and serious long-term health problems are common).[18] Isn't this just the kind of sacrifice that we generally applaud in developed countries, when a loving parent gives up a kidney to save a child with a life-threatening kidney disease?

There is often something to this charge of hypocrisy. However, philosophers who make this charge should take more care to distinguish the arguments that might incline one to sell an organ—such as Kantian notions of a duty to family—from the utilitarian argument that enfranchising the practice would lead to the greater social acceptance of similar transactions. By way of analogy, consistency does not require that entertaining the proposition "A parent may save the life of her child by cutting off a leg or selling herself into slavery" commits one to accept an effort to legalize, let alone facilitate, dismemberment or slavery. Two different questions are being asked here: what actions are morally understandable under conditions of desperation, and what social institutions or policies might be ethically justified to accommodate "choices" made under such desperate circumstances?

Another objection to philosophical arguments concerns what might be called the "rescue obligation." Proponents of incentives—whether arguing for *inter vivos* sales or for cash rewards for cadaveric organs (including tax rebates and funeral "stipends" as well as cash paid outright for each organ taken)—frequently argue that the number of persons who die before an organ is available for them presents a compelling moral case for shifting the burden of argument back onto those who support the preservation of the current altruism-based system.[19] Recitations of the statistics on the ever-increasing gap between those awaiting organs and the number of organs available typically preface rhetorical charges of avoidable tragedies, of life-saving body parts being left for the worms, and even of criminal liability for refusals to donate.[20] A letter to the *British Medical Journal* puts the underlying claim clearly: "We all have a moral duty to do everything we can to give the living the best possible quality of life."[21]

What's wrong with this claim? First, there is precious little legal or custom-based support for an obligation to rescue those whose organs have failed. Courts in the United States, for example, have repeatedly found that there is no duty to aid a person in need: "The common law has consistently held to a rule which provides that one human being is under no legal compulsion to give aid or rescue or to take action to save another.... The rule is founded upon the very essence of our free society."[22] This rule has traditionally been applied to living persons, but the mandate that organs may be removed for transplantation only with consent—expressed or presumed—would indicate that even after death, the default assumption is that there is no presumptive obligation to rescue.

Indeed, it is precisely the absence of an obligation to rescue that gives the decision to donate organs its positive moral weight. If this presumption were reversed, say by conscripting cadavers for their organs regardless of dissent, then no moral value would attach to the persons from whom organs are extracted, or from their next of kin. This would introduce a crass instrumentality into organ transplantation that is directly at odds with its longstanding ethos.

The claim that society as a whole has a positive duty to rescue those on transplant waiting lists is actually weakened by utilitarian calculation: there are immense numbers of other persons whose lives could more easily be improved or saved with the financial resources required for organ replacement. Even as strong a defender of organ transplantation as Richard Evans must admit that "from a public health perspective, more harm than good has already been done [by organ transplantation]"; in the United States, "nearly $6 billion is spent [annually] on a handful of solid organ transplant recipients."[23] We might contrast this expenditure, for example, to the $0.26 per vaccine to immunize against measles, which kills 900,000 children around the world.[24] In a world of finite resources for health care, it is hard to argue that the extraordinary expenditure associated with organ transplantation constitutes the best possible way to serve the needs of the living.

A third problem with the rescue claim is that organ transplantation is not the medical miracle it claims to be. Given the severity of the diseases from which transplant candidates suffer and the stubborn reality of organ rejection, many of those who die before receiving an organ might very well have died within several years even with a replacement organ. Survival rates vary significantly by the organ replaced, but the average 20 percent loss of life at the one-year point increases significantly after 5 years. Furthermore, the profession of transplant medicine has consistently overstated recipients' quality of life and understated the long-term toll of powerful antirejection medications.[25]

A final problem with the "rescue obligation" is that high-technology medicine is, more often than not, unavailable to persons whose bank accounts or insurance status are inadequate to the expense. In all of Africa, between 1978 and 1994, only 163 transplant surgeries were performed; during the same period, over 124,000 transplants were performed in the United States alone.[26] Even within developed countries, the "green screen" determines who gets to the waiting list for organs and who can afford the medications after surgery.[27] If society has a moral duty to rescue, the obligation surely is not limited to rescuing those of means.

Science and Superstition

Many medical professionals believe that the body-as-self conception—especially when it is extended to include the recently dead—is a superstition that must eventually disappear as "scientific" understandings of the body penetrate ever more deeply into the general culture. They point to the growing number of body fluids and parts that are openly marketed—from gametes to skin and corneas—as evidence that, at least in the United States, we are witnessing a shift toward property conceptions of the body and an acceptance of bodily commodification. If this is the case, then one could predict an inevitable trend toward incentives in organ procurement, first for cadaveric and then for living "donations." Indeed, advocates of commerce frequently claim that incentives would cross no new or substantially relevant threshold, since other body parts are already treated as commodities.[28]

But this modernist view of how medical science influences the general culture may be out of step. Physicians and other health professionals come to a disembodied view of the self—if in fact they do—only after the desensitizing socialization of medical school, where the curriculum promotes a Cartesian distinction between mind and body that accords well with the objectification of organ systems.[29] Rather than treating this way of thinking as the inevitable endpoint of a progressive culture, it would be just as reasonable to see it as a clinically useful but culturally aberrant view.

This alternative interpretation is supported by evidence that even those most fully immersed in the world view of modern medicine appear to have difficulty reconciling their scientific understandings of the body with their intuitive responses. How else can one explain why physicians often do not sign organ donor cards,[30] or the ambivalent responses by health care staff to persons declared brain dead or in a persistent vegetative state?[31] The strong dissent voiced at the AMA over the incentive proposal might be taken as additional evidence that even doctors are yet to be fully persuaded by the body-as-property view.

There are other indications that the corpse continues to be treated as integral to the self. Consider the extraordinary investment of time and money in the recovery of the smallest of body parts from the ruins of the World Trade Center, or the public horror occasioned by news of bodies left uncremated at a Georgia facility. Persistent accounts of organ recipients who express concern about the identity and character of the donor, and of donor kin who believe that the deceased lives on in the recipient, also show how firmly rooted in common intuition is the idea that a person's identity is embodied.

Clearly, the AMA's proposal entails much more than an innocent experiment. Rather than doing ethics by pilot study, it would be better to reflect more deeply on where the "is" and the "ought" of incentives line up. There is more at stake than encouraging donation.

Discussion Questions

1. Proponents of providing incentives to potential donors have advanced several critiques to the current altruism-based approach. Which of these three critiques seem to be especially significant?
2. What are some of the major worries about the commidification of buying and selling human organs?
3. What arguments are made by those who advocate the commercialization of human organs?

4. What does the author mean by the statement "We know from a massive ethnographic record that the cessation of biological functions is rarely seen as being commensurate with the separation of the self from the body"?
5. What is wrong with the claim "We all have a moral duty to do everything we can to give the living the best possible quality of life"?
6. What statistical evidence is there to support the claim that organ transplant is not the miracle it claims to be?
7. What evidence is there to suggest that even those fully immersed in the worldview of modern medicine appear to have difficulty reconciling their scientific understanding with their intuitive responses?
8. What are some indications that the corpse continues to be treated as integral to the self?

Endnotes

1. H.R. 2090, Help Organ Procurement Expand Act of 2001 (U.S. Rep. C. Smith, NJ) and H.R. 1872 Gift, of Life Tax Credit Act of 2001 (U.S. Rep. J. Hansen, Utah).
2. S.R. 1949, Organ Donation and Recovery Improvement Act (U.S. Sens. W. Frist, Tenn., and C. Dodd, Conn.). The language of the bill is most clearly directed toward reimbursement for a wider range of expenses incurred as a result of cadaveric donations, but some believe that the bill would also permit waivers for studies of other forms of financial incentives. See A. Robeznieks, "Feds Have Final Say on Organ Donor Initiatives," Amednews.com, July 22, 2002, http://www.ama-assn.org/amednews/2002/07/22/prsc0722.htm.
3. As early as 1995, the AMA supported even more extreme proposals for compensating donors, specifically calling for future contracts. American Medical Association, Council on Ethical and Judicial Affairs, "Financial Incentives for Organ Procurement: Ethical Aspects of Future Contracts for Cadaveric Donors," *Archives of Internal Medicine* 155 (1995): 589–91.
4. CEJA Report 1:A-02, "Cadaveric Organ Donation: Encouraging the Study of Motivation" (paper presented at the 2002 American Medical Association House of Delegates Annual Meeting, Chicago, Ill., 15–20 June 2002).
5. See Robeznieks, "Feds Have Final Say on Organ Donor Initiatives." By contrast, the American College of Surgeons released a statement in opposition to any financial compensation for organ donations; see "News in Brief," *Amednews.com*, 29 July 2002.
6. CEJA Report 1:A-02, "Cadaveric Organ Donation."
7. Quoted in A. Robeznieks, "Boosting Organ Donations Ultimate Focus of Initiative," *Amednews.com*, 8/15 July 2002.
8. Robeznieks, "Boosting Organ Donations Ultimate Focus of Initiative."
9. See D. Joralemon, "Shifting Ethics: Organ Transplantation and the Question of Compensation," *Journal of Medical Ethics* 27 (2001): 30–35.

10. See D. Joralemon, "Organ Wars: The Battle for Body Parts," *Medical Anthropology Quarterly* 9 (1995): 335–56; and D. Joralemon, "The Ethics of the Organ Market: Lloyd Cohen and the Free Marketeers," in *Biotechnology and Culture*, ed. P. E. Brodwin (Bloomington: Indiana University Press, 2000), 224–40, for reviews of the arguments of both proponents and critics of organ sales.
11. Admittedly the removal of some organs—most prominently, one kidney—is much less "risky" than is often supposed. Some pro-commerce advocates argue that selling such an organ ought to be placed lower on a scale of activities that are risky but legal. Of course, in assessing risk, a lot depends on the economic and medical conditions surrounding the surgery, and advocates of organ commerce point out that these conditions would be less risky for the donor if the practice were legalized and regulated.
12. Thus, organ acquisition plans tend to cluster in the upper-left and lower-right quadrants of Figure 9.1, suggesting a powerful connection between incentives and property views of the body. Plans in the other two quadrants are possible. For example, the donor's kin might be offered incentives directly by recipients in a form that builds on the often-stated idea that the deceased lives on in the recipient's body. This plan would fall into the upper right of the figure.
13. See R. Rao, "Property, Privacy, and the Human Body," *Boston University Law Review* 80 (2000): 359; and M. J. Radin, "Market-Inalienability," *Harvard Law Review* 100 (1982): 1849–937. See also the Uniform Anatomical Gift Act.
14. See M. Bloch and J. Parry, eds., *Death and the Regeneration of Life* (New York: Cambridge University Press, 1982); G. Howarth and P. C. Jupp, eds., *Contemporary Issues in the Sociology of Death* (New York: St. Martins, 1996); C. Seale, *Constructing Death: The Sociology of Dying and Bereavement* (New York: Cambridge University Press, 1998); and P. Metcalf and R. Huntington, *Celebrations of Death: The Anthropology of Mortuary Ritual* (New York: Cambridge University Press, 1997).
15. Radin, "Market-Inalienability."
16. Quoted in B. Conklin, *Consuming Grief* (Austin: University of Texas Press, 2001), for a recent exploration of this theme in relationship to endocannibalism among an Amazonian people.
17. Rao, "Property, Privacy, and the Human Body," 459.
18. The case of India is instructive since it has been a major locale for kidney sales, which have continued despite belated criminalization. See L. Cohen, "Where It Hurts: Indian Material for an Ethics of Organ Transplantation," *Daedalus* 128 (1999): 135–65. However, many other countries either permit or fail to stop organ commerce. See a series of articles in the *National Post Online* (29 March, 30 March, and 2 April 2002) authored by journalists M. Jimenez and N. Scheper-Hughes, at http://www.nationalpost.com/search/story.html?f=stories/20020329.
19. See J. Radcliffe-Richards et al., "The Case for Allowing Kidney Sales," *Lancet* 351 (1998): 1950–52; J. S. Cameron and R. Hoffenberg, "The Ethics of Organ Transplantation Reconsidered: Paid Organ Donation and the Use of Executed Prisoners as Donors," *Kidney International* 55 (1999): 724–32; and R. Sade, "Cadaveric Organ Donation: Rethinking Donor Motivation," *Archives of Internal Medicine* 159 (1999): 438v42.

20. See M. Lysaght and J. Mason, "The Case for Financial Incentives to Encourage Organ Donation," *American Society for Artificial Internal Organs* 46, no. 3 (2000): 253–56; L. R. Cohen, *Increasing the Supply of Transplant Organs: The Virtues of an Options Market* (New York: Springer, 1995); and R. W. Evans, "How Dangerous Are Financial Incentives to Obtain Organs?" *Transplantation Proceedings* 31 (1999): 1337–41.
21. S. Cansdale and R. Cansdale, "We Know That Our Daughter Lives On," *British Medical Journal* 318 (1999): 1490.
22. J. Rutherford-McClure, "To Donate or Not to Donate Your Organs: Texas Can Decide for You When You Cannot Decide for Yourself," *Texas Wesleyan Law Review* 6 (2000): 241. While U.S. common law has not given rise to any establishment of a "duty to rescue," most European countries have passed such laws. In the United States, five states have legislatively enacted related statutes, though in four of them "duty to rescue" simply means "duty to report a crime," if such can be done without risk to the reporter. Only in Vermont is a person obligated to provide "reasonable assistance" when another person "is exposed to grave physical harm," but again only if such can be done without danger or peril to self or others. See E. Volokh, "Duties to Rescue and the Anticooperative Effects of Law," *Georgetown Law Journal* 88 (1999): 105–14.
23. R. W. Evans, "How Dangerous Are Financial Incentives to Obtain Organs?" *Transplantation Proceedings* 31 (1999): 1337–41.
24. WHO/UNICEF figure cited in *Business Recorder*, 12 April 2001.
25. See D. Joralemon and K. Fujinaga, "Studying the Quality of Life after Organ Transplantation: Research Problems and Solutions," *Social Science and Medicine* 44 (1996): 1259–69, for a review of outcome studies.
26. T. Harrison, "Globalization and the Trade in Human Body Parts," *Canadian Review of Sociology and Anthropology* 36, no. 1 (1999): 21–35.
27. For a discussion of postsurgical costs and variable ability to pay, see L. Sharp, "A Medical Anthropologist's View on Post-Transplant Compliance: The Underground Economy of Medical Survival," *Transplantation Proceedings* 31, no. 4, suppl. 1 (1999): 315–35.
28. According to this claim, whatever justifies the selling of one's blood, for example, would also justify the selling of other body parts, unless these parts are different in kind. Some critics argue that solid organs are different in kind because they are nonreplenishable (removal of a lobe of the liver is an exception, since the liver will restore the missing segment) and because their removal represents a greater risk to the donor.
29. The relevant literature is reviewed in D. E. Gordon, "Tenacious Assumptions in Western Medicine," in *Biomedicine Examined*, ed. M. Lock and D. Gordon (Dordrecht: Kluwer Academic, 1988), 19–56.
30. Margaret M. Lock. *Twice Dead: Organ Transplants and the Reinvention of Death*, California Series in Public Anthropology, vol. 1. (Berkeley: University of California Press, 2002).
31. S. R. Kaufman, "In the Shadow of 'Death with Dignity': Medicine and Cultural Quandaries of the Vegetative State," *American Anthropologist* 102, no. 1 (2000): 69–83. See D. Joralemon and P. Cox, "Body Values: The Case against Compensating for Transplant Organs," *Hastings Center Report* 33, no. 1 (2003): 27–33.

Autonomy, Constraining Options, and Organ Sales

10

JAMES STACEY TAYLOR, PhD
*Department of Philosophy and Religious Studies,
Louisiana State University, Baton Rouge, Louisiana*

Contents

Preliminary Remarks	144
Dworkin's Case for Organ Sales—and the First Objections to It	145
Is the Option to Sell an Organ an Autonomy-Undermining Constraining Option for the Individual Who Chooses It?	148
Responses to Hughes	150
Organ Sales, Aid, and Group-Affecting Constraining Options	152
Conclusion	155
Discussion Questions	156
Acknowledgments	156
Endnotes	156

Although the recent development of immunosuppressive drugs such as cyclosporine-A and OKT3 have greatly increased the success rate of organ transplantation, there is still a chronic shortage of suitable organs available for transplantation.[1] Although various remedies for this shortage have been proposed,[2] the suggestion that it should be alleviated through legally allowing a current market in organs to exist has received almost universal moral condemnation.[3] Much of this condemnation is based on the view that allowing such a current market will undermine the autonomy of those who would participate in it as vendors.[4] Against this, Gerald Dworkin has recently argued that rather than undermining the autonomy of those who would participate in them as vendors, such markets will actually enhance it, for to allow persons to sell their organs will enable them to exercise a greater degree of control over their bodies.[5]

Dworkin's arguments in favor of allowing a current market in human organs have become the most prominent expression of this position within the philosophical literature—although this is no doubt partly owed to the

---

[*] First published in *Journal of Applied Philosophy* 19 (3) 273–285, 2002.

scarcity of the defenders of this view. Since this is so, Dworkin's arguments have attracted considerable attention from those opposed to allowing current markets in human organs. Of particular note are two recent and highly innovative criticisms of his position that have been developed by Paul Hughes and T. L. Zutlevics.[6] Hughes and Zutlevics both agree that Dworkin's claim that providing a person with additional options as to how she can control her life will typically enhance her autonomy is correct. Despite this, they argue that the option to sell an organ is unusual in that it is likely to be an autonomy-undermining "constraining option." Hughes argues that the choice of such an option is likely to undermine the autonomy of the individual, while Zutlevics argues that allowing the poor to have this option is likely to reduce the possibility that their autonomy will be promoted in the future through the provision of aid.[7] Both of these arguments are highly persuasive—but, as I will argue here, both are seriously flawed.

However, the argument in this chapter is not entirely negative. In arguing that Hughes's and Zutlevics's criticisms of Dworkin's arguments are mistaken, I will show that none of the most persuasive objections to a current market in organs that are based on the value of autonomy are successful. Instead, those arguments (such as Dworkin's) that favor allowing a current market in human organs on the grounds that respect for autonomy requires that such markets be allowed should hold sway. And this is important, for insofar as autonomy is still the preeminent value in contemporary medical ethics, the success of these arguments provides a strong *prima facie* case for recognizing the moral legitimacy of current markets in human organs.[8]

Preliminary Remarks

Before I move on to consider the arguments of Zutlevics and Hughes, it should be noted that the arguments in this chapter should not be taken to support the moral permissibility of a current market in all human organs. Instead, they should only be taken to support a current market in those bodily parts that are either renewable (such as blood, plasma, semen, and ova) or those solid organs (such as kidneys) whose loss will not affect the vendor's ability to live as he or she did prior to the sale. This narrowing of the focus of these arguments is not, however, peculiar to this contribution to the debate over the moral permissibility of organ sales. This is because in all of the autonomy-based arguments that this chapter will consider, it is implicitly assumed that the sale of an organ will not itself result in the compromising of the vendor's autonomy, but, instead, that the vendors will at least have the potential to be as autonomous after the sale as they were before it. (Thus, when these arguments refer to *organs*, they should be understood to refer to those bodily parts whose loss will not itself compromise the vendor's autonomy.) Since this is so, then, the autonomy-based arguments of this chapter should not be generalized to support current markets in either organs (such as hearts) or certain bodily appendages (such as hands) whose sale would itself adversely affect the future autonomy of the vendor.

Dworkin's Case for Organ Sales— and the First Objections to It

In "Markets and Morals: The Case for Organ Sales," Gerald Dworkin provides one of the very few positive arguments for the moral permissibility of a current market in human organs. Dworkin notes that it is considered morally acceptable for a person noncommercially to donate a kidney and to sell blood, semen, ova, and hair. The moral legitimacy of these practices, he claims, indicates that "we respect the bodily autonomy of individuals," where "bodily autonomy" is understood as persons' "ability to make choices about how their body is to be treated by others."[9] Dworkin also notes that allowing persons to engage in market transactions "is one way of recognizing their sphere of control" with respect to the goods that they are trading. So, because it is accepted that persons should be allowed to exercise control over their bodies, they should be allowed to sell their organs. Allowing a current market in human organs, then, will enhance personal autonomy through removing a prohibition that currently restricts persons' control over their own bodies.[10]

Dworkin's argument rests on the premise that a market transaction in which one sells one of one's organs is a voluntary transaction, one that the vendor is autonomous with respect to. Dworkin recognizes that this claim is precisely that which is standardly attacked by those opposed to allowing such markets on the grounds that they will allow the autonomy of the vendors to be diminished, and he attempts to rebut their arguments by demonstrating that they have counterintuitive implications. Those opposed to organ sales point out that the vendors would (typically) be forced to sell out of economic necessity. They then note that it is generally accepted that a person who is forced to perform an action out of necessity will suffer from a diminution in her autonomy with respect to that action.[11] If these two (widely held) views are correct, then those who are forced to sell their organs out of economic necessity will suffer from a diminution in their autonomy with respect to their vending action.[12] In response to this standard objection to allowing a current market in human organs Dworkin argues that if the poor should be prohibited from selling their organs for this reason then they should also be prohibited from joining the army, engaging in hazardous occupations such as high-steel construction, or being paid subjects in medical experiments, since these decisions are also often made out of economic necessity, and thus should also be considered to exhibit diminished autonomy. Yet to prohibit the poor from engaging in such activities, Dworkin claims, would be considered morally impermissible because such prohibitions would be "paternalist in the extreme." Since this is so, he concludes, by parity of reasoning the standard objection to the moral permissibility of allowing a current market in human organ has impermissibly paternalistic implications—and so it should be rejected.[13]

Yet although Dworkin's response to this "objection from exploitation" appears to be a plausible defense of the moral permissibility of a free market in human organs this appearance is misleading. This is because the force of this response rests on two implicit claims: that the only way to protect the poor from exploitation is to prohibit them from working in those occupations that are deemed exploitative, and that such prohibitions are impermissibly paternalist.[14] The first of these claims is false, for it is not true that the only possible way one might protect the poor from exploitation is to prohibit them from engaging in hazardous activities such as high-steel construction or kidney vending. Instead, one might protect the poor from exploitation by requiring that all employers (and traders in human organs) "ensure, so far as is reasonably practicable, the health, safety and welfare at work of all ... [their] ... employees."[15] Thus, rather than having to prohibit the poor from selling their organs to protect them from exploitation one need only regulate the way in this market operates. Furthermore, it is not clear that preventing the poor from working in unnecessarily hazardous conditions through subjecting employers (and organ traders) to regulatory legislation (such as the Health and Safety at Work Act) would be impermissibly paternalist. This is because in imposing such regulation, one is not adversely affecting either the quantity of the number of options that the poor possess (i.e., they do not have any fewer options than they did prior to its imposition) or the quality of the options that they possess.[16] Indeed, one is improving the quality of their option set by replacing a less attractive option (working in hazardous conditions) with a more attractive one (working in safer conditions). Thus, since such regulation is likely to serve to increase the well-being of the poor without any decrease in their autonomy, its imposition will be unobjectionable to those who are concerned with the protection of the autonomy of the poor.

However, even though Dworkin's response to the objection from exploitation fails as a defense of a free current market in human organs, a version of it can be used successfully to defend a regulated current market in human organs. This is because just as it seems to be impermissibly paternalistic to prohibit the poor from engaging in hazardous activities such as high-steel construction when they are protected from unnecessary hazards through legislative regulation, so too does it seem impermissibly paternalistic to prohibit them from participating as vendors in a similarly regulated current market for organs. And one can accept that this prohibition would be impermissibly paternalistic without having to accept either of the two claims that underlie Dworkin's original argument.

Dworkin's argument is thus defensible when it is understood as an argument in favor of a regulated current market in human organs. Moreover, when understood in this way it is immune to Zutlevics's first criticism of it. In developing this criticism Zutlevics points out that Dworkin's response to the objection from exploitation rests on the intuition "that most people would be reluctant to deny the poor the opportunity to join the army, to engage in hazardous occupations, or to receive financial remuneration for participation in medical experiments."[17] She then notes that most people would only agree that the poor should be allowed to engage in the hazardous activities that Dworkin lists if two conditions are met: that their employers did not exploit their financial necessity to expose them to levels of risk that the nonpoor were not exposed to, and that they could secure certain benefits and enhanced social standing from participation in these activities. Since this is so, Zutlevics argues, deciding whether a person's financially necessitated choice to perform an action is one that she is autonomous with respect to does not merely depend upon the risk associated with the chosen activity, as Dworkin holds. Instead, it also depends on whether the person choosing it could expect to secure benefits from it that would also be attractive to the nonpoor. Thus, if the sale of an organ were an option that did not meet these two additional conditions (and so was an option that was only attractive to the desperate poor), it would be disanalogous to the other hazardous activities that Dworkin considers. This is because, Zutlevics argues, if the option of selling an organ were attractive only to the desperate poor, then unlike the other activities Dworkin considers the only persons who would choose this option would be those who were economically forced to do so, and so who would not be autonomous with respect to this choice. And since this is so, she concludes, Dworkin's attempt to respond to the objection from exploitation fails, because this objection does not have the impermissibly paternalistic implications that he is concerned about.

If Dworkin's response to the argument from exploitation were best understood as favoring a free current market in human organs, then Zutlevics's objection here might be sound. However, as we argued above it is instead best understood as favoring a regulated current market in human organs. Since this is so, then even if Zutlevics's "guess" that most people would only allow the poor to engage in hazardous occupations such as military duty or high-steel construction on the conditions that they received acceptable financial and social compensation is correct, this does not undermine Dworkin's response to the objection from exploitation. This is because all that can be inferred from Zutlevics's guess is that for it to be as morally acceptable for the poor to sell their organs as it is for them to engage in the other hazardous activities that Dworkin lists, the market for human organs must operate in such a way that the compensation received by the vendors is comparable to that which they would receive were they to engage in these other hazardous activities. Since this is so, then, if the vendors in a current market for human organs receive enough compensation from the sale of an organ for this to be an option that is attractive not only to the desperate poor Dworkin's response to the objection from exploitation will hold. And while this level of compensation might not be forthcoming in an unregulated free current market for human organs (although, of course, it might) steps could be taken to ensure that it would be forthcoming in a regulated trade in human organs. (One might, for example, establish a monopsonistic market in which there is only one buyer, and that buyer pays an acceptable level of compensation for the organs it purchases.)[18] And a regulated market is, of course, precisely the sort of market that Dworkin's autonomy-based arguments best support. Rather than supplying the basis for an objection to Dworkin's response to the objection from exploitation, then, Zutlevics's "guess" actually serves to support his position.

Is the Option to Sell an Organ an Autonomy-Undermining Constraining Option for the Individual Who Chooses It?

So far, then, it appears that Dworkin's autonomy-based arguments in favor of allowing persons to sell their organs in a current market are successful. However, to accept the moral permissibility of such markets would be premature, for Paul Hughes has developed a highly persuasive (and highly original) objection to Dworkin's position. Hughes's argument is based on the recognition that merely providing a person with an addition to his set of options need not enhance his autonomy, for the addition of certain options might instead compromise it. To illustrate this, Hughes uses the example of "the legal option of refraining from pressing charges against one's assailant."[19] Although the possession of such an option is typically held to enhance the control that its possessors have over their own lives, Hughes notes that out of fear of their assailants some persons refuse to press charges, a refusal that condemns them to the possibility of yet more abuse at the hands of the original perpetrators. The option not to press charges is thus a "constraining option." This is because it serves to lock some of those who choose it into a continued cycle of autonomy-undermining abuse; a cycle that could have been broken (and their autonomy restored) had this option not been open to them.[20]

Having thus established that the possession of certain "constraining options" might serve to undermine a person's autonomy rather than enhancing it, Hughes draws on a neo-Marxist account of exploitation to argue that the option to sell one's organs is just such a constraining option. On this account of exploitation a person is exploited when her background set of options is constricted in such a way as to force her to perform the action that her exploiter requires of her,[21] (such as, for example, to work in his factory—or to sell him one of her kidneys). If a person is in a situation where she is faced with such a constricted range of options, Hughes argues, then anything that "presupposes and/or reinforces" this situation for her will perpetuate the undermining of her autonomy. So, if a person is provided with an addition to her choice-set that, if chosen, will result in her continuing to remain in her present autonomy-undermining circumstances, such an option will not be one whose possession necessarily serves to enhance her autonomy. Instead, her possession of this option might only serve to perpetuate its undermining.

In order to show that the option to sell one's organs in a current market is an autonomy-undermining constraining option of this sort, Hughes notes that it will typically be the poor who will be the vendors in such a market. From this, Hughes infers that for a current market in human organs to exist "it is necessary that there be poor people and that we allow them to participate in such a market."[22] Since this is so, Hughes concludes that the introduction of a current market in human organs presupposes that some persons live in autonomy-undermining economic circumstances. And if a system that "presupposes and/or reinforces" a person's presence within an autonomy-undermining situation perpetuates the undermining of her autonomy, then the introduction of a current market for human organs will only serve to undermine further the autonomy of potential vendors, rather than enhance it.

Furthermore, one of Zutlevics's arguments also suggests that allowing current markets in human organs might serve to reinforce the position of poor individuals in their autonomy-undermining economic circumstances, for there is "evidence which suggests that poverty is not significantly alleviated by selling organs."[23] In support of this claim, Zutlevics cites Sanjay Kumar, who has noted that the Chennai suburban slum colony Villivakkam is so full of poor persons who have sold a kidney that it has become internationally known as "Kidney-vakkam."[24] Rather than helping the poor escape from their autonomy-undermining economic circumstances, then, allowing them to sell their organs might only serve to enable them to continue to live in poverty, perhaps to sell other nonvital body parts in the future. And, since this is so, a current market in human organs might only serve to reinforce the continued existence of the poor in their autonomy-undermining economic conditions.

Responses to Hughes

It is indeed plausible to hold that if a system presupposes and/or reinforces an autonomy-undermining situation, then that system should also be regarded as being autonomy undermining. However, this neo-Marxist claim cannot be used to object to the introduction of a current market for human organs. This is because such a market neither presupposes nor reinforces the autonomy-undermining situation of the poor in the way that is needed for it to be an autonomy-undermining system.

To show this one must first distinguish between two senses in which the introduction of a system B "presupposes" the existence of a situation A. In the first sense, a system B "presupposes" the existence of a situation A if B is introduced in order to alleviate A, such that some time after B is introduced A might cease to exist. In the second sense a system B "presupposes" the existence of a situation A if B is introduced in the belief that A exists, and A and B are mutually dependent and will continue to coexist.[25] It is clear that Hughes cannot be using the first sense of "presuppose" in his argument for he denies that the introduction of a current market for human organs would alleviate the autonomy-undermining economic situation of the poor. Instead, he is using the second sense of "presuppose," such that a current market for human organs presupposes the autonomy-undermining situation of the poor as it is introduced in the belief that there are poor persons who live in such a situation, and that the introduction of this market both depends on their being in such a situation and contributes to their continued existence within it. However, neither of these two aspects of the second sense of what it is for a system B to presuppose the existence of a situation A holds true for the introduction of a current market into the autonomy-undermining economic situation of the poor. Since this is so, the introduction of such a market does not presuppose the existence of autonomy undermining. First, it is not necessary for the introduction of such a market that are "poor people and that we allow them to participate" in it. This is because all the proponents of such a market need presuppose is that some persons will be willing to purchase organs for transplantation, that others (of any economic standing) will be willing to sell them, and that the vendor and the purchaser will be able to agree on a price. Of course, no doubt almost all the vendors in such a market will be drawn from the ranks of the desperate poor, and so more organs would be sold if the poor did exist and were allowed to participate in such a market. But this point concerns the differential volume of trade that would take place in a current market for human organs with the participation of the poor, rather than the feasibility of such a market itself. In addition to this, the introduction of such a market does not meet the second condition needed for it to "presuppose" the autonomy-undermining situation of the poor in the second sense of "presuppose" outlined above, for it will not contribute to the continued existence of the autonomy-undermining economic situation of the poor.

To show that the introduction of a current market for human organs does not meet this second condition for it to presuppose (in the appropriate sense) the autonomy-undermining situation of the poor is, of course, to show that the introduction of such a market does not reinforce the autonomy-undermining situation of the poor. This being so, then, once it has been shown that the introduction of a current market for human organs does not reinforce the autonomy-undermining situation of the poor, it will have been shown that the introduction of such a market meets neither of the conditions required for it to presuppose the autonomy-undermining situation of the poor, nor does it reinforce the situation. And, since this is so, Hughes cannot hold that the option to sell an organ is a constraining option, for the introduction of a market for human organs will neither presuppose nor reinforce the autonomy-undermining situation of the poor.

It was noted above that Zutlevics's observation, that although the poor of Villivakkam could sell their kidneys they were still unable to escape their autonomy-undermining economic situation, could be used to argue that allowing them this option serves to reinforce their impoverished situation. However, that the typical organ vendor might continue to suffer from her autonomy-undermining economic impoverishment if she were to sell an organ provides scant grounds for objecting to such sales on the basis of respect for autonomy. This is because prohibiting the poor from selling their organs will be to prohibit them from pursuing the only option that they have of securing a small sum of capital. Thus, even if this sum is not enough for them to extricate themselves from their autonomy-undermining impoverishment, the alternatives for such persons are, at worst, the elimination of their enjoyment of their autonomy through death, and, at best, lives in which they have even less opportunity to exercise her autonomy that they would have possessed had they been allowed to sell an organ. Thus, even if such vendors are unable to escape from their poverty their autonomy will be enhanced, not diminished, through their vending actions.

Hughes, however, might object that his understanding of what it is for a system to "reinforce" a person's presence in her autonomy-undermining situation differs from that which underlies this argument drawn from Zutlevics's observation. Instead of understanding a system as reinforcing a person's presence in her autonomy-undermining situation if it is one that merely enables her to continue to exist in it, Hughes's understanding of what it is for a system to "reinforce" a person's presence in her autonomy-undermining economic circumstances seems to be that the situation of the person concerned vis-à-vis her autonomy would be more likely to improve were this system not in place. Yet even with this understanding of what it is for a system to "reinforce" a person's presence in place, the option of selling a kidney cannot be considered a constraining option. This is because it is not the case that allowing a person to sell an organ will make it less likely that she will secure a situation that is more conducive to the exercise of her autonomy. Indeed, rather than reinforcing the economic status quo, allowing a current market in human organs might in some cases actually subvert it. This is because allowing such a market might provide the poor with the opportunity to acquire amounts of capital that they would otherwise not have access to, the possession of which might allow them to finally escape their economic constraints. For example, in the Philippines vendors consider the sale of an organ to be an important way to raise money to start up a new business, while a similar practice exists also in India.[26] Instead of reinforcing the status quo, then, allowing a current market in human organs might enable the poor to transcend it.[27]

Organ Sales, Aid, and Group-Affecting Constraining Options

In arguing that the possession of the option to sell one's organs does not serve to reinforce one's presence in one's current economic circumstances, it was claimed that for some persons this option would be the best that was available to them, and so its removal from their choice-set would make them worse off than they were with it.[28] Zutlevics, however, argues that this claim is false, contending instead that the best option that these persons have is to be the recipient of aid.[29] Zutlevics argues that it is important to recognize this, for once one does so one will also see how it is that allowing the poor to sell their organs in a current market will only be to provide them with an option that is a constraining option for them as a group.

Zutlevics is correct to note that recognizing that the best option that the poor have is to be the recipients of aid is the key to developing the argument that providing the poor with the option to sell their organs is to provide them with an option that might be a constraining option for them as a group. However, she is wrong to argue that this recognition undermines Dworkin's view. This is because this aid-based antimarket argument is caught on the horns of a dilemma. On one hand, if the poor do not receive sufficient aid to allow them to escape from their poverty, then the proponents of current markets in human organs are right to hold that the best option that they actually have might be to sell an organ. On the other hand, if sufficient aid is provided to allow the poor to escape the economic deprivation that would otherwise

Autonomy, Constraining Options, and Organ Sales 153

drive them to sell an organ it is unlikely that persons would wish to participate as vendors in a current market for human organs, and so there would be no need to prohibit this. (And, of course, it would be "paternalist in the extreme" to prohibit those few persons who for reasons of their own wish to sell their organs from doing so.) Since this is so, then, it appears that a current market for human organs should be allowed whether or not aid is forthcoming.

Zutlevics, however, has a way out of this dilemma. Zutlevics argues that allowing the poor of impoverished countries to participate as vendors in a current market in human organs now might lead to less aid being forthcoming to them in the future. This might be so, she argues, since if a current market in human organs is allowed it is likely that there will be a flow of organs from impoverished non-Western countries to the affluent West. And this, she continues, will provide a reason for the Western countries not to provide aid to the impoverished countries from which they are purchasing their transplant organs, for the provision of such aid would rescue the poor of the impoverished countries from the economic desperation that leads them to sell their organs to the West. Thus, if a current market in human organs is allowed it will provide a disincentive for the affluent West to give aid to the impoverished countries from which it purchases its organs. So, Zutlevics concludes, a current market for human organs should be prohibited on the grounds that allowing the poor of non-Western countries to sell their organs to the West is likely to reinforce their presence in their autonomy-undermining economic situation through providing the West with a disincentive to supply them with the aid that they require to escape this.

Zutlevics's argument is both highly insightful and very persuasive. As Hughes does, Zutlevics argues that the option to sell one's organs is not an autonomy-enhancing option, as Dworkin claims, but, instead, is an autonomy-undermining constraining option. Unlike Hughes, however, Zutlevics does not claim that the option to sell an organ is likely to be an autonomy-undermining constraining option for the person who chooses it. Instead, she argues that the possession by the poor of the option to sell their organs is likely to undermine the overall degree of autonomy that is enjoyed by the poor as a group—even if such sales might enhance the autonomy of the vendors themselves. Moreover, unlike Hughes, Zutlevics is able to provide an account of why allowing such sales will reinforce the autonomy-undermining social conditions in which the poor find themselves.

Before I move on to criticize Zutlevics's argument I should note that it is not an argument against allowing current markets in human organs per se, but only an argument against any market whose existence might provide a reason for the affluent to curtail their provision of aid to the needy. Since this is so, then, this argument does not oppose a current market in human organs in which the poor are allowed only to sell to their fellow poor, not does it oppose a market in which only the nonimpoverished are allowed to sell their organs.

Recognition of this last point leads directly to the first criticism of Zutlevics's argument. In "Markets and Morals," Dworkin explicitly addressed arguments opposed to allowing a current market in human organs that, like Zutlevics's, focused on the possibility that such markets might lead to the exploitation of the poor. Dworkin rhetorically asks whether one would be more or less inclined to favor organ sales if individuals whose average income was less than 80 percent of median family income were prohibited from selling their organs—a move that would have the effect of removing persons in the lower 40 percent of income distribution from the market.[30] Here, Dworkin is attempting to draw out the intuition that such a move would be considered to be highly unjust, prohibiting as it would those who would be most likely to benefit from the sale of their organs from doing so.

Zutlevics, however, has a ready response to this objection. Dworkin's rhetorical objection to antimarket arguments such as hers is based on the view that restricting the class of vendors to exclude the poor is of no benefit to them. As Zutlevics has persuasively argued, however, this might not be true, for such a restriction might serve to eliminate one reason that the affluent might have to refuse to provide aid to the poor. Rather than focusing on the short-term disadvantages that such a restriction might impose upon those poor individuals who would have otherwise sold their organs, then, one should instead focus on the long-term benefits that it might have for the poor as a class—and once this is done, such a restriction might not seem to be as unjust as Dworkin holds it to be.

Provided that one accepts Zutlevics's consequentialist approach to moral reasoning, then, her argument is defensible against Dworkin's objection. However, it is not so readily defended against the challenge that its basic premise is mistaken. Zutlevics holds that the possibility that autonomy-enhancing aid to the impoverished countries of the world would decrease if current markets in human organs were allowed is high enough to justify their prohibition. This premise of Zutlevics's argument is, of course, a speculative one—and there are several factors that undermine its plausibility. Firstly, the affluent countries of the West might wish the poorer countries of the world to attain wealth and financial stability to provide additional markets for Western goods. Furthermore, they might wish to aid them to avoid the possible political instability which their economic deprivation might generate, and which might subsequently adversely affect Western interests in the international arena. Similarly (and especially in the wake of the September 11, 2001, terrorist attacks on New York City and Washington, DC), Western countries might be motivated to provide aid to developing countries simply to dampen anti-Western sentiment.

Of course, these considerations are, like Zutlevics's own premise, speculative, so although recognizing them militates against a too-ready acceptance of Zutlevics's premise it does not decisively refute it. However, even though these considerations are speculative there is evidence to suggest that Western countries would be unlikely to refuse to provide aid to impoverished countries in order to maintain them as suppliers of organs for transplant into Western citizens. As G. V. Tadd has noted, when it became public knowledge that Turkish nationals were selling their kidneys for transplantation to persons in Britain, the resulting public outcry was largely responsible for the passing of the Human Organ Transplants Act of 1989 prohibiting this trade.[31] Rather than forming their policies concerning foreign aid to ensure the continuance of an international trade in human organs, then, it seems that Western countries will actually move to prohibit it, with the desire to avoid the opprobrium of both their own citizens and the international community heavily outweighing the desire to secure a supply of cheap transplant organs for a subset of their citizens.

Given both the speculative considerations outlined above and the British government's actual reaction to the public opposition to the international trade in human organs, there are good reasons to reject Zutlevics's claim that allowing such a trade would encourage the Western countries to withhold aid from those impoverished countries who would become net suppliers of cheap transplant organs. And since this claim provided the basic premise for her argument that allowing the poor to sell their organs would only provide them with a constraining option that, if chosen, would be likely to diminish the degree of autonomy that they enjoyed as a group, these considerations provide good reasons for rejecting her argument outright.

Conclusion

I have not provided in this chapter any arguments for the moral acceptability of a current market for human organs—except indirectly, insofar as I have defended Dworkin's autonomy-based arguments for the permissibility of such markets against the criticisms of Hughes and Zutlevics. However, showing that Dworkin's autonomy-based arguments in favor of allowing a current market in human organs can be defended against these criticisms is important, for this shows that if one genuinely values personal autonomy one should favor such markets rather than oppose them, even if one believes that the poor should be provided with aid. Since this is so, then, given that personal autonomy is the preeminent value in contemporary medical ethics, the possibility of using a current market in human organs to procure organs for transplantation should be welcomed by medical ethicists, rather than condemned by them.[32]

Discussion Questions

1. What is the almost universal reaction to the suggestion that the shortage of organs could be alleviated by the allowing a universal market in organs to exist?
2. What pro and con arguments were presented in reaction to allowing a universal market in organs?
3. What arguments are presented by Hughes and Zutlevics in opposition to those posed by Dworkin?
4. When the author referred to *organs*, just exactly how did he define it to avoid any ambiguity?
5. What rationale was presented by Dworkin for organ sales?
6. According to those opposed to the sale of organs, they have concluded the vendors would typically be forced to sell out of economic necessity and this would have certain negative consequences. What are these consequences?
7. What does Dworkin mean when he asserts that to not permit someone to sell their own organs would be "paternalistic" in the extreme?
8. Why does Zutlevics argue that allowing the poor of impoverished countries to participate as vendors in a current market in human organs might lead to less aid being forthcoming to these countries in the future?
9. What kind of arguments were made by the author to refute the assertion by Zutlevics about aid being reduced to the impoverished countries in the future if the poor were allowed to sell their organs?

Acknowledgments

I thank Paul Hughes and two anonymous referees for their exceptionally helpful comments on an earlier draft of this chapter.

Endnotes

1. As of August 23, 2002, there was a total of 5,682 patients on the United Kingdom's national transplant waiting list, with only 1,347 transplants having been performed. At the end of December 2001, there was a total of 6,842 patients on the waiting list with 2,717 solid organ transplants having been performed that year; and in December 2000, there was a total of 6,779 patients on the waiting list with 2,708 solid organ transplants having been performed that year. Statistics prepared by UK Transplant Support Service Authority (UKTSSA) from the National Transplant Database maintained on behalf of the UK transplant community.

2. Such measures include publicity campaigns to encourage people to carry donor cards, facilitating registration on the NHS Organ Donor Register, using organs from non-heart-beating donors, and initiating a system of presumed consent on which it is assumed that the individual wishes to be a donor unless he or she had previously registered an objection. These measures are outlined in Michael Wilks, et al., *Organ Donation in the 21st Century: Time for a Consolidated Approach* (London: British Medical Association, 2000). See also Arthur Caplan and Daniel H. Coelho, eds., *The Ethics of Organ Transplants: The Current Debate* (Amherst, N.Y.: Prometheus, 1998), 140.

3. There are three ways in which such a market for transplant organs might operate; a futures market (in which persons sell their organs for transplantation on their death), a current market (in which persons sell their organs for transplantation while they are still living), and a market for the organs of cadavers (in which the "owners" of a cadaver sell its organs.) Of these three possible markets, the current market in organs is usually held to be the most morally objectionable. Those few persons who have argued in favor of allowing a current market in human organs include Gerald Dworkin, "Markets and Morals: The Case for Organ Sales," in *Morality, Harm and the Law*, ed. Gerald Dworkin (Boulder, Colo.: Westview Press, 1994), 155–61; Mark J. Cherry, "Is a Market in Human Organs Necessarily Exploitative?" *Public Affairs Quarterly* 14, no. 4 (2000): 337–60; and Richard A. Epstein, *Mortal Peril: Our Inalienable Right to Health Care?* (New York: Perseus, 1997). See also Janet Radcliffe Richards, "Nephrarious Goings On: Kidney Sales and Moral Arguments," *The Journal of Medicine and Philosophy* 21, no. 4 (1996): 375–416, for arguments against the standard objections to allowing a current market in human kidneys—although Radcliffe Richards does not explicitly endorse allowing such a market.

4. The British Transplantation Society and the Renal Association object to allowing a current market in kidneys on this basis, stating that one of the necessary conditions that must be met prior to a living donor kidney transplantation's being performed is that the donor's decision to donate was "entirely voluntary and not due to coercion *or the offer of an inducement*." British Transplantation Society and the Renal Association, *United Kingdom Guidelines for Living Donor Kidney Transplantation* (London: British Transplantation Society, 2000), 9, emphasis added.

5. Dworkin, "Markets and Morals," 156.

6. Paul M. Hughes, "Exploitation, Autonomy, and The Case for Organ Sales," *International Journal of Applied Philosophy* 12, no. 1 (1998): 89–95; and T. L. Zutlevics, "Markets and the Needy: Organ Sales or Aid?" *Journal of Applied Philosophy* 18, no. 3 (2001): 297–302.

7. Although Zutlevics does not use the term "constraining option" to refer to the option of selling one's organs, it is clear that she believes it to be one, for she holds that the possession of it by the poor is likely to reinforce their presence within their autonomy-undermining economic circumstances (Zutlevics, "Markets and the Needy," 299). It should also be noted that since Zutlevics and Hughes claim that allowing the poor the option of selling their organs would reinforce

their impoverishment, their arguments might also be read as arguments that address the effectiveness (or lack thereof) of organs sales in improving the well-being of the poor.

8. Even a cursory glance at the bioethics literature will support this claim, as noted in Janet Smith, "The Preeminence of Autonomy in Bioethics," in *Human Lives: Critical Essays on Consequentialist Bioethics*, ed. David S. Oderberg and Jacqueline A. Laing (New York: St. Martin's Press, 1997). However, it must also be recognized that such a cursory glance might not reveal the very significant challenges to its preeminence that autonomy is now facing. Feminists, for example, are criticizing the value of autonomy, holding it to be based on an unrealistic ideal of personhood. See, for example, Carolyn Ells, "Shifting the Autonomy Debate to Theory as Ideology," *Journal of Medicine and Philosophy* 26, no. 4 (2001): 417–30; and S. Sherwin, "A Relational Approach to Autonomy in Health Care," in *The Politics of Women's Health: Exploring Agency and Autonomy*, ed. S. Sherwin (Philadelphia: Temple University Press, 1998), 19–47. In addition to this, communitarians are starting to argue against what they perceive to be the excess respect accorded to autonomy in recent bioethics. See Willard Gaylin and Bruce Jennings, *The Perversion of Autonomy: The Proper Uses of Coercion and Constraints in a Liberal Society* (New York: Free Press, 1996). Similarly, Carl Schneider argues that medical ethicists accept the primacy of autonomy too uncritically in the face of empirical evidence that demonstrates that patient rights and welfare could be better promoted by a return to a more paternalistic approach. Carl E. Schneider, *The Practice of Autonomy: Patients, Doctors and Medical Decisions* (Oxford: Oxford University Press, 1998).
9. Dworkin, "Markets and Morals," 156.
10. Ibid.
11. See Harry G. Frankfurt, "Coercion and Moral Responsibility," in *The Importance of What We Care About*, ed. Harry G. Frankfurt (Cambridge, Cambridge University Press, 1988), 26–46; and Gerald Dworkin, "Acting Freely," *Nous* 4 (1970): 367–83. For the dissenting view, see Michael J. Murray and David F. Dudrick, "Are Coerced Acts Free?" *American Philosophical Quarterly* 32, no. 2 (1995): 147–61.
12. Those who have offered versions of this argument include Hughes, "Exploitation, Autonomy, and the Case for Organ Sales," 89–95; Robert Audi, "The Morality and Utility of Organ Transplantation," *Utilitas* 8, no. 2 (1996): 141–58; John B. Dossetor and V. Manickavel, "Commercialization: The Buying and Selling of Kidneys," in *Ethical Problems in Dialysis and Transplantation*, ed. C. M. Kjellstrand and J. B. Dossetor (Dordrecht, Kluwer Academic, 1992), 61–69; and Pranlal Manga, "A Commercial Market for Organs? Why Not," *Bioethics* 1, no. 4 (1987): 321–38.
13. Dworkin, "Markets and Morals," 157.
14. I thank an anonymous referee for drawing my attention to the implicit claims that underlie Dworkin's response.
15. The Health and Safety at Work Act, 1974, 2 (1).
16. This, of course, assumes that the number of jobs available to the poor will not decrease as a result of the imposition of such regulation. If this assumption is mistaken (as conventional economic wisdom holds it to be), then one will have

to consider whether the degree of well-being and autonomy that is forfeited by those who lose their jobs outweighs that which is gained by those whose jobs are made less hazardous.

17. Zutlevics, "Markets and the Needy," 298.
18. For arguments for a monopsonistic market in human organs, see John Harris and Charles Erin, "An Ethically Defensible Market in Organs," *British Medical Journal* 325, no. 7356 (July 20, 2002): 114–15; and John Harris and Charles Erin, "A Monopsonistic Market," in *The Social Consequences of Life and Death Under High Technology Medicine*, ed. I. Robinson (Manchester: Manchester University Press, 1994): 134–54.
19. Hughes, "Exploitation, Autonomy, and the Case for Organ Sales," 92. For a fuller discussion of this, see Paul M. Hughes, "Paternalism, Battered Women and the Law," *Journal of Social Philosophy* 30, no. 1 (1999): 18–28.
20. Hughes, "Exploitation, Autonomy, and the Case for Organ Sales," 92.
21. As Hughes puts it, exploitation "is not just what happens when a worker labors in a factory for a wage, it's what happens to make that happen." Hughes, "Exploitation, Autonomy, and the Case for Organ Sales," 92.
22. Hughes, "Exploitation, Autonomy, and the Case for Organ Sales," 94.
23. Zutlevics, "Markets and the Needy," 300.
24. Sanjay Kumar, "Curbing Trade in Human Organs in India," *The Lancet* 344, no. 8914 (July 2, 1994): 48–49. Cited by Zutlevics, "Markets and the Needy," 300.
25. I thank an anonymous referee for clarifying these two different senses of the term *presuppose*.
26. Angeles tan Alora and Josephine M. Lumita, *Beyond a Western Bioethics* (Washington, DC: Georgetown University Press. 2001), 89; Patricia A. Marshall, David C. Thomasma, and Ardallah S. Daar, "Marketing Human Organs: The Autonomy Paradox," *Theoretical Medicine* 17, no. 1 (1996): 10.
27. Although see Zutlevics, "Markets and the Needy," 300.
28. This point is argued for in I. Kennedy, et al., "The Case for Allowing Kidney Sales," *The Lancet* 351, no. 9120 (June 27, 1998): 1899 the 972, cited by Zutlevics, "Markets and The Needy," 300.
29. Zutlevics, "Markets and the Needy," 300.
30. Dworkin, "Markets and Morals," 157.
31. G. V. Tadd, "The Market for Bodily Parts: A Response to Ruth Chadwick," *Journal of Applied Philosophy* 8, no. 1(1991): 95 the 102. The relevant section of the Human Organ Transplants Act is Section 1(1)(a), under which it is inter alia "an offence to make or receive any payment for the supply of, or offer to supply, an organ removed from a living person which is intended to be transplanted into another individual whether in Great Britain or elsewhere."
32. Of course, it is a very different question as to whether or not a market system should be used to *distribute* the kidneys that are procured through the use of a current market. The useful distinction between using a market for procurement and using it for distribution was noted by Henry Hansmann, "The Economics and Ethics of Markets for Human Organs," *Journal of Health Politics, Policy and Law* 4, (1989): 60. For suggestions concerning how to distribute organs procured through a market by nonmarket means, see Dworkin, "Markets and Morals,"158; and Harris and Erin, "A Monopsonistic Market," 114–15.

Markets and the Needy Organ Sales or Aid?

11

T. L. ZUTLEVICS, PhD
Philosophy Department, Flinders University, Adelaide, Australia

Contents

Introduction	161
The Moral Viability of a Current Organ Market	162
Discussion Questions	166
Acknowledgments	166
Endnotes	166

Introduction

For well over a decade, bioethicists have noted that the drastic shortage of organs for transplantation has rendered the procurement of organs a crucial issue.[1] As Emmanuel Thorne notes, the recent "proposal by a prominent organ transplant center … to hasten the death of potential organ donors" clearly conveys the desperation of the situation.[2] Moreover, as is widely acknowledged, the problem is not a shortage of potential organ donors but rather actual ones.[3] The challenge facing policy makers in this area is to increase organ donation from potential donors without transgressing moral boundaries. Suggestions have been various and include altering the criteria for death to increase the pool of potential donors, changing donor policy from "opting in" to "opting out," demoting autonomy from its place in bioethics as the principal moral value, xenotransplantation, tissue engineering, and creating a market in organs.[4]

My focus in this chapter will be on the moral viability of the last option—a market in organs. Support for this option is steadily increasing. As Thorne notes, the ban on such markets has been blamed for shortages of organs and increased waiting lists.[5] Whilst many have argued for a market in organs, it is Gerald Dworkin who most persuasively defends the ethicality of a market in organs.[6] As Dworkin points out, there are two possibilities here—a futures market and a current market.[7] I will follow Dworkin in focusing on a current market in the sale of organs from living donors, as this is generally

---

* First published in *Journal of Applied Philosophy* 18 (3) 297–302, 2001.

considered more difficult to justify. One of the most pressing concerns here is that such a market will exploit the poor. In the following section, I outline this concern and scrutinize Dworkin's and others' rejection of it. Briefly, I argue that the arguments Dworkin employs for allowing the poor to sell their organs fail, and in fact better support an argument for increasing aid to the needy.

The Moral Viability of a Current Organ Market

As Dworkin acknowledges, the people most likely to sell their organs will be those who are in dire need.

> Those who have alternative sources of income are not likely to choose an option which entails some health risk, some disfigurement, some pain and discomfort. The risks of such sales will certainly fall disproportionately by income class.[8]

The concern is that choices made under nonoptimal conditions are insufficiently voluntary and are exploitative of the poor. According to Dworkin, if this line of reasoning is valid, it would have wider implications. For instance, it would imply that poor people should not be allowed to join the army, engage in hazardous occupations, or be paid subjects in medical experiments.[9] Dworkin at this point assumes that most people would be reluctant to deny the poor the opportunity to join the army, to engage in hazardous occupations, or to receive financial remuneration for participation in medical experiments. At this stage, Dworkin's argument is based on intuition—an intuition, moreover, which would not necessarily be widely held.

My guess is that most people would look favorably on the poor joining the army on the proviso that they were treated on a par with other members of the army and not given dubious assignments. In many societies, the army represents a reputable career that provides people with income, status, and other benefits such as health care, food, shelter, and education. Our response to Dworkin's second suggestion, namely, engaging in hazardous occupations, would depend on the exact nature of the work. Dworkin's suggestion of high-steel construction, where adequate safety standards were met, would most likely meet with general approval as such an occupation would afford some social standing as well as income. Conversely, many would be less sanguine about hazardous occupations that did not accord social respect or meet satisfactory safety standards. For example, companies who sent the poor, inadequately trained and clothed, into areas with hazardous levels of radioactive material would most likely meet with general disapproval. Finally, with regard to participation in medical experiments, I think, once again, our intuitions are likely to be less straightforward than Dworkin assumes. For instance, we would need to know the precise nature of the experiments before we could pass judgment. Controlled, well-designed experiments that had passed an ethics committee would be acceptable to most people. In contrast, poorly designed experiments that would never pass an ethics committee would most likely meet with disapproval.

These considerations suggest that Dworkin's attempt to undermine the concern that it is exploitative to allow the poor to sell their organs does not succeed as the wider implications he is concerned about do not follow. Risk in and of itself is not the sole concern. Importantly, we are concerned with the wider context of the risk. This includes, amongst other things, what we expect of other groups (in this case, the nonpoor), associated benefits, and social standing.

Dworkin next tries to put living organ donations into context by citing one study that estimated that the increased risk of death to a 35-year-old from giving up one kidney is roughly the same as that associated with driving a car to work 16 miles a day. Dworkin then asks us,

> Imagine saying to a poor person either that her choice to commute such a distance is not voluntary, or if it is, she still ought not to be allowed to commute such a distance, although we will allow middle class persons to do so.[10]

What Dworkin is saying is that it would be absurd to disallow poor people to commute, and so, since commuting has the same risks as kidney donation, it would be absurd to disallow poor people to sell their kidneys. However, once again it is not obvious that the cases are straightforwardly analogous. Whilst the actual operation may have the same risk associated with it as commuting, there are other risks that the analogy fails to take into account—most obviously the risk of future vulnerability for members of the community to which the donors belong. As Dworkin himself notes, most well-off people would be extremely reluctant to donate their organs unless it were for the benefit of a friend or relative. Organs are not things we readily give up. Hence, organ markets will primarily be supplied by needy people in poor countries—a point Dworkin is also aware of. This is of concern as such countries may begin to be viewed as resources for wealthier nations. Once this happens, respect is likely to be diminished, and perhaps the door will be opened for more exploitative practices. Western societies have certainly exploited poorer nations for goods far less significant than body parts.

Dworkin would most likely dismiss this concern. He may argue that we could put in place legislation to prevent people from poorer countries being viewed merely as resources for wealthier nations.[11] However, it is doubtful that such legislation would succeed. What is primarily at issue is an attitude, and attitudes are difficult to legislate against. This is particularly so when they result in certain omissions. The real concern is not that the West will go in and actively plunder organs from people in poorer countries. Rather, the concern is that in seeing poorer countries as resources, we will be less motivated to offer alternative avenues of aid. For example, imagine that such a market did exist and that as a result the shortage of organs was rectified.[12] Would wealthier nations really be interested in helping poorer countries attain financial stability and wealth, when doing so would most likely result in a loss of supplies to the organ market?

There is another concern with Dworkin's strategy that should make us wary of accepting a current market in organs. According to Dworkin, "There are certainly objections of justice to the current highly unequal income distribution. But it seems to me paternalistic in the extreme, given that injustice, to deny people choices which they perceive as increasing their well-being."[13] On the face of it, Dworkin's basic point seems intuitively right—who would deny someone the opportunity to better their situation? But I think this is too simplistic and misses an important point. The reasoning appears to be as follows.

1. The poor experience extreme hardships.
2. We should allow people to engage in activities that would alleviate their hardship.
3. Selling organs would alleviate the poor's hardships. Therefore,
4. We should allow the poor to sell their organs.[14]

Whilst initially appealing, this argument is problematic as it justifies a great deal more than allowing the poor to sell their organs. The situation of the poor can be so desperate that even actions that cause extreme harm would constitute an improvement in their situation. We know this is true because communities exist where parents seek to alleviate the hardships of their children by mutilating them so that they can beg for food more effectively and hence not starve. We know this is true because women, children, and some men prostitute themselves, not for a decent living wage, but so that they and their families can afford a little food. And we know this is true because some families sell their daughters into slavery and prostitution so that they can afford to eat.

Dworkin would most likely respond by pointing to the fact that in most of these cases the harm experienced is not autonomously chosen as the decision to be harmed is made by someone else. As we know from his other writings, personal autonomy is something highly valued by Dworkin—functioning in many cases as a moral constraint on what others can do to us.[15] However, it is not difficult to think of examples where the agent does in fact choose to be harmed in order to alleviate hardships. For example, a woman in straitened circumstances may expose herself to HIV by prostituting herself in order to feed her children or provide them with medicine. Another example would be someone who continued to work in a hazardous industry devoid of safety standards because they needed the income. Furthermore, as most autonomy theorists note, we do make decisions on behalf of our children. Such decisions are generally viewed as justified so long as they serve to better the opportunities of our children. This would rule out the third case—selling a child to benefit other family members—but it would not necessarily rule out the first case.

It is true that some people's lives are so bad that selling their organs would improve their lives and those of their family. But should we encourage such policies when there are other options for help—extensive aid programs and so on? If a person's life really would be drastically improved by selling a kidney or a section of their liver, then it is arguable that they are entitled to help. After all, as many moral theorists have argued, we have an obligation to help protect the needy—or at least not use their vulnerability for our own advantage.[16]

In a similar vein to Dworkin, Kennedy and coauthors have recently argued,

> If our ground for concern is that the range of choices is too small, we cannot improve matters by *removing the best option that poverty has left*, and making the range smaller still. To do so is to make subsequent choices, by this criterion, even less autonomous.[17]

This passage warrants close scrutiny. The argument rests on the assumption that the best chance the poor have to alleviate their poverty is to sell their organs. But surely there are other options. As I have suggested, increased aid is another option.[18] Furthermore, one has to take into account evidence that suggests that poverty is not significantly alleviated by selling organs. For example, Sanjay Kumar has noted that "[s]o rampant is the trade in Madras that its suburban slum colony Villivakkam—teeming with poor people who have sold one of their kidneys—has come to be known internationally as 'kidney-vakkam.'"[19] It would therefore appear that selling one's organs does not provide sustained relief from poverty. If this is correct, the claim that allowing a current market in organs represents the best option to alleviate poverty is further discredited.

Consequently, I would suggest that Dworkin's, and indeed Kennedy and coauthors', arguments more naturally support the conclusion that we should help the desperately needy (perhaps through aid), not the conclusion that a current market in organs should be developed. The intuitive appeal of Dworkin's argument is that we feel it would be a good thing if the situation of the poor were rectified. However, this does not support a current market in organs.

Finally, a recent study by Burroughs et al. found that people who didn't feel that they should be paid for their organs were more likely to donate.[20] It is possible that those disinclined to donate would be prepared to sell their organs. Yet it is also possible that many people who are currently prepared to donate their organs, or those of deceased family members, would be disinclined to either sell or donate them if a market for organs were in existence. If this were the case, we would be more reliant on organs from poorer nations, which would be strategically as well as ethically less than ideal. The point is that we cannot assume that a market in organs would increase availability—it may be counterproductive to the attempt to turn potential donors into actual ones. The issue requires further investigation.

Discussion Questions

1. What was the principal focus of this chapter?
2. What example does the author give for the assertion that the situation of the poor can be so desperate that even actions that cause extreme harm would constitute an improvement in their situation?
3. What alternative arguments were presented by the author to the statement of Dworkin and Kennedy in which they conclude the best chance the poor have to alleviate their poverty is to sell their organs?
4. What were the findings of the study conducted by Burroughs et al.?

Acknowledgments

I am greatly indebted to Ian Ravenscroft for many helpful discussions. Thanks are also due to Suzanne Uniacke, and to Karen Reynolds who invited me to speak at the School of Informatics and Engineering at Flinders University on the ethical issues surrounding organ donation.

Endnotes

1. See for example, Kenneth Einar Himma, "A Critique of &UNOS Liver Allocation Policy," *Cambridge Quarterly of Healthcare Ethics* 8, no. 3 (1999): 311–20; Jean-Christopher Meele, "A Kantian Argument for a Duty to Donate One's Own Organs: A Reply to Nicole Gerrand," *Journal of Applied Philosophy* 17, no. 1 (2000): 93–101; Aaron Spital, "The Shortage of Organs for Transplantation: Where Do We Go from Here?" *The New England Journal of Medicine* 325, no. 17 (October 24, 1991): 1243–46; and Robert Veatch, "Routine Inquiry about Organ Donation:—An Alternative to Presumed Consent," *The New England Journal of Medicine* 325, no. 17 (October 24, 1991): 1246–49.

2. Emmanuel Thorne, "The Shortage in Market-Inalienable Human Organs: A Consideration of 'Nonmarket' Failures," *The American Journal of Economics and Sociology* 57, no. 3 (July 1998): 247–60.
3. For example, K. Bart et al., "Cadaveric Kidneys for Transplantation: A Paradox of Shortage in the Face of Plenty," *Transplantation* 31, no. 5 (May 1981): 379–82.
4. These suggestions have been advocated by various writers, but see for example Spital, "The Shortage of Organs for Transplantation"; D. Thomasa, "Ethical Issues and Transplantation Technology," *Cambridge Quarterly of Healthcare Ethics* 1, no. 4 (1992): 333–34; J. Portman, "Cutting Bodies to Harvest Organs," *Cambridge Quarterly of Healthcare Ethics* 8, no. 3 (1999): 288–98; and G. Dworkin, "Markets and Morals: The Case for Organ Sales," *The Mount Sinai Journal of Medicine* 60, no. 1 (1993): 60–69.
5. Thorne, "The Shortage in Market-Inalienable Human Organs," 247.
6. Dworkin, "Markets and Morals." See also A. Barnett and D. Kaserman, "The Shortage of Organs for Transplantation: Exploring the Alternatives," *Issues in Law and Medicine* 9, no. 2 (1993): 117–37.
7. A futures market involves individuals selling the rights to their organs after their death. In a current market, individuals sell their organs whilst alive.
8. Dworkin, "Markets and Morals," 67.
9. Ibid.
10. Ibid.
11. Perhaps along similar lines to the legislative solution advocated by Dworkin in response to possible unjust distributional consequences of a market. See Dworkin, "Markets and Morals," 67.
12. Many have argued this. See, for example, A. Barnett and D. Kaserman, "Comment on 'The Shortage in Market-Inalienable Human Organs': Faulty Analysis of a Failed Policy," *The American Journal of Economics and Sociology* 59, no. 2 (April 2000); and D. Kaserman and A. Barnett, "Organ Transplants: Free Market Can Solve Shortage," *The Atlanta Constitution*, September 10, 1991.
13. Dworkin, "Markets and Morals," 67.
14. Argument 1–4 in fact differs from that given by Dworkin. Dworkin's argument is couched in terms of choices perceived to increase well-being. Argument 1–4 is stated in terms of choices that actually alleviate hardships. However, this alteration strengthens Dworkin's argument. It is more difficult to argue against the right of people to engage in risky behavior that will actually increase their well being than it is to deny them choices that they merely perceive as bettering their situation. This is especially so if we have good reason to believe them to be mistaken.
15. See for example G. Dworkin, *The Theory and Practice of Autonomy* (Cambridge: Cambridge University Press, 1988).
16. See G. Brock, *Necessary Goods: Our Responsibilities to Meet Others' Needs* (Lanham, Md.: Rowman and Littlefield, 1998) for a useful collection of papers defending the legitimacy of positive rights claims and our duty to help the needy. See also R. Goodin, *Protecting the Vulnerable* (Chicago: The University of Chicago Press, 1985).
17. J. Radcliffe-Richards et al., "The Case for Allowing Kidney Sales," *The Lancet* 351, no. 9120 (June 1998): 1950–52.

18. Moral weight is added to this option when one adds into the calculation that, arguably, many poor people are as badly off as they are because of Western interference. Policies pursued by Western societies have contributed to the poverty and hardship experienced by people in the Third World. On this point, see C. Card, "Caring and Evil," *Hypatia* 5 (Spring 1990): 101–8.
19. S. Kumar, "Curbing Trade in Human Organs in India," *The Lancet* 344, no. 8914 (July 1994): 48–49.
20. T. Burroughs et al., "The Stability of Family Decisions to Consent or Refuse Organ Donation: Would You Do it Again?" *Psychosomatic Medicine* 60, no. 2 (1998): 156–62.

12

Selling Bits and Pieces of Humans to Make Babies
The Gift of the Magi Revisited*

CYNTHIA B. COHEN, PhD, JD
The Kennedy Institute of Ethics, Georgetown University, Washington, DC

Contents

Introduction	169
Ethical Concerns about Selling Human Organs for Transplantation	171
Ethical Concerns about Selling Human Gametes for Reproduction	176
Ethical Concerns about Selling Fetal Eggs and Ovaries for Reproduction	179
Ethical Concerns about Selling Human Cells and Eggs for Cloning	181
The Human Significance of Reproduction	184
Discussion Questions	185
Acknowledgments	185
References	186

Introduction

O. Henry, in *The Gift of the Magi* (1992), relates a tale of a poor woman who sells her shining long hair to purchase a watch fob for her husband for Christmas. Meanwhile, her husband sells his heirloom gold watch to buy combs for his wife's hair for Christmas. Each sacrifices something dear to obtain funds for a gift for the other. We regret that financial need has driven them to sell precious items in order to express their love, but we do not condemn either of them for their acts. Selling hair and watches is ethically acceptable. Indeed, there is a wide range of products, from housewares to cars, that we consider it appropriate to exchange on the open market for money. The distribution of certain goods in this way can foster an incentive for productivity and creativity that will ultimately benefit society.

---

* First published in *Journal of Medicine and Philosophy* 24 (3) 288–306, 1999.

Significant changes in the delivery of health care are in progress today that would add health care itself to the range of marketable products. As this move toward the marketization of health care gathers force, reproductive medicine is increasingly sliding toward the sale of certain human bits and pieces to generate babies. The commodification of human gametes to enable women to become pregnant is now an established practice in reproductive medicine and the sale of human cells and fetal ovaries and eggs to achieve reproductive ends is in the offing. Such fresh avenues for the sale of bits and pieces of human beings could not only assist those who need medical care to create babies, but enable those who are poor to obtain funds to express their love and meet their needs.

What if Della, the impoverished wife in the O. Henry tale, were to sell some of her eggs to a woman who cannot ovulate? The latter wishes to engage in cloning by nuclear substitution, replacing the nuclei of Della's eggs with some from her own mammary cells, so that she can have a child with her own genetic makeup. Or what if Della were to sell some of her mammary cells to a woman with a heritable genetic disease? That woman plans to clone these cells in order to have children free of that serious disease. Fetal egg and ovary transfer are on the horizon. Perhaps Della might become pregnant and sell the ovaries of the resulting fetus to a woman with no ovaries. These ovaries, once matured, would be implanted in the woman and the eggs they provide could be used to produce a child. Or if the couple involved preferred not to wait, they might purchase fetal eggs from Della and use them to generate a baby. In all of these instances, Della would receive funds that she could use to provide her husband with a token of her love and have a surplus to use for other important purposes.

Would we accept these sales with the same equanimity that we displayed toward the commodification of hair and watches in O. Henry's tale? Would we view human bits and pieces as appropriate products to enter into a stream of commerce that ultimately flows through the reproductive area of the health care system? Or would such sales transform that touching story into a darker ethical tale reflecting a denial of human dignity and worth? Would they display that we have lost our view of reproduction as an essentially human activity in the face of increasing commodification of reproductive health care?

It is fair to say that most of us are leery about selling certain human bits and pieces in order to create babies. The sale of fetal eggs and ovaries strikes many as ethically repulsive. Indeed, we are sufficiently wary of selling human eggs that we talk instead about "donating" them, despite the tenor of newspaper advertisements indicating that money is the chief inducement for stranger oocyte "donation." Selling mammary cells initially seems as ethically unproblematic as selling hair, for these minute human bits and pieces appear to be of no ethical consequence. Yet when such sales are carried out for purposes of human reproduction, they become more troubling. Why do many of us tend to bridle at selling fetal parts, human eggs, and even simple human cells to those who are infertile when we do not object to selling hair? What is it that makes the sale of human bits and pieces in order to generate babies ethically disturbing?

The problem is that to sell human body parts and products is not simply to insert physical bits and pieces of human beings into the stream of commerce. These bits and pieces bear meanings of deep significance to us, and the act of selling them therefore has consequences of ethical import. Thus, we reject the sale of kidneys, hearts, and other organs because this compromises certain extra-economic values that are extremely important to us as a community. As Tom Murray asks, "Do people really think that organs are like cars and so on, such that they will respond to money for organs in the same manner as for those other objects?" (1996, 103). We are similarly troubled about the sale of human eggs. There is something ethically distinctive about these gametes on which we find it hard to put our collective finger, a distinctiveness that makes us ethically queasy about their sale. Thus, as Ruth Macklin notes, "A presumption appears throughout the literature that … it would be wrong to pay donors for their eggs.… However, nowhere is an explanation offered for why payment for eggs is ethically suspect" (Macklin 1996, 107).

In this chapter, we will parse out the concerns of those who object ethically to the sale of human bits and pieces to generate babies. First, we will pay close attention to what it is about human body parts or products in general that makes their sale "ethically suspect"—even when this is done for ethically admirable purposes. Then we will fathom why many claim that the sale of human body parts or products for reproductive purposes, in particular, is ethically disturbing. The ethical force of the sale of human bits and pieces to generate babies is not well defined within our shared value system, and whether such sales can be justified as part of the increasing marketization of health care needs closer evaluation. In what follows, we will find that the objections that some raise to the sale of human body parts and products within the health care sector for reproductive purposes are grounded in more than a feeling of repugnance. They are supported by sound ethical claims.

Ethical Concerns about Selling Human Organs for Transplantation

What if Della, instead of selling her hair, decided to sell one of her kidneys? This would not only enable her to buy her husband a present for Christmas, but also leave over enough money to meet their food expenses for the next 2 years. Despite this desirable outcome, such a sale would strike many as wrong. Kidneys, as Murray observes above, are not cars. They are not the sorts of things that should be put on the open market in exchange for money.

This view is reflected in the federal law barring the sale of human organs for transplantation. Why do we, as a society, pass such laws and think that it is wrong to sell human kidneys when we are not much bothered by the sale of human hair?

Human kidneys are qualitatively different sorts of human bits and pieces from human hair, for they sustain life. Hair, in contrast, serves mainly as personal adornment. The preservation of life is a greater value than that of exterior beautification. Kidneys, consequently, are ethically more significant to us than human hair. Yet the reason that we reject the sale of human kidneys cannot be that we think it wrong to sell something that can be used to keep people alive. We have no ethical qualms about selling other materials and procedures that are designed to save lives, such as respirators, oxygen tanks, intensive care services, and transplant surgery. The reason we are reluctant to exchange money for human kidneys is that this would deny something distinctly valuable about human beings: their human dignity and worth.

Although ours is a pluralistic society, a basic ethical premise that underlies and allows this pluralism is that human beings have a certain dignity and worth. We are not disembodied beings, but complex combinations of intellect, emotion, appetite, spirit, and body. Our body has special value because it is the medium through which we express ourselves. Thus, our special value as human beings extends to our bodies. Yet it does not extend to all parts of our bodies. We do not ordinarily consider that hair, spit, or fingernail parings carry human dignity and worth, for these generally function as inessential human bits and pieces unrelated to what it is that makes human beings of special value. It is those parts of the body that are integral to the functioning of human beings, such as kidneys, livers, brains, hearts, and eyes, that we take to bear special dignity and worth because of their role.

When we or our integral body parts are sold, our dignity as human beings is denied. Many other practices, such as slavery, prostitution, and the sale of military draft call-up notices, are wrong for the same reason—they deny the respect due to human beings as creatures with special worth. Indeed, we believe so strongly that organs integral to human functioning have a certain dignity that we are reluctant to sell them even after we have died and no longer need them. This is reflected in state laws barring such sales, as well as the careful rules governing the procurement of human bodies for dissection in medical schools. To set a market price on humans, their whole bodies, or integral parts of their bodies, is to deny the special value of human beings.

Kant can be instructive here, although we need not become full-fledged Kantians to benefit from his thought. Dignity, for Kant, is an unconditioned worth that all persons have just in virtue of being human (Kant 1964, 94). It is unconditioned in that it does not depend on their particular needs, the consequences of their actions, or any other contingent facts about them. Human dignity, however, is not a Platonic form hovering over humans in a

Kantian sky; it is an attribute of particular persons. Still, according to Kant, it is not an attribute of isolated individuals, but of individuals who belong to a community, "the realm of ends." In that community, each member is suffused with dignity.

Let us grant that we attribute dignity to persons as psychophysical entities. Must we also ascribe dignity to parts of them? How are human organs related to whole bodies, selves, and persons? Kant emphasizes the integration or "togetherness" of the various aspects of the human person. He states that "the body is part of the self; in its togetherness with the self it constitutes the person" (Kant 1963, 166). Thus, Kant rejects dualism. We are organic wholes whose kidneys, hearts, and eyes are a part of us, not isolated organs. Dignity does not just accrue to certain distinctive features of humans, such as self-consciousness, freedom, and rationality, but to all of their integral aspects. Our embodied integrity is not an object that we own in the way that we own such discrete things as cars. It is not something that can be separated off and sold while leaving our self intact. Thus, any body part that is necessary for the functioning of the whole person, Kant asserts, is endowed with the dignity of that person (Munzer 1993). Kidneys and testicles are such essential body parts; hair is not.

Kant goes on to distinguish between things that have a price and things that are beyond price (Kant 1964, 96). The price of a thing is a relative measure of its value; for example, relative to supply and demand. Human beings, in contrast, are of incomparable ethical worth and admit of no equivalent. Each has value that is beyond the contingencies of supply and demand or of any other relative estimation. They are priceless. Consequently, to sell an integral human body part is to corrupt the very meaning of human dignity. Since that dignity is "exalted above all price," of incalculable worth, he maintains, we cannot compensate for an offense against it by offering money (Hill 1992). For this reason, the human community should not permit individuals to give over integral parts of their bodies for money.

Kant was reacting to a tradition represented by Hobbes in which dignity was identified with price and a person's value was set by the commonwealth. Hobbes stated that "[t]he value or worth of a man is as of all other things, his Price; that is to say, so much as would be given for the use of his Power" (1968, 151). He went on to insist that "as in other things, so in men, not the seller, but the buyer determines the Price." Thus, different persons have different values or prices, depending on the market, according to Hobbes. Kant objected to this view because it denied that all humans equally have a basic dignity and worth that are beyond any price.

This does not mean that Kant would have rejected donating, rather than selling, a non-renewable organ that is not absolutely essential to human functioning, such as a single kidney. It is true that for Kant this organ contributes to our ability to act in the world as embodied selves, and is therefore endowed with the dignity of the whole person. Kant was not sufficiently prescient to consider the possibility of human transplantation, but had he known about it, he would have maintained that gifts of the body whose loss would not wholly destroy their donor's integrity as an embodied self do not deny human dignity. Indeed, they can be taken to uphold that dignity just because they allow the donor to share something of him or herself as a gift to another member of the realm of ends. Donation is a gesture of altruism and of solidarity with other human beings. It is an implicit acknowledgment that we value other human beings as worthy of respect, admiration, and love. However, gifts of the body that involve dismemberment and destruction of the integrated bodily self, such as the gift of a heart or liver, would be ethically unacceptable to Kant, for the dignity of human beings would also be dismembered by such gifts.

Radin is a contemporary thinker who, while not a Kantian, objects to selling body parts on similar grounds. Bodily integrity, she maintains, should not be conceived of as fungible—by which she means the body and its integral parts should not be treated as though they can be replaced with money. Radin observes,

> A fungible object can pass in and out of a person's possession without effect on the person as long as its market equivalent is given in exchange.... To speak of personal attributes [that which "has become identified with a person, with her self-constitution and self-development"] as fungible objects—alienable "goods"—is intuitively wrong". We feel discomfort or even insult, and we fear degradation or even loss of the value involved when bodily integrity is conceived of as a fungible object ... if my bodily integrity is an integral personal attribute, not a detachable object, then hypothetically valuing my bodily integrity in money is not far removed from valuing me in money ... that is inappropriate treatment of a person. (Radin 1987, 1937)

For Kant and Radin, human beings and their integral parts are not the sorts of objects that can become the property of others, even if their market equivalent is given in exchange. Human bodily integrity is an intimate personal attribute, not a detachable object. To sell human beings and those bits and pieces integral to them as embodied selves is to violate that which is essential to them. Radin would agree with Kant that, as it violates human dignity to sell whole persons, so, too, it violates that dignity to sell body parts integral to whole persons. Thus, it is ethically acceptable to sell human hair, for this accoutrement is not integral to the functioning of the whole person, but it is not ethically acceptable to sell vital organs which have become identified, in Radin's words, with our "self-constitution and self-development."

Yet it is logically possible for an entity to have both dignity or worth and a market value. We attribute special worth to our homes as places in which our families grow and thrive, and yet we also put a commercial value on them. Similarly, some might argue, we could value our integral body parts as suffused with human dignity and still sell them on the open market without diminishing that dignity. Kant, however, does not think this is possible. We cannot think of an entity as simultaneously having both dignity and market value, and still retain the attitudes we typically exhibit toward entities we regard as possessing human dignity. Ultimately, the existence of a market in human body parts would transform our attitudes toward ourselves and others in the realm of ends so that we would come to think of one another, not so much as moral agents with a special dignity, but as repositories of organs and other bodily bits and pieces. If people were to turn themselves and their body parts into commodities, their very humanity and that of all of us would be demeaned.

This argument against selling human organs seems to contradict the view so closely associated with Kant that we ought to respect the autonomous choices of individual human beings. If people freely and rationally choose to sell parts of their bodies, some might argue, they should be allowed to do so. How does this putatively Kantian position square with his view that it is ethically wrong for the human community to allow its members to sell body parts?

Since the body is the medium through which the whole person acts, its integrity is essential to Kant's view of autonomy. Respect for autonomy entails respect for the fullness of the person, including our bodies. To sell an integral part of ourselves is to misuse our autonomy in the same way that selling ourselves into slavery does so. Autonomy is an important ethical limit, but is itself limited in scope and weight. It meets one of its limits when the sale of human body parts is at issue. Even though we respect the freedom of individuals to do what they want with their lives, we draw certain lines based on human dignity beyond which we do not give effect to their free choices. Think of Della in O. Henry's story selling an eye to a blind person and thereby restoring his vision. Della would still see and function normally with one eye, and it would have been her autonomous choice to go through with the sale. Moreover, she would have provided a great benefit to the person who was blind. Yet Kant would not accept this transaction as ethical. People should not sell their eyes, for these are part of who they are. To treat their eyes as commodities is to alienate their dignity as human beings, to consider human beings as of calculable worth.

It is this sort of argument, not necessarily the specific Kantian version of it, that has led us as a society to conclude that it is wrong to sell integral human body parts. To sell an organ necessary to the functioning of a human being is to deny its special worth and dignity as an integral aspect of our very selves. Even when that organ would save a life or would buy a precious gift and food enough for two years, it would be wrong to sell it. Donating it would seem the only ethical way in which to provide it to another. On this view of human dignity and worth, which is essential to our shared value system, it would be wrong for Della to sell her kidney in order to buy her husband a present and meet some of their food expenses.

Ethical Concerns about Selling Human Gametes for Reproduction

What if instead of her hair, Della decided to sell some of her oocytes? This act would provide her with enough money to buy her husband a gift and would leave enough extra to meet their household needs for several months. She could sell her eggs to an infertile couple who would use them in what has come to be known as egg "donation." Meanwhile, her husband, Jim, might sell some of his sperm to an infertile couple to buy Della a present. Should we view the sale of human gametes for reproductive purposes in the same ethical light that we view the sale of human organs?

Human gametes do not contribute to integral bodily functioning in the same way as human organs. Indeed, Della's and Jim's gametes appear to be extra human bits and pieces that make no distinctive contribution to their embodied selfhood. Most of their gametes will not be used for any special purpose over the course of their lifetimes, but will be sloughed off into oblivion or else reabsorbed. Gametes, therefore, would not appear to fall under the Kantian prohibition against the sale of integral body parts. Yet, as Ruth Macklin observes, there is something "unsavory" about selling human eggs, even though the practice does not appear to violate such principles of bioethics as nonmaleficence and beneficence or the rights of any person (Macklin 1996, 106). What is it about the sale of human gametes that does not sit right with us?

Human gametes are not merely insignificant physical bits and pieces produced by the human body. They have a special worth and dignity that is grounded in five interrelated features that they bear. First, human gametes are necessarily derived from human beings. Even if we should learn to clone animals that produce human gametes, those gametes would ultimately have to be derived from human beings; pigs will not spontaneously produce human eggs or sperm, thus, human gametes have a certain derivative dignity because they must be obtained from human beings, creatures with a special dignity and worth. Second, gametes can be used for a significant human function. While they are not life-sustaining body parts integral to the functioning of human beings, they are life-giving bodily bits and pieces integral to a function of special import to human beings, reproduction. When united with the gamete of a person of the opposite sex, they are transformed into embryos that can grow into living children. That they are necessary for human reproduction therefore also contributes to their derivative worth, for they bring valuable human beings into the world.

Third, unlike kidneys, human gametes cannot be interchanged for each other without losing something of the unique identity of those from whom they come. They serve as vehicles through which some of the distinctive physical attributes, personal characteristics, and some of the family traits of their biological possessors are expressed. Their uniqueness also gives gametes a certain derivative dignity and worth, for they each convey the distinctiveness of the human being who produces them. Fourth, when gametes are united in reproduction, they bring unique human beings to life. Each person born is a distinctive individual who has properties and characteristics that, in combination, belong to no other person. Without the contribution of two gametes from two different progenitors, such persons could not come into existence. This power of gametes to contribute to the creation of distinctive individual human beings further enhances their derivative dignity.

Finally, gametes introduce these new human beings and those who have brought them into being into a special biological, ethical, and social relation. Part of what gives meaning and cohesiveness to our lives and helps us to feel recognized as individuals is our biological connectedness to others. The biological tie relates children not only to parents, but to a larger family that is linked by a set of enduring relationships. The most significant of these relationships are affected by conception and birth. Elizabeth Anderson observes that

> the principle of respecting genetic ties…places children in a far wider network of associations and obligations than the consent-intent rule sanctions. It supports the role of grandparents and other relatives in the nurturing of children, and provides children with a possible focus of stability and an additional source of claims to care if their parents cannot sustain a well-functioning household. (1990, 80)

The biological connection between gamete providers and children born of their gametes thus has special social and ethical import. While the practice of adoption indicates that we do not consider biological ties essential to parenthood, it also reveals that we take them as sufficiently important to require birth parents explicitly to renounce such ties before adoptive couples can acquire parental status over their children.

The significance of this fifth feature is confirmed by some sperm "donors" who report that their fairly casual sale of sperm eventually had a greater personal, ethical, and biological significance than they had anticipated at the time of sale (Achilles 1989, 105–19). They now understand that vending their sperm led to the creation of children who are linked to them by ties of biology; because of this they now feel a certain sense of responsibility to them. These "donors" are concerned about the welfare of their biologically connected children and are receptive to learning about how they are doing (Daniels 1989). Many egg "donors" also express an interest in those who receive their gametes and want to know about the children who result from them (Schover et al. 1991; Power et al. 1990). Some even want to meet the children and their nurturing parents and are willing to donate blood or organs to assist them medically, if necessary. Those who donate kidneys for transplantation, in contrast, feel no similar sense of responsibility for the outcome of their donation. While they may feel camaraderie with those whom they assist, they do not maintain that they have a familial bond with them, nor do they often feel personally responsible for their welfare. Thus, the special relation that is initiated between gamete providers and the children who result from use of their gametes further imparts a certain dignity and worth to these human bits and pieces.

Because human gametes are the medium through which unique human beings are created who stand in a special relation to their unique progenitors, who themselves have dignity and worth, gametes have a derivative dignity and worth. Are they the sorts of objects that Della and Jim in the O. Henry story should exchange for money?

Imagine literally selling your face (not a photo of it) to someone who wanted a new face after a terrible accident in which his original face had been disfigured. This would also involve irrevocably giving up for money something that is an integral and distinctive part of you and through which you and your family are uniquely revealed. It would be as wrong to expose this significant aspect of your embodied integrity to market forces as it was to sell your eyes and your kidneys.

Similarly, to sell your gametes would be to trade something that is distinctively expressive of you and no other person in the world for money. This, too, seems wrong, for it is to commodify a life-giving part of you that is deeply reflective of you as an individual with dignity and worth. Further, it is to sell something that is expressive of the children who result from your gametes. Purchasers receive a product of your body that can be manipulated to create, not just a generic child, but a particular child with certain distinctive features and characteristics derived from you. Today, sperm "donors" and, increasingly, egg "donors" are labeled and categorized so that purchasers can choose those gametes that will enable them to have children with certain characteristics and behaviors. The derivative dignity of human gametes is being denied as they come to command varying prices in the marketplace, depending on the value of certain features of their progenitors. In effect, this amounts to the purchase of children. It also involves purchasing parenthood, for it exchanges for money that special relation between the gamete provider and the child who results from his or her gamete that providers recognize cannot be denied.

Thus, to buy and sell human gametes for reproductive purposes is wrongly to treat them as fungible objects that can pass in and out of a person's possession without effect on that person or others. It is to deny the derivative dignity and worth of these life-giving human bits and pieces. It is this derivative dignity that makes selling them not merely "unsavory," but ethically wrong. Therefore, it would be wrong for Della to sell her eggs and Jim his sperm in order to express their love for one another. To do so would be to exchange for money that which is beyond price.

Ethical Concerns about Selling Fetal Eggs and Ovaries for Reproduction

Perhaps instead of her hair, Della might sell some of her fetal ovaries or eggs. She could use the money to buy her husband a present for Christmas and have funds left over for serious emergencies. To do this, she would have to become pregnant and then abort the fetus she carried so that its ovaries and eggs could be extracted. If Della sold the fetal ovaries to a woman who lacked functional ovaries, this woman could have them transplanted into her own body and, once they matured, could produce eggs. The reproductive process would then proceed using the purchaser's husband's sperm. If the infertile couple elected instead to purchase some of the eggs of the fetus from Della, these would be matured in vitro, fertilized with sperm from the husband of the infertile woman, and, as embryos, would be implanted in the purchasing woman's uterus.

These possibilities, which have not yet been carried out in human beings, would bring children into the world whose immediate biological parents were dead human fetuses. Is our ethical squeamishness at this prospect an unthinking response that can be corrected by reflection—or is it well founded? Let us set aside the difficult issue of the morality of elective abortion in responding, for our focus here is on the ethics of selling fetal eggs and ovaries to create children. The question at issue is whether the eggs and ovaries of human fetuses have some special value that ethically forecloses their sale for reproductive purposes.

The eggs and ovaries of human fetuses lack at least two of the features that give human gametes a derivative worth and dignity: they are not uniquely expressive of the person who creates them, and the children who result from their use do not stand in a special relation to the person who provided them—because there is no such person. The literal genetic mother of the resulting child is not Della, but her fetus. A generation of living maternal entities would be skipped. There would be no maternal progenitor with unique attributes, selfhood, and personal identity capable of forming a significant relation with the resulting child. There would be no living person who could extend to fetal gametes the same sort of derivative dignity and worth that living persons convey to their gametes.

This does not mean, however, that fetal gametes and ovaries have no worth and that it is ethically acceptable to put them up for sale. Many people, even those who hold that abortion at all stages of pregnancy is ethical, maintain that human fetuses are deserving of a certain degree of respect. This is because they have the potential to become persons who can stand in relation to others. This became evident from the consternation created in the early 1970s by the revelation that human fetuses had been subjected to untoward medical experiments (Fletcher and Ryan 1987). Concern about respect for human fetuses led to the creation of a federal commission whose charge, in part, was to bar such inappropriate uses of fetal material. This same concern leads us to treat even aborted dead fetuses as we do human bodies: we view them as deserving of respect and do not allow them to be discarded casually. Fetal gametes and ovaries are considered essential parts of the fetus, integral fetal material, that is deserving of respect. To sell fetuses or their integral parts is to violate this ethical norm and to treat them as property that can be used and disposed of in any way we choose. Thus, because human fetuses and their integral parts have a certain dignity as potential human beings, we should refrain from selling them for reproductive purposes.

There is an additional reason for not selling human fetal parts: to do so is irretrievably to violate the paradigm of human reproduction. It is to replace that paradigm with an act that has a wholly different meaning. In human reproduction, a man and woman enter into a personal and physical relationship; their gametes are merged during sexual intercourse; the resulting embryo grows within the woman's uterus and emerges at birth; some of the distinctive characteristics of those involved are intermingled and revealed in the unique children who are born; and a special parent–child bond is initiated between this man and woman and the resulting children. These defining features of reproduction give it its very meaning.

When we replace sexual intercourse with in vitro fertilization in order to assist infertile couples to have children, we modify this reproductive paradigm in an important way. Yet, by and large, we tend to accept this change because reproduction still retains many of its essential features and its human significance. The question is how much we can modify this model in order to accommodate the needs of the infertile and yet continue to view what is involved as human reproduction? When we use dead fetuses as the source of material to produce children, we lose most of the defining features of the human reproductive paradigm. To employ fetal eggs and ovaries to create children does not involve initiating sexual intercourse between a man and a woman who are in a personal partnership, uniting their gametes to create a unique child, and engendering a special parent–child relation between the couple and the resulting child. This practice therefore lacks most of the essential characteristics of the reproductive paradigm and represents a change in kind, not just of degree, in the way that humans have children.

Using dead fetuses as raw material for reproductive purposes moves the creation of children within the ambit of the manufacturing paradigm. Here materials are employed to produce a marketable product in the most efficient way to achieve financial gain. It is not that the process of human reproduction is forever bound by biology, but that any changes we make in it ought not eliminate that which makes it distinctively human. When we manipulate fetal bits and pieces in order to create children, we move outside the realm of the human mode of reproduction and transform it into the manufacture of children by means of any available bits and pieces associated with human beings. To convert the creation of children into a form of manufacture in this way is to render the role of human contributors insignificant and to lose that which makes this an essentially human activity.

Because of this, a practice of using bits and pieces of dead fetuses for reproductive purposes would have negative ethical import. And, because fetuses are potential persons to be treated with respect, it is ethically dubious to treat them as mere objects of use to be entered into the stream of commerce. Della, therefore, should refrain from selling her fetal eggs and ovaries to buy Jim a present for Christmas and should find some other means of obtaining funds to express her love for him that are ethically acceptable.

Ethical Concerns about Selling Human Cells and Eggs for Cloning

What if Della, who has no known inherited genetic diseases, were to sell some of her mammary cells to be cloned into a new human being? That would allow her to buy Jim a present for Christmas. In this process of cloning, the nucleus of one of Della's mammary cells would be removed and fused with the enucleated egg of the purchasing woman; the resulting embryo would be implanted in the latter's uterus. If all went well, a child with Della's genetic makeup would result. Or perhaps Della might contemplate selling one of her own eggs for cloning. That egg would be enucleated and fused with the nucleus of a cell from an infertile woman and the same process would ensue. In this case, a child would result with the buyer's genetic profile.

Would the sale of human cells and eggs for purposes of cloning be more akin ethically to the sale of human organs? Human gametes? Fetal eggs and ovaries? Or does it not resemble any of these sales ethically, and therefore fall under a different ethical rubric—one that would allow it?

Individual human cells are differentiated. That is, they have different structures and disparate roles to play in the way that the human body functions, depending on their type. Mammary cells and liver cells each perform certain tasks and cannot be exchanged for one another without losing what is distinctive to each kind. Yet no single cell is essential to human functioning. We shed and discard them without notice, leaving our embodied selves intact. Thus, at first glance, single cells of the human body seem more akin to superfluous human bits and pieces such as hair, urine, and fingernail parings, than to human organs. If this is the case, they do not appear to have the sort of dignity and worth that would lead us to conclude that they should not be sold.

Yet when a single mammary cell is cloned for reproductive purposes, it loses its status as a differentiated cell and now takes on a new and important function. It is transformed by the process of cloning from a cell that merely contributes to the production of milk into one that is essential to the production of a child. Della's cloned mammary cell, should it be fused with an enucleated egg and become an integral part of that egg, would thereafter have the potential to create new human life. Much as Della's egg was a life-giving bodily bit and piece, a medium for the expression of her selfhood, and, when fertilized, the bearer of a special bond between her and the unique resulting child, so the single mammary cell, when cloned, would do the same. It would also serve the life-giving reproductive function, express Della's identity, and, if fertilized, her parental relation to the resulting unique child. Thus, that cell, as an essential part of a human egg, would take on a derivative dignity akin to that of a gamete. That dignity would make it ethically ineligible for sale as a commercial product.

Were Della's egg used for purposes of cloning, it would still retain its function as a gamete, even though it acquired a different nucleus. It would still have the derivative worth that it had when used for paradigm reproductive purposes and, because of this, would be ethically ineligible to be sold on the open market. We must conclude that because of the derivative worth of Della's transformed cell and her egg, it would be wrong for Della to sell them for purposes of cloning.

Our story does not end here, however. We must step back and ask whether cloning itself is ethically objectionable, for if it is, that establishes a firm ethical barrier against selling human bits and pieces to be cloned. To respond to this question, let us return to our earlier exploration of the ethics of using of fetal eggs and ovaries for reproductive purposes. In that context, we observed that just because certain human bits and pieces can enable human beings to create children, it is not ipso facto ethically justifiable to use them for that purpose. The paradigm of human reproduction requires the use of human bits and pieces derived from persons whose unique identity they express and who stand in a special relation to the children they produce. The problem we found with the use of fetal eggs and ovaries for reproductive purposes was that there are no such persons.

A related difficulty arises when a single cell or egg is cloned for reproductive purposes. It is not that there is no living person who stands as the progenitor of the resulting child. Della stands in that capacity when her single cell is used, and the purchaser of Della's egg does when that egg is used for cloning. In both these cases of cloning, however, there is a missing person. When Della sells her cell to be cloned, neither Jim nor any other contemporaneous male contributes something of himself to the very constitution of the resulting child. Della alone provides the essential component that will be transmitted to the child through cloning, for her nucleus controls the development of the egg. When Della's egg is used, only its purchaser contributes the nucleus; no contemporaneous male makes a contribution to the offspring. Cloning can be engaged in by an individual person as an isolated subject who has no significant relation to another person who also contributes to the very being of the resulting child. Thus, cloning does not express something of the separate and unique identities of two persons in one child, a significant feature of the reproductive paradigm.

Nor does cloning aim at allowing the resulting child his or her own unique identity, another important feature of the reproductive paradigm. Instead, it attempts to establish an identity for the resulting child that belongs to someone else. While the child cloned from Della's mammary cell will develop in different ways than did Della because of environmental and mitochondrial influences, the point is that the child is deliberately created to be closely imitative of his or her forebear, Della. Even identical twins, who are often cited as equivalent to cloned persons, differ from them in this respect, for they are the outcome of the union of two different people. They are not called by the very means used to bring them into the world to be duplicates of someone else. The child who results from cloning, in contrast, is not invited from the very beginning to develop his or her own capacities for individuality and uniqueness.

As was the case in the use of fetal eggs and ovaries for reproduction, cloning lacks most of the significant features of the reproductive paradigm. It does not involve sexual intercourse between a man and woman who stand in a physical and personal partnership; it does not merge the gametes of a man and woman; it does not create unique children; and it does not initiate a special bond between the couple and the resulting child. Moreover, there are no features of cloning that can be viewed as substituting for these missing features of the reproductive paradigm in the way that in vitro fertilization, for instance, can be viewed as substituting for sexual intercourse. Cloning cannot offer a replacement for sexual intercourse or for the merging of gametes, for these features require the cooperation of two persons, and this is excluded by the very concept of cloning. Consequently, cloning falls outside the reproductive paradigm. It, much like the use of fetal eggs and ovaries to produce a child, loses that which is distinctively human about having children.

Cloning does not fall within the paradigm of human reproduction, but instead comes within the parameters of the manufacturing paradigm. Its goal is to manipulate human bits and pieces in the most efficient way to bring children into the world. It therefore treats human eggs and cloned cells as objects of mere use, rather than as human bits and pieces with a derivative human dignity. Thus, cloning diminishes the significance of the role of human contributors. Further, when human cells and eggs are sold in order to be cloned, their employment as marketable products denies their derivative human dignity. They become demeaned by being treated as fungible objects to be sold to the highest bidder. We conclude, therefore, that Della should find some other way to earn the funds to buy Jim a present for Christmas, rather than sell her eggs and cells to be cloned.

The Human Significance of Reproduction

For want of a better term, we have been backed into discussing whether human "bits and pieces" should be sold on the open market for reproductive purposes. We have no smoother language to use because never before have we had to cope with the possibility of creating human beings from eggs extracted from the human body, from any cell in the human body, or from dead human fetuses. The appearance on the reproductive horizon of egg donation, fetal egg and ovary use, and cloning poses a linguistic challenge that, in turn, reveals an underlying ethical challenge. The sale and use of human "bits and pieces" for reproductive purposes is not to be evaluated solely in terms of its efficacy in producing children. It is also to be judged in light of its effects on our vision of the meaning of human reproduction and on our very humanity.

The distinctive significance of human reproduction and of human persons as embodied beings is jeopardized when we move the creation of children out of the ambit of the reproductive paradigm into that of the manufacturing paradigm. Reproduction is not a technical process whereby human "bits and pieces" of no particular value are manipulated to form a child. It is an intensely personal and intimate physical activity and, at the same time, a deeply interpersonal and value-laden social practice. When this activity is forced into a manufacturing mode, it is cut off from its biological, personal, social, and ethical moorings. Reproduction becomes depersonalized and disembodied and it loses its significance as a distinctively human activity.

We should not deny the dignity and worth of human beings by transforming human parts that can be used for reproduction into commodities whose production and distribution is regulated by market norms in an increasingly commercialized health care system. It is ethically unacceptable to transform these means of procreation into objects or widgets similar to loads of cement or bales of hay. To ignore the worth of these human "bits and pieces" is to risk losing not only our understanding of the meaning of human reproduction, but also our vision of the dignity and nonfungibility of human beings themselves. And to risk such loss would be to chance destroying a primary thread in the fabric of our common life.

Discussion Questions

1. What was the rationale given by the author for our reluctance to exchange money for a kidney?
2. What is dignity, according to Kant?
3. How does Kant distinguish between things that have a price and things that are beyond price?
4. How was dignity identified by Hobbs?
5. What was the rationale provided by Raden to the opposition to selling body parts?
6. What does the author mean when she says, "Unlike kidneys, human gametes cannot be interchanged for each other without losing something of the unique identity of those from which they come"?
7. What conclusion did the author come to regarding the sale of the integral parts of the human fetus for reproduction purposes?
8. Why would a child cloned from the mammary cell of the fictional character Della be different than her?
9. In what ways does cloning lack most of the significant features of the reproductive paradigm?

Acknowledgments

I would like to thank the Senior Research Fellows and Scholars of the Kennedy Institute of Ethics at Georgetown University for their perceptive comments on an earlier draft of this chapter. I am especially indebted to Margaret Little, Robert Veatch, Rihito Kimura, and John Hasnas. None of these individuals is responsible for the conclusions I draw here.

References

Achilles, R. "Donor Insemination: The Future of a Public Secret." In *The Future of Human Reproduction*, ed. C. Overall. Toronto: Women's Press, 1989.

Anderson, E. S. "Is Women's Labor a Commodity?" *Philosophy and Public Affairs* 19 (1990): 71–92.

Daniels, K. R. "Semen Donors: Their Motivations and Attitudes to Their Offspring." *Journal of Reproductive and Infant Psychology* 7 (1989): 121–27.

Fletcher, J. C., and K. Ryan. "Federal Regulations for Fetal Research: A Case for Reform." *Law, Medicine and Health Care* 15 (1987): 126–38.

Henry, O. *The Gift of the Magi and Other Short Stories*. New York: Dover, 1992.

Hill, T. E., Jr. *Dignity and Practical Reason in Kant's Ethical Theory*. Ithaca, NY: Cornell University Press, 1992.

Hobbes, T., C. B. MacPherson, eds. *Leviathan*. Harmondsworth, UK: Penguin, 1968.

———. *Lectures on Ethics*, trans. L. Infield. Indianapolis, IN: Hackett, 1963.

Kant, I. *Groundwork of the Metaphysics of Morals*, trans. H. J. Paton. New York: Harper and Row, 1964.

Macklin, R. "What Is Wrong with Wommodification?" In *New Ways of Making Babies: The Case of Egg Donation*, ed. C. Cohen, 106–21. Bloomington: Indiana University Press, 1996.

Munzer, S. R. "Kant and Property Rights in Body Parts." *Canadian Journal of Law and Jurisprudence* 6 (1993): 319–41.

Murray, T. H. "Organ Vendors, Families, and the Gift of Life." In *Organ Transplantation: Meanings and Realities*, ed. S. J. Younger, R. C. Fox, and L. J. O'Connell. Madison: University of Wisconsin Press, 1996.

Power, M., R. Baber, H. Abdalla, A. Kirkland, T. Leonard, and J. W. W. Studd. "A Comparison of the Attitudes of Volunteer Donors and Infertile Patient Donors on an Ovum Donation Programme." *Human Reproduction* 5 (1990): 352–55.

Radin, M. J. "Market Inalienability." *Harvard Law Review* 100 (1987): 1849–1937.

Schover, L. R., R. L. Collins, M. M. Quigley, J. Blankenstein, and G. Kanoti. "Psychological Follow-Up of Women Evaluated as Oocyte Donors." *Human Reproduction* 6 (1991): 1497–501.

A Theological Perspective

A Catholic Perspective on Organ Sales. In this article, the author addresses the issue of the sale of human organs and the moral implications of a market in human organs under the aegis of *Christian Bioethics*. He argues that moral issues of this kind cannot be adequately addressed from the point of view of moral frameworks that point exclusively to procedural norms. Rather, a moral perspective must embody some substantive norms derived from a particular content-full moral or theological perspective. The substantive norms to which he appeals in this article are those of Roman Catholicism. The most important sources cited include the works of Pius XII (1956) and the works of John Paul II (1985 and 1991). The conclusion he reaches is that not only is it morally permissible for Catholics to participate in a market in organ sales, but also it may be prudent public policy.

Body Parts and the Marketplace: Insights from Thomistic Philosophy. With rare exception, Roman Catholic moral theologians condemn the sale of human organs for transplantation. Yet, such criticism, while rhetorically powerful, often oversimplifies complex issues. Arguments for the prohibition of a market in human organs may, therefore, depend on a single premise, or a cluster of dubious and allied premises, which when examined cannot hold. In what follows, the author examines the ways in which such arguments are configured. For example, Thomas Aquinas' (1224–1274) understandings of embodiment and moral uses of the body are usually interpreted as, and cited in support of, foreclosing a market in human organs. Aquinas' principle of totality requires that one preserve the wholeness of the human body. In approaching Aquinas' texts, the author assumes the role of a revisionist who takes seriously his core commitments, while at the same time indicating that one can further develop his understanding of the body in ways which are supportive of the sale of human organs while remaining in conformity with the author's core concerns. Such considerations will provide significant grounds for concluding that a market in human organs for transplantation appreciates the embodied nature of the human person; respects the body and its parts as personal, rather than as mere things; is consistent with acknowledging God's dominion over our lives and bodies; and constitutes an appropriate utilization of God's gifts to us. Moreover, such a market would likely create significant opportunities charitably to help others, to enhance human dignity, and to protect against the serious dehumanization of current national bureaucratic procedures for organ donation.

The Commercialization of Human Body Parts: A Reappraisal from a Protestant Perspective. The idea of a market in human organs has traditionally met with widespread and emphatic rejection from both secular and religious fronts alike. However, as numerous human beings continue to suffer an uncertain fate on transplant waiting lists, voices are beginning to emerge that are willing at least to explore the option of human organ sales. Anyone who argues for such an option must contend, however, with what seem to be largely emotional rejections of the idea. Often it seems that rebuffs offered on a secular ground are rooted in nothing more than vague discomforts. The author suspects that these discomforts are often based in religious sentiments that have wound their way into the fabric of secular American culture. Therefore, he concluded that in order to contribute further to those voices heard in favor of human organ sales, it is worthwhile to show that, from a religious perspective, it is just as possible to affirm the appropriateness of human organ sales as it is from a secular basis. Since Protestantism has historically had a powerful influence in American society, it is a proper starting point for such an investigation.

A Catholic Perspective on Organ Sales[*]

13

NICHOLAS CAPALDI, PhD
University of Tulsa

Contents

The Catholic Church's Position on Transplantation and the Sale of Human Organs	189
The Ideal Public Policy	192
A Second-Best Policy: A Tax Reduction or Tax Credit in Support of the Ideal Public Policy	194
A Third-Best, but Prudential, Policy: Catholic Participation in an Organ Market	195
Discussion Questions	201
Endnotes	201
References	201

The Catholic Church's Position on Transplantation and the Sale of Human Organs

The position of the Church on the transplantation of body organs has both positive and negative dimensions. The positive dimension may be summarized as follows.

1. Transplantation between species, from animal to human, in general, is not morally forbidden.
2. Transplantation from a corpse to a living being is permissible.

   From the moral and religious aspect, there is no objection to the removal of a cornea from a corpse.... For the patient who receives them ... they represent a restoration and a correction of a defect, suffered from birth or brought on by accident.... As to the corpse from which the cornea is taken, nothing is done to affect either goods to which he has a right or his right to these goods. A corpse no longer is a subject of a right in the strict sense of the word. (Pius XII 1960, 379)[1]

---

[*] First published in *Christian Bioethics* 6 (2), 139–151, 2000.

However, physicians

> should not be permitted to undertake excisions or other operations on a corpse without the permission of those charged with its care, and perhaps even in the face of objections previously expressed by the person in question. (Pius XII 1960, 382)

3. Persons may choose in their wills to dispose of their bodies for legitimate medical purposes.

> [M]edical science and the training of future physicians demand a detailed knowledge of the human body, and that cadavers are needed for study.... It also follows from this that a person may will to dispose of his body and to destine it to ends that are useful, morally irreproachable and even noble (among them the desire to aid the sick and the suffering). (Pius XII 1960, 381)

As Pope Pius XII argues,

> [T]he public must be educated. It must be explained with intelligence and respect that to consent explicitly or tacitly to serious damage to the integrity of the corpse in the interest of those who are suffering, is not a violation of the reverence due to the dead since it is justified by valid reasons. In spite of everything, this consent can involve sadness and sacrifice for the near relatives, but this sacrifice is glorified by the aureole of merciful charity toward some suffering brothers. (1960, 382)

4. Organ transplantation from a live donor is also permissible. Some had interpreted a 1930 remark by Pope Pius XI (*Casti Connubii*) to rule out this possibility:

> [P]rivate individuals ... are not free to destroy or mutilate their members, or in any other way render themselves unfit for their natural functions, except when no other provision can be made for the good of the whole body.

However, everything turns upon how one understands the meaning of rendering oneself unfit for one's natural functions. Pope John Paul II makes clear that this obligation does not rule out live organ donation for transplantation, provided that one does not seriously endanger one's own health, identity, or adequate biological functioning.

> Furthermore, a person can only donate that of which he can deprive himself without serious danger or harm to his own life or personal identity, and for a just and proportionate reason. It is [also] obvious that vital organs can only be donated after death. (1991, 12–13)

5. Organ donation is neither a duty nor an "obligatory act of charity" (Pius XII 1960, 381).
6. Specifically regarding organ sales, compensation is not in principle ruled out.

   [I]t would be going too far to declare immoral every acceptance or every demand of payment. The case is similar to blood transfusions. It is commendable for the donor to refuse recompense; it is not necessarily a fault to accept it. (Pius XII 1960, 381–82)

   In short, Pius XII concludes that, from the perspective of Roman Catholicism, whereas organ donation is commendable, the for-profit sale of human organs for transplantation is permissible.
7. Although either the donor or the recipient may not share Catholic beliefs that the human being is formed "in the image and likeness" of God, it would seem important that Catholic medical personnel who participate in the transplantation of a "bought and sold" organ do; this follows from an analogy with blood transfusions, where one does not inquire into the religious beliefs of patients in order to determine if they are worthy of giving or receiving such a transfusion.
8. All other things being equal, potential recipients who share Christian beliefs about the dignity of the body might be preferred under conditions of scarcity in order to promote ends that are useful, morally irreproachable and even noble, such as the desire to aid the sick and suffering, while upholding the dignity and divine origin of life.

The negative dimension may be summarized as follows.

1. The following conditions would render the sale of human organs morally impermissible: (a) if the transaction were carried out in a manner that obfuscates, denies, or undermines the belief in the divine origin of human life or the dignity thereby due a corpse; or (b) if the transaction, and the compensation gained, is motivated by or used for illegal, immoral, or irreligious purposes.
2. Transplantation from a corpse requires that the corpse be treated with the respect due to "the abode of a spiritual and immortal soul, an essential constituent of a human person whose dignity it shared" (Pius XII 1960, 380).
3. The transplantation of the sexual glands from animals to humans is to be rejected as immoral (Pius XII 1960, 374), because to so transplant would straightforwardly deny the sacred element in humanity and the goods of human procreation.

4. As Pope John Paul II has expressed the concern, if a particular sale promotes a "reductive materialist" conception of human life, it is unacceptable:

> The body cannot be treated as a merely physical or biological entity, nor can its organs and tissues ever be used as items for sale or exchange. Such a reductive materialist conception would lead to a merely instrumental use of the body, and therefore of the person. In such a perspective, organ transplantation and the grafting of tissue would no longer correspond to an act of donation but would amount to the dispossession or plundering of a body. (1985, 221)

> Yet, the for-profit sale of an organ or the acceptance of recompense does not of itself reduce organ donation to a mere instrumental use of the body; it thus does not in itself render the donation less morally praiseworthy.

5. Society, specifically in the form of its political organization, the state, may not commandeer the organs of one human being without the permission of that individual person. The relation of individual human beings to the larger body politics is moral, not organic.

> [T]he total organism which is humanity has no right to impose on individuals demands in the domain of physical being on the grounds of any natural right of the "whole" to dispose of the parts. (Pius XII 1960, 376)

Moreover,

> [E]very moral association of men, if we look to its ultimate usefulness, is in the end directed towards the advancement of each and every single member, since they are all persons. (1960, 377)

This circumstance rules out any form of coercive donation, including organ procurement strategies such as presumed consent, in which, absent specific refusal, one is presumed to have consented to donation.

The Ideal Public Policy

From a Catholic perspective, the ideal public policy would be one in which everyone voluntarily donated their organs, especially to private medical-charitable agencies and preferably to those with a Christian commitment honoring the divine origin of human life.

It is important to spell out why there ought not to be a government agency involved in the process other than to prevent force or fraud. In a secular society, or a society not committed to the Judeo-Christian tradition, government neutrality cannot guarantee that transplantation will be conducted with larger moral and theological purposes in mind. Government-sponsored and -run programs are notoriously inefficient; they inevitably undermine the independence and integrity of private, charitable intermediate institutions, especially those committed to religious values.

Government programs discourage private charity, partly because everyone assumes that someone else is responsible for taking care of the problem. Given such circumstances, the commendable aspects of charity evaporate. It is inherently impossible for the government or a governmental agency in a modern liberal culture, such as the United States, to formulate an objective policy to promote a canonical, content-full account of human good. One difference between the classical world (including medieval Christendom) and the modem or post-Renaissance/post-Reformation world is that the former believed in a collective good, whereas we as moderns do not. A collective good, as opposed to a common good, is a larger holistic good that transcends and encompasses individual good. Modern liberal cultures, in large part because of the influence of Christianity, believe in the unique value of individuals whose personal autonomy cannot be overruled or "trumped" by any notion of a larger collective good. Moderns can and do subscribe to a notion of a common good understood as the background conditions that promote personal autonomy and integrity. This common good can never require, for example, the sacrifice of any individual or his organs for a larger good. The common good is negotiated in politics but always with the understanding that some things like individual autonomy cannot be negotiated away or contravened. This view is reflected in doctrines of rights, in the rule of law, and in the presence of a constitution. There is no organization that can either formulate or delegate to others the formulation of a policy of the collective good, for such a good simply does not exist.

Governments and their agencies can arrive at political resolutions of largely economic conflicts; what governments cannot do is canonically resolve moral dilemmas. Attempts to establish government programs to resolve ethical issues involving organs or anything else (1) ignore the absolute inability of governments to perform this task, (2) abdicate responsibility for moral decisions, and (3) transfer such responsibility to a group that in the end can only voice its own private interests or mask those interests in the name of a mythical collective good.

For the same reason, namely, the absence of any objective collective good, no other lay body, such as a group of physicians, has moral authority to determine and enforce a policy of organ donation, sales, and transplantation. Training as a physician confers technical skill rather than moral expertise or moral authority. Technical scientific skills are necessary and important, but they are never sufficient conditions for determining moral decisions. Physicians themselves often recognize this circumstance; this explains, for example, why medical ethics has become such a large and autonomous discipline.

Catholic medical institutions, under this policy, should be more actively involved in promoting organ donation and in establishing elaborate protocols for guaranteeing the moral integrity of transplantation. Since there will be serious transaction costs involved in this process, such as significant overhead, some consideration must be given to how such costs will be covered.

A Second-Best Policy: A Tax Reduction or Tax Credit in Support of the Ideal Public Policy

On the assumption that an ideal policy of voluntary donation will not produce the requisite supply of organs for transplantation, the need for a second-best or supplementary policy is indicated. Such a policy might call for the creation of a limited market in human organs in which the government offered tax credits to those who donate. There are many advantages to such a program. First, the government would not be involved in administering the program of transplantation, so the disadvantages of government–run programs are evaded. Second, many individuals would like to donate their organs but do not and cannot know the specific individuals who will benefit from the transplantation. They find it difficult to imagine a generalized beneficiary, and hence the cultivation of the commendable aspect of donation for them is lost. In such circumstances, many individuals are less likely to donate. By having a system of tax credits for organ donation, individuals can at least imagine the benefits that will accrue to the heirs of their estate. Third, among the heirs one might count newly created Catholic centers for organ transplantation. Such centers might be the beneficiaries both of direct tax credits and additional donations of those newly educated about the importance of organ transplantation.

At some point, the question will be raised: how much of a tax credit? Economics will inevitably demonstrate that it should be equal to the market value of the organ. Without some sense of the market value of an organ, including the costs of transplantation, the amount set would be arbitrary and likely counterproductive. Something similar already operates with regard to the donation of works of art. That is, some knowledgeable person estimates the market worth of the charitable donation. In short, without some kind of market in human organs, a tax credit system that encourages organ donation, even for the right reasons, probably will not adequately function or even come into existence. It is commendable for the donor to refuse recompense; it is not necessarily a fault to accept it.

A Third-Best, but Prudential, Policy: Catholic Participation in an Organ Market

In an imperfect world, one may use markets morally to promote noble ends. In fact, markets may be the best means for accomplishing such ends. The following argument moves through two stages: (1) establishing a market where none exists, and (2) operating within a preexisting market.

If there is to be a market, then for reasons already enumerated it should not be run by a governmental agency. In a private (i.e., nongovernment) market, sales of organs would originate with individuals selling organs to other individuals, to brokers, or to quasi-charitable medical agencies operating within that market. Further sales or transactions would occur when organs are resold or transmitted from the agencies to individuals. There is no reason why any of the parties involved in these transactions need show disrespect for the divine origins of human life. The market can be viewed simply as a device for fostering noble ends in the most expeditious manner.

It may be objected that some individuals who sell their organs do so from either nonreligious motives or even immoral motives. Aside from the difficulties of determining the motives of specific sellers, those agencies that buy the organs will have the right motives for so doing. In short, a quasi-charitable Catholic transplantation agency can help to render the process sacred by treating the organ in the right spirit despite the intentions of the original or even intermediate sellers. There seems to be no difference here from the purchase of blood supplies. One does not refuse to buy plasma without first investigating the motives of the original person who produced the blood.

Moreover, if the supply were large enough one would not refuse a transplant to someone who lacked faith in the divine origin of life anymore than one would refuse a transfusion to a nonbeliever. There is always the possibility that carrying out the transplant under religious auspices may have an effect on the recipient. On the other hand, given the finite supply, potential recipients who took the sacred nature of the process seriously would certainly seem entitled to some preference in keeping with the moral and theological dimensions of the process.

Finally, the existence of a market would allow such agencies to engage in differential pricing; that is, charging less to some and more to others depending on any number of variables, including income status. Organs could then become available to many who would otherwise not be able to afford them or even have them in the first place. Agencies in a market could thereby add a noble dimension to the world of medicine that would otherwise not exist. Rather than favoring the rich, such a market would make treatments available to the poor that otherwise would likely not exist. This circumstance seems to be true of markets in general, namely, they expand the availability of services and commodities. There is nothing in the existence of a market that in itself undermines belief in the divine origin of human life and the respect due to the body.

This brings us to the second set of circumstances, namely, what should one do with a market that already exists. In large secular societies, there already exist and will continue to exist markets in health care resources and services. Everything that I have argued for so far applies to this market. We should lobby for tax incentives for organ donations, and Catholic agencies should be organized and energized to see that the process remains as close as possible to its sacred intentions. As Pope John Paul II reminds us in his reference to the fourth-century Doctor of the Church, Saint Basil the Great: "As regards medicine, it would not be right to reject a gift of God (that is, medical science), just because of the bad use that some people make of it; we should instead throw light on what they have corrupted" (Great Rules 55:3; John Paul II 1985, 221).

It is often argued, naïvely, that a market in organ sales adds additional expenses: acquisition costs (compensation to the original donor or "owner") and transaction costs for administering the program. The reason such arguments are naïve is that without compensation, there would be no market and the supply would be all too low. The analogue to this argument would be that paying farmers for producing food merely adds costs without offsetting benefits. Rather than simply adding costs, compensation creates the motivations that in turn tend toward the production of a much greater organ supply than would otherwise exist. Those who argue against a market in human organs presuppose that there are other ways to obtain organs, such as through government coercion or a state-sponsored program of publicity; yet such programs also cost money. Moreover, any form of government coercion or enforced donation would violate Catholic teachings that organ donation must be voluntary; while commendable, organ donation is neither a duty nor an obligatory act of charity.

It is often assumed within the medical community and elsewhere that markets are immoral or amoral at best. By and large, this reflects both ignorance of how markets operate and misconceptions about the alternatives to markets. While I do not have time here to dwell at length on economics, I note in passing that markets always presuppose a larger cultural and moral context; that explanations of markets based upon human selfishness are just that, explanations; and that these latter explanations can and have been rejected as inadequate. The only alternative to a market is a system of centralized allocation. As I have already argued, centralized allocation presupposes a by now discredited mythical conception of a collective good.

A large part of our educational system, including the education of physicians, since the Enlightenment has focused on technical expertise. One of the great myths that has haunted us for the past 200 years is the belief that there can be a social technology (including decisions about how to deal with organs) based upon science in the same way that there is physical technology based upon science. This myth is now largely discredited (see, for example, Capaldi 1998). Any centralized system, as opposed to a market system, will invariably be governed by purely political considerations or the coercive imposition of a particular content-full moral code on everyone, whether individuals subscribe to that code or not.

Physicians and medical personnel, who resist this line of argument, should perhaps examine their own motives. How many medical personnel mistake their technical medical expertise for moral expertise? How many are motivated by the unfounded and highly questionable belief that their personal control of the transplantation process produces more good than a market system? Are these people assuming the same role that should be denied to governments? Perhaps such medical personnel would do well to consider that a market economy is the best foundation for the advancement of science and technology, that this point has been recognized about the economy in general, and that there is no reason to assume that it does not apply to medicine.

An additional common objection to a market in organs is concern about exploitation of those in poor countries selling their organs for the benefit of rich people in rich countries. Force, fraud, and medical misrepresentation aside, there are several responses to this legitimate concern. To begin with, there is a misuse here of the term *exploitation*. To "exploit" people is to use them for one's own selfish ends, that is, without consideration of their interests. It is not exploitation when people are given compensation for an organ. Perhaps what is meant is that the exchange is uneven in that the seller gets "less" from the exchange than the buyer or the intermediaries. This would be difficult if not impossible to determine because the value of income from the sale of a kidney might make an extraordinary difference in the lives of the seller and the seller's family.

Moreover, a market in organs may provide poor people with the resources to help their families and eventually even to climb out of poverty. Perhaps this is one of those occasions in which while it is commendable for the donor to refuse recompense, it is not necessarily a fault to accept it. As serious economic studies have shown (Berger 1986), many Third World countries began to climb out of poverty precisely this way; that is, by supplying something that wealthier economies needed. Again, there seem to be stages of economic growth in which development at first accentuates the gap between the rich and the poor but that gap later narrows. The system, moreover, does not work in just one direction. Poor countries are the recipients of benefits from technology largely developed and paid for by richer countries, who absorb the costs of research and development. Start-up costs are also less when poorer countries borrow the latest technological advances. It is not capitalism or a global economy that causes poverty; rather, the free market economy appears to be the only real hope of escaping mass poverty.

We must never forget that the question is not whether this is "fair" but whether given historical and empirical realities there is a better alternative. The only alternative to a market is a centrally controlled system of production and distribution, and, as I have repeatedly stressed, such systems simply do not work and are frauds to boot. The issue is not whether it is fair, anymore than whether we are concerned with whether the genetic lottery is "fair." The issue is how best to minimize suffering in a way that does not compromise our religious commitments. There is nothing in Christianity that entails or requires centralized governmental economic control.

There is an almost Alice in Wonderland quality about this objection. Is it really "fair" that those of us who grew up in the United States and who became professionals do not have to sell our organs to send our children to college? Should all PhDs and MDs in the United States be forced to provide one kidney free of charge in order to make up for the unfair advantages they have enjoyed because of genetic or demographic lotteries? Where would this line of argument end?

What is being suggested by this line of objection is the following: we do not really want the government to supervise the process of organ transplantation. An alternative, which some people seem to want, is a body of professionals (presumably medical doctors) who have autonomous control of the organ transplantation process. And just how would that operate? Would the "professionals" determine cases based upon merit? Who ought to define *merit* or *desert*, and on what grounds? Would the "professionals" determine cases based upon what would maximize benefits in the long run? Who ought to determine long-run "benefits," and given what criteria? As Hayek demonstrated, such calculations are beyond human capacity. Would the "professionals" strive for equality? If so, then either an equal redistribution would in a very short time progress to a market with unequal results or such equality would have to be maintained by a totalitarian despotism the likes of which we have never seen.

It is also sometimes claimed that the autonomy and dignity of being human are undermined by organ sales. Yet, it is difficult to see how rendering it illegal for someone to sell an organ constitutes respect for the denied seller as opposed to just being an example of outright paternalism. Note, however, that a significant percentage of those who object to organ "sales" are perfectly comfortable with "compensation" for donation. Objections based on supposed autonomy and dignity costs are thus likely in large measure rhetorical.

A similar objection concerns the notion that a market in organs constitutes commercialization and thereby denies the inherent dignity of the individuals involved. Sometimes this objection reflects a general repugnance about commerce. There are a number of bizarre aspects to this objection. When a kidney is donated and the recipient pays for the transplant (via insurance or other means), the hospital and physicians "profit" from performing the transplant. Does this sully the act of donation? Should all transplant operations be performed gratis? What about all other medical services? Why should physicians be compensated but not donors? Such an objection either displays ignorance of the importance of commerce for human societies or expresses preference for a feudal-hierarchical society. More serious is the assumption that "commercial" transactions are indifferent to any values other than material greed. Surely those committed to medical values in general and Catholic values in particular would rightly object to commerce in organs that ignored important moral and spiritual considerations. Indeed, there is nothing that precludes Catholic participation in an organ market for the express purpose of seeing to it that these moral and theological values and goals are given serious consideration.

Many are concerned that a market in organs would lead to a slippery slope in which some individuals would consider donating all of their organs (a form of suicide) under economic duress. Yet, the existence of such a market does not preclude outlawing some forms of commercial transaction. Similarly, others express concern that a market in organs would undermine or discourage those who wish simply to donate. Individual cases aside, this is an empirical question. The proponents of a market can fairly reply that a market would increase availability. In short, it provides neither sound argument nor significant rationale for forbidding a market in human organs. Empirical questions should be settled empirically: let us try a market and see what happens to the organ supply.

Opponents of a market in organs are rightfully concerned about fraud and the raising of undue concerns in the minds of those who are terminally ill about the quality of care that they will receive. None of this precludes the usual legal safeguards, and all of this seems to provide a space for injecting Catholic or Christian values into the market.

Markets introduce their own inherent positive values. A market will improve access because it permits demand to be equated with supply at equilibrium price levels. Considerations of profit also encourage management efficiency. In a modern liberal society that is religiously "neutral" and has a market economy, there will and ought to be a market in human organs. It is precisely such a larger context that permits and guarantees that Catholic institutions can participate and that Catholic values will be honored. This should be viewed as a great opportunity. By entering the market, Catholic medical institutions can within their own confines render the process sacred and, by example, help to promote the sacramentalization of the process. The presence of religious institutions within the larger market acting as nonprofit commercial entities will lead to the establishment of standards in comparison to which we can make meaningful judgments about regulating the for-profit part of the market.

The existence of a market could conceivably raise additional funds that could be used to render Catholic medical institutions more solvent and thus more able both to promote Catholic medical values as well as to help many of those who cannot be adequately assisted under present financial circumstances. This argument can be broadened to encompass the notion of Catholic sponsored health insurance. The more Catholic institutions operate within a market context, the more independent they can become of government intrusion and eventual secularization. Individuals who are poor or who have limited resources have the most to gain from a large-scale market in organs: they would have greater access to organs because there would likely be more organs available; moreover, they or their relatives or heirs would have access to financial resources that would otherwise not exist.

The following self-test[2] is suggested as a way for readers to locate their own position. The test provides a way of determining at what level some moral consensus can be formulated:

1. An adult donates a kidney for transplantation to a family member.
2. An adult, who cannot donate directly to a family member, engages in a tissue exchange with a tissue bank that can supply the needs of the sick family member.
3. An adult donates a kidney in exchange for medical care for a seriously ill family member, care that could otherwise not be available for financial reasons.
4. An adult accepts compensation for a kidney donation and uses the compensation in order to provide other family members with substantial education or economic opportunities that would otherwise not be available.
5. An adult accepts compensation for a kidney donation (notice how I avoid the term *sells*) in order to obtain substantial education or economic opportunities that would otherwise not be available for himself in order to support a family.
6. An adult accepts compensation for a kidney donation in order to buy lottery tickets.

Once the existence and moral legitimacy of the larger market in organ sales are recognized, there will be additional ethical issues raised within Catholic medical transplantation agencies. Such issues would form the substance of the next stage of this discussion.

Discussion Questions

1. What are the positive dimensions of the Catholic Church as it relates to organ sales?
2. What are some of the negative dimensions of the Catholic Church as it relates to organ sales?
3. From a Catholic perspective, what would be the ideal policy regarding the transplantation of organs?
4. According to the author, why should there not be a government agency involved in the organ donor process?
5. What is the difference between the classical world (medieval Christendom) and the modern or post-Renaissance/post-Reformation world?
6. What are the problems involved in attempting to establish government programs to resolve ethical issues involving organs or anything else?
7. What was the "second-best" policy advocated by the author?
8. What was the "third-best" policy advanced by the author?
9. What was the author's position as it relates to the existence of an open market in human organs?

Endnotes

1. Pius XII's position has been reaffirmed by Pope John Paul II (1985).
2. Adopted from B. M. Dickens (1990, 905).

References

Berger, P. *The Capitalist Revolution: Fifty Propositions about Prosperity, Equality and Liberty*. New York: Basic Books, 1986.

Capaldi, N. *The Enlightenment Project in the Analytic Conversation*. Dordrecht: Kluwer Academic, 1998.

Dickens, B. M. "Human Rights and Commerce in Health Care." *Transplantation Proceedings* 22, no. 3 (1990): 905.

John Paul II, Pope. "Blood and Organ Donors, August 2, 1984." *The Pope Speaks* 30, no. 1 (1985): 1–2.

John Paul II, Pope. "Many Ethical, Legal, and Social Questions Must Be Examined in Greater Depth." *Dolentium Hominum* (June 1991): 12–13.

Pius XII, Pope. *Papal Teachings: The Human Body*, sel. and arr. Monks of Solesmes. Boston: The Daughters of Saint Paul, 1960.

14 Body Parts and the Marketplace
Insights from Thomistic Philosophy*

MARK J. CHERRY, PhD
Department of Philosophy, Saint Edwards University, Austin, Texas

Contents

Introduction	203
The Tradition	205
Totality and Charity	208
Markets and Charity	215
Conclusion	217
Discussion Questions	218
Endnotes	219
References	222

Introduction

With rare exception, Roman Catholic moral theologians condemn the sale of human organs for transplantation. Unlike the market, most systems of voluntary organ donation are based on the implicit assumption that the procurement of organs for transplantation is only appropriately characterized as a gift. Gift giving is generally marked by altruism, personal concern for the other, love, and, in some cases, intimacy. The encouragement of gift giving, in short, is core to the development of important areas of character and virtue involved in personal regard and love for others. Gift giving at the very least requires personal concern for identifiable others or identification with the community to which the gift is addressed. Gift giving is tied closely with concerns of compassion and charity, including the root notion of *caritas*, or love. Such compassion, it is argued, reaffirms that "not all of life depends on efficient, large scale organizations and a productive economy. [It helps to] create a space in which to think about our dependence on one another, the needs that can never be fulfilled by bureaucracies and material

---

* First published in *Christian Bioethics* 6 (2) 171–193, 2000.

goods, and the joys that come from attending to those needs" (Wuthnow 1991, 304). Policies that encourage gift giving, altruism, or charity express in part the concern that individuals develop a sense of love and concern for others. Arguments for the gift of human life, it is contended, lose their force when it is a question of sales (see, for example, Ashley and O'Rourke 1994, 175).[1]

A market in human organs, it is argued, would corrupt organ procurement and transplantation protocols and quality medical care, and important modes of human interaction would be sullied by greed. Consider, for example, John Haas's argument regarding commercialization of organ procurement. His conclusions, while couched in somewhat rhetorical language, advance important criticisms:

> The proposal to allow individuals to sell their own organs betrays an incorrect understanding of the human person. It suggests that the body or its component parts is a "thing" which we own and that we are entitled to dispose of it as we see fit. This overlooks the fact that we are bodies; we do not possess bodies. If the need is great, then we may justifiably sacrifice one part of ourselves out of love if such a sacrifice does not render us physically less functional. However, to determine a "price" for one of our organs would be to suggest our bodies are something over which we have absolute dominion and can dispose of in whatever manner we wish. Such an act would also blur the fact that God has ultimate dominion over our lives and bodies which He has freely given us as a gift. It would be appropriate, in imitation of Him, to sacrifice something of ourselves on behalf of others, but not to sell ourselves or parts of our bodies. This line of reasoning would also hold for those who would presume to gather organs from the dead and then market them. (1990, 1)

It is important to note the special moral costs that Haas identifies: a market in human organs would (1) fail adequately to appreciate the embodied nature of the human person; (2) treat the human body, and its constitutive parts, as mere things; (3) blur God's dominion over our lives and bodies; and (4) inappropriately utilize God's gift to us of our bodies. As Haas concludes, "There is already the danger in a market oriented economy of viewing human beings as a commodity whose price must be factored into business decisions. To develop a market in human organs would contribute even more to this dehumanizing tendency" (1990, 2). Such a market would, therefore, (5) dehumanize organ vendors. Moreover, (6) it is clear that love and charity are not regarded as consistent with financial profit.[2]

Such criticism, while rhetorically powerful, often oversimplifies complex issues. Arguments for the prohibition of a market in human organs may, therefore, depend on a single premise, or a cluster of dubious and allied premises, which when examined cannot hold. In what follows, I will examine the ways in which such arguments are configured. For example, Thomas

Aquinas's (1947, 1224–1274) understandings of embodiment and moral uses of the body are usually interpreted as, and cited in support of, foreclosing a market in human organs. Aquinas' principle of totality requires that one preserve the wholeness of the human body. In approaching Aquinas's texts, I will assume the role of a revisionist who takes seriously his core commitments, while at the same time indicating that one can further develop his understanding of the body in ways that are supportive of the sale of human organs while remaining in conformity with the author's core concerns. Such considerations will provide significant grounds for concluding that a market in human organs for transplantation appreciates the embodied nature of the human person; respects the body and its parts as personal, rather than as mere things; is consistent with acknowledging God's dominion over our lives and bodies; and constitutes an appropriate utilization of God's gifts to us. Moreover, such a market would likely create significant opportunities charitably to help others, to enhance human dignity, and to protect against the serious dehumanization of current national bureaucratic procedures for organ donation.

The Tradition

When Western Christianity explicitly articulated its notions of proper medical deportment, it had already articulated its own beliefs and culture. Especially among Western Christianity of the high Middle Ages, as exemplified by Thomas Aquinas, these moral understandings were incorporated in Christian theological doctrine. This defended the ability of persons generally to understand the natural law: that there is an objective good for human beings (*ST*, I–II, q94, a.2c), which reason can articulate, thus justifying the general canons of moral behavior.[3] Despite significant secularization following the Reformation, Western Christian reflection continued to have considerable influence. There remained in the West the attempt to fashion rational justification for the general lineaments of Christian culture and moral intuitions as well as its fundamental social structures.

Aquinas's arguments regarding the principle of totality reflect a commitment to the coincidence between faith and natural theology. He gives arguments that he takes to be binding on all persons as such, even though it is clear that the character of the argument and the content he engages can only be fully appreciated within a set of Western Christian presuppositions. It is important to appreciate that Aquinas, and later Thomists, do not recognize that theirs is a particular moral rationality. Instead, Western Christian moral reflections are often posited in terms of general discursive rationality; their conclusions are argued to be justifiable through reason alone.[4] Rather than asking, "What do we know to be true in the fullness of Christian faith, practice and revelation?" the question has been "What are those principles governing human action to which no rational human being can deny his or her assent?" (MacIntyre 1988, 176).

In particular, Aquinas held that it is morally impermissible to remove a part of the body as long as it is healthy and retains its natural disposition (*ST*, II–II, q65, a). He argued as follows: the life of a human being as a biologically functioning whole is a natural good.[5] Anything that damages this good, endangering or attacking parts of the bodily whole, is *prima facie* morally impermissible. Therefore, only insofar as one can show that the intervention or removal of the part is in fact intended to preserve the natural good can the *prima facie* impermissibility be defeated. Given such an argument, the challenge for organ donation and sales using living donors is precisely the same: cutting away healthy organs from living persons violates the natural good of the wholeness of the body and is, therefore, *prima facie* morally impermissible.

With the development of blood, tissue, and organ transplantation, as well as empirical evidence pointing to the significant good created by such activities, this commitment to rational discourse led contemporary Thomists to reinterpret the principle of totality as implying an obligation to preserve human biological functioning, rather than anatomical wholeness. The basic good that must be respected is not the fulfillment of the good of this or that organ, but of the whole human person. That person's bodily health is integral, rather than instrumental, to the fulfillment of this good, a good that ought to be measured in terms of the functional organic whole (Finnis 1991, 79).[6]

The historical roots of Aquinas's concern for the natural good of human biological wholeness are found in ancient Christian canons bearing on the preservation of men and women as embodied and gendered beings. Certain heretical sects, such as the Valesians, interpreted Christ's teaching that "if thy right eye offend thee, pluck it out ... likewise if thy right hand or foot offend thee, cut it off" (Matthew, 18: 8–9) as implying that one ought to amputate parts of the body that incite one to sin (Nicodemus and Agapius 1957, 84). Such sects often encouraged castration to avoid sexual sins and to achieve spiritual purity. In response, the Church promulgated canons prohibiting the practice of voluntary, nonmedically indicated, castration, holding that persons were to master their sinful passions rather than mutilate their bodies as a physical shortcut. Consider, for example, canon I from the First Council of Nicaea (A.D. 325):

> If anyone has been operated upon by surgeons for a disease, or has been excised by barbarians, let him remain in the clergy. But if anyone has excised himself when well, he must be dismissed even if he is examined after being in the clergy. And henceforth, no such person must be promoted to holy orders. But as is self-evident, though such is the case as regards those who affect the matter and dare to excise themselves, if any persons have been eunuchized by

barbarians or their lords, but are otherwise found to be worthy, the Canon admits such persons to the clergy. (Nicodemus and Agapius 1957, 163)

Apostolic canons XXII, XXIII, and XXIV, considered to have arisen from first-century A.D. moral commitments, tied purposeful self-mutilation to moral and spiritual condemnation. Individuals who castrate themselves are castigated as self-murderers, plotters against their own lives, and enemies of God's creation.

> Let no one who has mutilated himself become a clergyman; for he is a murderer of himself, and an enemy of God's creation. (Apostolic canon XXII, in Nicodemus and Agapius 1957, 84)
>
> If anyone who is a clergyman should mutilate himself, let him be deposed from office. For he is a self-murderer. (Apolistic canon XXIII, in Nicodemus and Agapius 1957, 85)
>
> Any layman who has mutilated himself shall be excommunicated for three years. For he is a plotter against his own life. (Apostolic canon XXIV, in Nicodemus and Agapius 1957, 85)

On the one hand, castration that results from hatred of being male, or as a physical means to help one control sinful passions, is mutilation that inappropriately rejects the fundamental sexual and gendered nature of God's creation; it thereby constitutes a grave moral evil.

On the other hand, as canon VIII of the First and Second Regional Synod, held in Constantinople (A.D. 861), clarifies, castration for medical reasons, such as to prevent the spread of disease, requires no such intention. It, therefore, can be free of moral and spiritual condemnation.

The divine and sacred Canon of the Apostles judges those who castrate themselves to be self-murderers; accordingly, if they are priests, it deposes them from office, and if they are not, it excludes them from advancement to holy orders. Hence it makes plain that if one who castrates himself is a self-murderer, he who castrates another is certainly a murderer. One might even deem such a person quite guilty of insulting creation itself. Wherefore the holy Council has been led to decree that if any bishop, presbyter, or deacon be proved guilty of castrating anyone, either with his own hand or by giving orders to anyone else to do so, he shall be subjected to the penalty of desposition from office; but if the offender is a layman, he shall be excommunicated; unless it should so happen that owning to the incidence of some affliction he should be forced to operate upon the sufferer by removing his testicles. For precisely as the First Canon of the Council held in Nicaea does not punish those who have been operated upon for a disease, for having the disease, so neither do we condemn priests who order diseased men to be castrated, nor do we blame laymen either, when they perform the operation with their own hands. For we consider this to be a treatment of the disease, but not a malicious design against the creation or an insult to creation (canon VIII, First and Second Regional Synod, in Nicodemus and Agapius 1957, 465).

Castration may licitly be performed as a necessary means to preserve the health or good of the individual's body.[7]

Totality and Charity

Aquinas recasts these concerns, focused on castration and rejection of one's gendered embodiment, articulating a more general obligation to preserve the wholeness of the body. According to Aquinas, human persons exist as a physical unity, composed of integral parts. Each part exists for and is subordinated to the good of the whole. The body was created as a whole for the natural good of the person. One is obligated to respect the body's integrity and develop its capacities so that it is conducive to moral virtue. Voluntarily maiming or mutilating the body, understood as the removal or functional destruction of parts of the body, violates the natural good of the biological whole, and is, therefore, *prima facie* morally impermissible.

As Aquinas argues,

> Since a member is part of the whole human body, it is for the sake of the whole, as the imperfect for the perfect. Hence a member of the human body is to be disposed of according as it is expedient for the body. Now a member of the human body is of itself useful to the good of the whole body, yet, accidentally it may happen to be hurtful, as when a decayed member is a source of corruption to the whole body. Accordingly so long as a member is healthy and retains its natural disposition, it cannot be cut off without injury to the whole body. (*ST*, II–II, Q.65, a.1)

Insofar as the body is healthy and functioning normally, it is *prima facie* morally illicit to remove or destroy its parts.

However, if mutilation is necessary to preserve the health and integrity of the body, the *prima facie* moral impermissibility is defeated.

> If, however, the member be decayed and therefore a source of corruption to the whole body, then it is lawful with the consent of the owner of the member, to cut away the member for the welfare of the whole body, since each one is intrusted with the care of his own welfare. The same applies if it be done with the consent of the person whose business it is to care for the welfare of the person who has a decayed member: otherwise it is altogether unlawful to maim anyone. (*ST*, II–II, Q.65, a.1)

Just as the ancient Christian canons permit castration to treat disease, Aquinas concludes that body parts may be removed to preserve the good of the whole, such as the amputation of a gangrenous limb to prevent the spread of disease and decay.

Three general conditions govern the moral licitness of anatomic or functional mutilation. First, the continued presence or functioning of the organ is causing serious damage or constitutes a menace to the body as a whole. Second, this damage is remediable, or at least measurably lessened, by the surgical removal in question, and there is significant assurance that the operation is efficacious in this regard. Third, the expected positive outcome, in terms of eliminating danger to the whole organism, easing of pain, and so on, compensates for the negative effects created by the mutilation and potential harmful side effects of surgery (Pius XII 1960, 277–78). It need not be that the amputated organ is itself diseased so long as its continued presence or functioning directly or indirectly causes a serious menace for that individual's body.

Persons possess a stewardship or useful, rather than absolute, dominion over their bodies and its parts.[8]

> As far as the patient is concerned, he is not absolute master of himself, of his body, or of his soul. He cannot, therefore, freely dispose of himself as he pleases. Even the motive for which he acts is not by itself either sufficient or determining. The patient is bound by the immanent purposes fixed by nature. He possesses the right to use limited by natural finality, the faculties and powers of his human nature. Because he is the beneficiary, not the proprietor, he does not possess unlimited power to allow acts of destruction or of mutilation of anatomic or functional character. (Pius XII 1960, 198–99)

Maiming the body is, therefore, morally impermissible. Moreover,

> The decisive point rests not in the fact that the organ which is amputated or paralyzed be itself infected, but that its continued presence or functioning cause either directly or indirectly a serious menace for the whole body. It is quite possible that in functioning normally a healthy organ could cause harm to one which is unhealthy, in such a way as to aggravate the evil and the repercussions of this last on the organism as a whole. Or it can happen that the removal of a healthy organ and the paralyzing of its function remove from the evil—cancer, for example—the possibility of extending further, or else change the effect of this evil on the body. If there is no other alternative available, in both cases a surgical operation on the healthy organ is permissible. (Pius XII 1960, 278)

The potential harms of surgery are justified in terms of their effect on preserving the natural good of the biologically functioning whole and the overall well-being of the individual. More broadly applied, the principle requires that diagnostic and therapeutic procedures be judged in terms of their efficaciousness for producing the good of the particular patient on whom they are used (Kelly 1960, 246).

As Aquinas articulates the position, however, the principle of totality is fully consistent with a market in human organs procured from cadaver sources. Taking such organs is not itself incompatible with respect for the human body; with death, obligations to preserve the natural good of the biologically functioning whole, or the well-being of the individual, lose their salience. Once an individual has died, organs removed from the cadaver become much like other types of things. This is why transplanting organs from cadaver sources to living persons does not offer any intrinsic moral problem (see Ashley and O'Rourke 1994, 75). Similarly, a futures market, in which one contracts now for the sale of organs after one's death, would likewise satisfy the principle of totality. On such grounds, it seems plausible to view certain markets in human organs as consistent with Roman Catholic moral theological conceptions of embodiment and God's dominion as well as respecting human dignity.

On the other hand, in itself the principle of totality rules out the procurement of healthy blood, tissue, and organs from living donors. It, therefore, in turn *proscribes both donation and selling of healthy organs from living persons*. Since the principle requires any removal of a part of the human body to be justified in terms of preserving that person's bodily wholeness, one cannot justify either the donation or sale of body parts in terms of preserving the wholeness of others. As Gerald Kelly argues, the principle of totality is only applicable in cases where there is the subordination of part to the whole in the natural body. There exists no such subordination between individuals and society as a whole. "Each person is a distinct entity, with a distinct finality" (1960, 247). Persons exist neither for the sake of others nor for the sake of society. Citizens may have certain duties to society, but this is quite different from asserting that they are parts of a quasi social organism in the same sense as the kidney is part of the body (1960, 247).

Moreover, the donation or sale of body parts cannot be justified by the fact that such parts, including blood, skin grafts, and bone marrow, are restored by the body. In itself, such reasoning would justify the useless letting of blood or the pointless removal of other regenerating tissues. This would violate the natural good of the biological whole for no reason whatsoever.

Instead, moral appeal must be made to a principle of charity: the donor or seller intends that the body parts be transplanted into another person and thereby wills that other's good. For such an argument to hold, however, it must be structured as follows. (1) Persons are charitable beings, and (2) such charity is a good. Moreover, (3) the good of being charitable is often more important than the good of preserving the wholeness of the body. However, (4) directly intending to kill oneself is forbidden (e.g., donating one's heart while still living). Therefore, often charity is sufficient to defeat the *prima facie* moral impermissibility of removing healthy human body parts, as long as this is not part of an act that intends directly to kill oneself.

Pius XII supports the premises of this argument in his praise of blood donors for their charity, comparing their behavior to the model of Christ:

> Model as He is of all charity. He is your model in a special way ... to give one's blood for someone unknown to us, perhaps someone ungrateful, who will forget or who will not even want to know the name and countenance of his savior; to donate something of one's own strength only to communicate it to others and give them back what they have lost; to restore one's lost energies only to repeat and renew the same gift and the same sacrifice: it is to this that you are generously dedicated. (1960, 105)

Pope John XXIII reiterated this view in 1959, saying, "Yours is truly, then, an apostolate. But to achieve its perfection it must be rooted and founded in charity, which is love of God and of brother" (p. 334).

The principle of charity, whereby one assumes a cost or burden, intending the good of others, provides sufficient reason to defeat the principle of totality's *prima facie* moral inappropriateness and justifies the removal of healthy tissue, blood, and organs.

However, since the principle of totality still holds, it must be reinterpreted as implying an obligation to preserve only a *de minimus* standard of human biological functioning. One must distinguish between the good of the adequately functioning body and the good of the full integrity of the anatomical whole. The principle of totality must be understood as only strictly requiring the former, not the latter. This reinterpretation of the principle of totality has significant appeal since transplantation of human tissue, blood, and organs has considerable potential for helping others, while still maintaining the adequate biological functioning of the donor.

This change, while departing from Aquinas, plausibly captures the biological circumstance that one must make distinctions even among body parts. Some parts are necessary for embodiment or existence (e.g., the higher brain), others parts are necessary for adequate human functioning (e.g., the heart), and there are those parts that are neither (e.g., the appendix). Certain parts of the body serve little role in effective human biological functioning. For example, the healthy appendix serves no known purpose in the human digestive system. Its removal, even while healthy, does not interfere with the integrity of the body; it neither suppresses nor otherwise harms any organic function of the body. Insofar as there is sufficient reason to subject the patient to the surgical risks (i.e., if it is already necessary to open the abdomen to perform another operation), the appendix may be excised prior to closing the incision. The relative unimportance of the appendix, the risk of future appendicitis, and the minimal additional risk to the patient together justify elective appendectomy (Healy 1956, 125; see also McFadden 1961, 267; Gallagher 1984).[9] Moreover, its incidental removal precludes the possible harms of future surgery if the appendix were ever to become diseased. As Charles McFadden argues, though, it would not generally be permissible for a person to arrange to have surgery solely for the removal of a healthy appendix. The risks of surgery outweigh the contingent good to be gained given the relatively small possibility that the individual might at some future date have appendicitis, and at that time not have access to medical interventions (McFadden 1961, 269; see also Kelly 1960, 253; Varga 1984, 223–24).[10]

With regard to organ procurement, while persons may not capriciously diminish the integrity of their own bodies, not all of one's organic parts are necessary to preserve adequate biological functioning. Insofar as procurement from living persons is limited to redundant organs, such as a kidney, or regenerating tissue, such as a liver slice, the functional wholeness of the body is maintained. The principle of charity provides a sufficient reason to justify the substantial mutilation and the risks of organ procurement surgery, insofar as the organ is to be provided to someone who vitally needs it (O'Rourke and Boyle 1993, 217–22; Cummings 1990, 66–67).[11] Assuming that donating one kidney for transplant does not lessen kidney function, with detriment to one's health generally, it is permissible, even though one accepts a risk to health in the event of contracting kidney disease later (Grisez 1993, 2:544).[12] It is morally licit to voluntarily give up an organ, or other body part, which is not needed and to assume the risk that the one remaining kidney will continue to function (see McFadden 1961, 268; Kenny 1962, 163; Kelly 1960, 251–52; Finney and O'Brien 1956, 233; Healy 1956, 139–42). In short, biological function as distinct from simple bodily integrity became the basis for justifying the removal of healthy organs from living donors for transplantation. Provided that functioning is not compromised, one who donates a redundant organ or regenerative tissue is merely accepting a risk to good functioning in the future for the sake of helping another in grave need.

Note, however, that this reinterpretation of the principle of totality is neutral with regard to whether one donates or sells the body part. If one can give away an organ, or regenerative tissue, with sufficient reason, one ought to be able to sell it for sufficient reason. A parent, for example, could donate a kidney to his son to save the child's life. The organ is removed for a good purpose consistent with the principle of charity, and he accepts the risks to his future health as a side effect. Similarly, it seems permissible for a parent to sell a kidney to purchase a life sustaining operation. The structure of the action in the second case is the same as in the first. The only difference is that the second has an additional step in the instrumental analysis: obtaining sufficient funds that save the child's life (see also Boyle 1999, 136). Moreover, the sale saves the purchaser's life directly, which is something the vendor might well have significant morally compelling reasons to do.

It is difficult to understand how giving organs can be permissible but selling organs always impermissible, unless one has some view that accepting payment intrinsically involves a wrong. Selling organs might involve such harm, for example, if done capriciously, without regard for one's welfare. One must, for example, consider the impact on the physical health of organ vendors in terms of mortality and morbidity costs. Yet, such costs are likely not significant. Long-term life expectancy for donors is not measurably lessened by the removal of the redundant internal organ (e.g., a single kidney) or regenerative tissue (e.g., a liver slice). The primary health risks for living donors are those associated with the operative procedure for harvesting the organ. For example, perioperative mortality for nephrectomy is approximately 3 deaths for 10,000 donors (0.03%), with other major complications occurring in less than 2% of cases. The occurrence of long-term morbidity risks, such as increased risk of hypertension or proteinuria after living-donor nephrectomy, is controversial (Ross et al. 1997, 1753). Other operations, such as harvesting a liver slice, can be somewhat more risky for the donor (see Najarian et al. 1992, 807–10; Bia et al. 1995, 322–27; Bay and Herbert 1987, 1–8). One concern is that an organ market would unduly impact the poor, or those in poorer health, who would be the most likely to become vendors. However, organ failure does not limit itself to the wealthier or healthier segments of the population. Yet, donation among family members is considered morally licit, even if those donating are poor and in poorer health than more affluent members of society. Provided redundant internal organs and regenerative tissues are procured in a suitably sterile environment, by a competent surgeon, selling redundant organs and regenerative tissues is less risky than many other occupations. Such mortality and morbidity risks exist wherever living donors are utilized, regardless of whether money changes hands. Therefore, presuming living donors will continue to be utilized, such risks are neutral with regard to the market. Insofar as such donation is morally justified, it is plausible that similarly intentioned sales ought to be understood as morally justified as well.

Moreover, forbidding organ sales may demean the poor and sick by closing off options for improving their lives (i.e., the one by procuring funds by selling a kidney, and the other by gaining health by transplantation). Insofar as a disproportionate number of poorer individuals would be exposed to such risks, the potential harms of organ donation would need to be weighed against the short- and long-term benefits attributable to increased income. As Angeles tan Alora and Josephine Lumitao document, in the Philippines redundant organ sales are considered by vendors to be an important means to raise resources to support fledgling businesses and to further family welfare (Alora and Lumitao 2000). While redundant organ sales were legal, Indian transplant teams documented the success of such transplantation programs, in terms of graft survival, lack of donor mortality, return of patients to productive lives, and assistance in resolving the great financial need of donors (Thiagarajan et al. 1990). Indeed, one such study from India suggested that graft survival from live unrelated donors at one year appeared to be moderately superior than from live related transplants (84% versus 81%, respectively) (Thiagarajan et al. 1990, 913; see also Reddy et al. 1990). Purchasing organs for transplantation, these physicians from the developing world conclude, is in keeping with ethical values, as well as appropriate understandings of fundamental commitments to medical care.[13]

A market in human organs may even lead to positive health benefits for vendors. A human organ market would increase the vendor's overall social and economic prospects, which would, in turn, lead to indirect health benefits. Individuals with higher salary, higher status jobs incur advantages: economic, social, and functional. For example, despite universal single-tier health care coverage, life expectancy in Canada varies according to income and status. In 1971 the difference in life expectancy in Canada between the highest and lowest earning was 6.3 years for men and 2.8 years for women. This deviation had only reduced in 1986 to 5.6 years for men and 1.9 years for women (Iglehart 1990, 563; see also Wilkins et al. 1989). Consider also the Whitehall II study conducted in Great Britain on civil service workers, which demonstrated an inverse association between employment grade and prevalence of angina, electrocardiogram evidence of ischemia, and symptoms of chronic bronchitis. Morbidity and mortality were both affected by employment grade (Marmot et al. 1991). The reasons cited to account for these differences include (1) "different attitudes to health," such as "the lower degree of belief among those with lower status jobs that they could take action to prevent a heart attack"; (2) "patterns of social activity differed, with clear indication of less, and less satisfactory, social support among those with lower status jobs"; and (3) "work environment [being] perceived differently between grades. Impressive evidence has accumulated that jobs characterized by low control, poor opportunity to learn and develop skills, and high psychological work load are associated with increased risk of cardiovascular disease" (Marmot et al. 1991, 1392; see also, Wright 1991, 285–87). Low job control was closely linked with position in the employment hierarchy. In a similar study among Czech men, it was also concluded that low job control was related to acute myocardial infarction in middle age (Marmot et al. 1997; see also Taylor 1991, 70; Goldstein 1995, 397; Fletcher 1988, 27; Monat and Lazarus 1991, 82). In addition, mortality from heart disease is higher in manual than in nonmanual occupational classes (Marmot and McDowall 1986; see also Locke and Taylor 1991, 140, 150–55).

Low income has also been consistently related to measures of unfavorable birth outcomes. Within lower income neighborhoods in urban Canada, there are higher rates of infant mortality, low birth weight, very low birth weight, prematurity, and small gestational age (Wilkins et al. 1991, 7). "From 1971 to 1986, infant mortality in urban Canada declined by 50%, but the ratio of rates in the poorest neighborhoods compared to the least poor neighborhoods diminished by only 8%" (1991, 8). These statistics point to indirect health benefits for children associated with the income level and job status of parents.

Market incentives encourage persons to raise resources to further personal as well as social interests and goals. Profits from organ sales would allow for the private pursuit of business and educational opportunities, or to further more public agendas. A market in human organs would create opportunities, which some may view as attractive, in securing resources for pursuing their own educational, business, political, and welfare interests. Increase in control over one's occupation (i.e., increase in status as well as increase in salary) leads to economic, social, and functional advantages, which in turn are indirectly associated with increased life expectancy, increased health, reduced infant mortality, and increased advantages for children. Morbidity costs and mortality risks lower with income level and professional status. Measured solely in terms of health care consequences, selling one's internal redundant organs may be a rational strategy to raise one's income, increase one's economic and social prospects, and thereby indirectly benefit oneself and one's family. Insofar as this is true, allowing the poor to market their organs will offer health advantages as well as empower them. It will give them control over their own lives and enhance personal dignity, which, given the foregoing data, should itself provide further economic, social, and health advantages.

Markets and Charity

Moreover, it is unclear that current organ procurement practices are accurately characterized as "altruistic" or that donation takes place in a spirit of "charity" or "gift giving." With the documented success of transplantation procedures and the advent of immunosuppressive drugs, such as Cyclosporine, that increased long-term survival rates, physicians and the general public quickly changed their view of organ transplantation from an experimental surgical procedure to a medically successful therapy (Fox and Swazey 1992, 8–30). This shift altered medical social reality to the extent that human organ transplantation has come to be regarded as a treatment to be offered whenever medically indicated. Human organs are often construed as a "scarce medical resource." This medical shift, in language, expectation, and practice, placed a greater perceived moral burden on family members and even strangers to make their organs available to others if needed. However, by bringing the considerable legal force of the government to bear against the very possibility of selling one's organs, one legislates the necessity of the "donation," thereby calling into question the "altruistic" character of such transactions. Rather than binding potential donors and recipients, as well as their physicians, in the solidarity of shared social values and caring human relationships, dying patients are disinterestedly recast as "sources" of needed medical resources, and their grieving families as "access barriers" to be overcome. It may be that it is the current system's blanket prohibition on selling, rather than the market, which in the context of organ procurement dehumanizes patients, treating their bodies as mere collections of useful parts, and thereby failing appropriately to understand the embodied nature of persons and the sovereignty of God.

Indeed, since the principle of totality must be outweighed by the significance of charity, this will rule out many donations. Persons who stand to be financially supported by a person needing an organ might have other motivations than "kindness" for donating an organ. Other donations might be premised on reciprocated love, friendship, guilt, or concern not to be stigmatized for failing to donate (Office of Technology Assessment 1987, 117). How pure must one's intentions be so as to transfer organs as an act of altruism?

On the other hand, it is possible charitably to intend the good of another through for-profit market transactions. While the virtue of charity is often understood as a benevolent disposition toward others and their welfare, the relief of suffering, the bestowal of gifts, and other similar actions, Christian charity traditionally focused on the love of others for God. As John McHugh and Charles Callan summarize this virtue, "charity refers to divine love, that is, to the love of God for man or the love of man for God. Here, we are considering charity as the virtue by which the creature loves God for His own sake, and others on account of God" (1960, 454). Charity, so understood, is consistent with the market. Among the examples of charity, McHugh and Callan list, "in a wide sense, almsgiving includes selling on credit as a favor to a poor customer; a loan granted at a low rate of interest or without interest, help in securing employment, etc." (1960, 495). Assisting someone through the market can be a significant act of charity.

Indeed, Pius XII specifically allowed that for-profit selling of human body parts could be consonant with the principle of charity.

> Moreover, must one, as is often done, refuse on principle all compensation? This question remains unanswered. It cannot be doubted that grave abuses could occur if a payment is demanded. But it would be going too far to declare

immoral every acceptance or every demand of payment. The case is similar to blood transfusions. It is commendable for the donor to refuse recompense; it is not necessarily a fault to accept it. (Pius XII 1960, 381–82)

Removal of a healthy human organ would be permissible even if one accepts or requests monetary compensation, or other valuable consideration, provided that one does not exploit those in need by demanding too great a fee; although, presumably, a poor individual could ask for greater compensation from a rich recipient. One could view this possibility as consonant with the reflections of certain theologians on the priority one should give the poor. (See, for example, Haas 1990; Hobgood 1997; Finn 1997; Beckley 1997; Robb 1997.) In short, as Pius XII expresses the position, there is nothing intrinsically evil about the for-profit sale of human organs (see also Moraczewski 1984, 3).

Rather than eroding charity, the market may enhance and draw together moral communities, opening significant opportunities for developing personal relationships and for charitably providing for the fundamental needs of others. Significant expressions of altruism may exist side by side with a for-profit market. For example, if it is altruistic for a parent to give a kidney to save his child's life, it is similarly altruistic for a parent to sell a kidney to pay for a life-saving operation (see, for example, Radcliffe-Richards 1996, 392).

Forbidding a market in human organs restricts persons from joining together with others to pool financial resources to purchase organs for the impecunious. It prevents altruistic donation of organs to nonprofit groups, who could then sell such parts to raise funds to purchase food, shelter, or health care for the poor. Indeed, a market may open significant new opportunities for the expression of altruism, for building solidarity and community, as well as for charitably providing for the fundamental needs of others. A market in human organs would likely be more successful on each of these grounds than current nationalized bureaucratic depersonalized donation procedures.

Conclusion

In summary, the principles of totality and charity are fully consistent with a market in human organs procured from cadaver sources as well as with a futures market. With death, body parts are no longer caught up in the life and good of the human person; they are much like other types of things, albeit things that, as their history, have been parts of a former person. Such markets neither degrade human dignity nor depersonalize or dehumanize living human beings. They are fully consistent with the embodied nature of persons, careful stewardship of God's gift to us of our bodies, and recognition of His dominion over creation.

On the other hand, presuming that one sells a healthy organ to a well-matched recipient, the requirement of a sufficient reason for removal of an organ may be satisfied with (1) the expected good to the recipient of the organ of an increase in quality and quantity of life, and (2) the good which the income will provide for the vendor. The vendor may, for example, have morally compelling charitable reason to sell an organ, such as to purchase medicine, food, or shelter for the vendor's family. Insofar as the principle of totality is satisfied in the case of organ donation, it is satisfied in the case of organ selling. As long as one markets only redundant organs, or regenerative tissue, the *de minimus* standard of adequate biological functioning is satisfied.[14]

Insofar as one's intention in removing the organ is not because one is attempting to destroy the natural good of human biological wholeness but because one wants to engage in a market transaction to (1) help others through the market and (2) to assist one's family through the provision of resources not otherwise available, the sale of redundant internal organs is not an example of mutilation which the canons contemplated, nor is it forbidden by the recast principle of totality. In removing the redundant organ, the natural good of the individual's bodily functioning wholeness is not set at risk. Moreover, it is an instance of an individual cooperating with others in society to provide for the needs of others, as well as for oneself. Given such conditions, it should not be considered a mutilation that offends the Deity or as destroying or reducing the natural good of biological functional wholeness. On such grounds, the organ market may be morally permissible. Indeed, given appropriate circumstances in which the charity of the sale is apparent, it may even be commendable.

Discussion Questions

1. What is the position of Roman Catholic moral theologians as it relates to the sale of human organs?
2. What are some of the major attributes associated with gift giving?
3. What special moral issues have been exposed by John Haas as they relate to the commercialization of organs?
4. What are the historical roots of Aquinas' concern for the natural good of human biological wholeness?
5. What is the Catholic Church's position on individuals who voluntarily mutilate themselves?
6. What are the three general conditions that govern the moral licitness of anatomic or functional mutilation?
7. What were the findings of the Whitehall II study conducted in Great Britain on civil service workers?

8. What positive outcomes were cited by the author of market incentives for individuals to sell their organs?
9. What happens when a market for the voluntary sale of one's organs is prohibited?

Endnotes

1. As Rev. Father Joseph Howard Jr. captures the position, "The body can never be treated as a mere biological entity; nor can its organs or tissues ever be used as items for sale or exchange ... love, communion, solidarity, and absolute respect for the dignity of the human person constitute the only legitimate context of organ transplantation" (1994, 58). Pope John Paul II summed up the essence of organ donation as a "decision to offer without reward, a part of one's own body for the health and well-being of another person. In this sense, the medical action of transplantation makes possible the donor's act of self-giving, that sincere gift of self which expresses our constitutive calling to love and communion" (*Dolentium Hominum* 1992, n. 3). Benedict Ashley and Kevin O'Rourke concur, holding that it follows from this moral theological position that a market in human organs is contrary to human dignity and deeply depersonalizing (1994, 175).
2. Haas also expresses concerns regarding the standard of care: "If there were a market for selling organs of the dead, there might be an incentive not to do whatever would normally be considered necessary to keep the person alive. In fact, there might even be an incentive to kill such persons by acts of commission or omission" (Haas 1990, 2).
3. Aquinas argues, "Consequently the first principle in the practical reason is one founded on the notion of good, *viz.*, that good is that which all things seek after. Hence this is the first precept of the law, that good is to be done and pursued, and evil is to be avoided. All other precepts of the natural law are based on this: so that whatever the practical reason naturally apprehends as man's good (or evil) belongs to the precepts of the natural law as something to be done or avoided.... Because in man there is first of all an inclination to good in accordance with the nature which he has in common with all substances; inasmuch as every substance seeks the preservation of its own being, according to its nature; and by reason of this inclination, whatever is a means of preserving human life, and of warding off its obstacles, belongs to the natural law. Secondly, there is in man an inclination to things that pertain to him more specifically, according to that nature which he has in common with other animals: and in virtue of this inclination, those things are said to belong to the natural law, which nature has taught to all animals, such as sexual intercourse, education of offspring and so forth. Thirdly, there is in man an inclination to good, according to the nature of his reason, which nature is proper to him: thus man has a natural inclination to know the truth about God, and to live in society: and in this respect, whatever pertains to this inclination belongs to the natural law; for instance, to shun ignorance, to avoid offending those among whom one has to live, and other such things regarding the above inclination" (*ST,* I-II, q94, a2).

4. As Alasdair MacIntyre documents, Thomists in the last hundred years have often ascribed to Aquinas a belief in a set of necessarily true first principles, which any truly rational person is able to evaluate as true. "For this kind of Thomist the rational superiority of Aquinas' overall system of thought does not lie both in its having transcended the limitations of its predecessor traditions, while preserving from them what has withstood dialectical objection, and in its since then having not similarly been transcended by any successor system of thought, but instead in its argumentative ability to encounter its modern rivals on *their* chosen ground for debate and to exhibit the rational superiority of its claims concerning first principles to theirs" (MacIntyre 1988, 175–76).
5. For a modern Thomistic defense of this view, see John Finnis, who argues, for example, that biological life is a natural basic good: "A first basic value, corresponding to the drive for self preservation, is the value of life. The term 'life' here signifies every aspect of the vitality (*vita*, life) which puts a human being in good shape for self determination. Hence, life here includes bodily (including cerebral) health, and freedom from pain that betokens organic malfunctioning or injury" (1980, 86; see also Finnis et al. 1989).
6. "So the transplantation of a duplicated organ such as the kidney, leaving the whole substantially unimpaired, need not be regarded as doing harm for the sake of good" (Finnis 1991, 79).
7. As Aquinas argues, "A member should not be removed for the sake of the bodily health of the whole, unless otherwise nothing can be done to further the good of the whole. Now it is always possible to further one's spiritual welfare otherwise than by cutting off a member, because sin is always subject to the will: and consequently in no case is it allowable to maim oneself, even to avoid any sin whatever. Hence Chrysostom, in his exposition on Mt. 19:12 (Hom, lxii in Matth.), 'There are eunuchs who have made themselves eunuchs for the kingdom of heaven,' says: 'Not by maiming themselves, but by destroying evil thoughts, for a man is accursed who maims himself, since they are murderers who do such things.' And further on he says: 'Nor is lust tamed thereby, on the contrary it becomes more importunate, for the seed springs in us from other sources, and chiefly from an incontinent purpose and a careless mind: and temptation is curbed not so much by cutting off a member as by curbing one's thoughts'" (*ST* II-II, Q65, a3).
8. The relationship persons have with their bodies, it is argued, is inappropriately characterized as a form of absolute "ownership." While an owner of a thing may use or destroy it at will, so long as he does not conflict with the rights of others, persons do not own their bodies in such a fashion. "Above all, he must conserve his body and his life, for they do not belong to him, but to God; man may not destroy needlessly his body or any part of his body" (Finney and O'Brien 1956, 207).
9. There is some dispute over whether the surgeon may simply remove the healthy appendix during the course of another abdominal procedure, or, whether to justify the incidental appendectomy, he must judge that the appendix's presence after an abdominal operation constitutes a probable danger from adhesions that may render the second operation necessary (Finney and O'Brien 1956, 229; see also Shiners 1958, 37–38; Nolan 1963, 28–44, 290–324; Regan 1965, 320–61; Connery 1954, 603; Connery 1956, 561; Kelly 1963, 628–29).

10. McFadden points out that in unusual cases where it is evident that surgical aid will not be available in the future, it may be permissible, but not obligatory, to undergo elective appendectomy, for example missionaries who will be venturing into primitive areas without significant contact with modern medicine (1961, 269; see also Kelly 1960, 254).
11. As Pope John Paul II addressed a group of blood and organ donors on August 2, 1984, "Above all I appreciate the purpose which has united you: namely, to promote and encourage such a noble and meritorious act as donating your own blood or an organ to those of your brothers and sisters who have need of it. Such a gesture is the more laudable in that you are motivated, not by a desire for earthly gain or ends, but by a generous impulse of the heart, by human and Christian solidarity—the love of neighbor, which forms the inspiring motive of the Gospel message, and which has been defined, indeed, as the *new commandment*" (1985).

    In 1991, while acknowledging the benefits of organ transplantation, the pope also encourages caution: "Among the many remarkable achievements of modern medicine, advances in the fields of immunology and of surgical technology have made possible the therapeutic use of organ and tissue transplants. It is surely a reason for satisfaction that many sick people, who recently could only expect death or at best a painful and restricted existence, can now recover more or less fully through the replacement of a diseased organ with a healthy donated one: We should rejoice that *medicine, in its service to life, has found in organ transplantation a new way of serving the human family,* precisely by safeguarding that fundamental good of the person.... Love, communion, solidarity, and absolute respect for the dignity of the human person constitute the only legitimate context of organ transplantation. It is essential not to ignore the moral and spiritual values which come into play when individuals, while observing the ethical norms which guarantee the dignity of the human person and bring it to perfection, freely and consciously decide to give a part of themselves, a part of their own body, in order to save the life of another human being" (1992; see also Michejda 1992).
12. For a discussion of the ways in which contemporary theologians have understood proportionate good to outweigh harmful effects, see Hoose (1987), McCormick and Ramsey (1978), and Cahill (1984). For a more traditional account of the doctrine of double effect, see Boyle (1984).
13. Indeed, Thiagarajan et al. lament that the greatest value lost is professional and academic respectability because of "those who have allocated to themselves the right to sit in judgment, based on their own environment and prejudices, and to exclude from scientific discussion those observations that come to alternative and controversial yet acceptable practices prevailing in other less fortunate areas of the world" (1990, 94).
14. Ashley and O'Rourke summarize permissible removal of organs from living persons for transplantation following five conditions:
    1. There is a serious need on the part of the recipient that cannot be fulfilled in any other way.
    2. The functional integrity of the donor as a human person will not be impaired, even though anatomical integrity may suffer.

3. The risk taken by the donor as an act of charity is proportionate to the good resulting for the recipient.
4. The donor's consent is free and informed.
5. The recipients for the scarce organs are selected justly (1996, 175).

Only the first four conditions address the removal of healthy organs from living persons. Moreover, each can be plausibly met while compensating donors for the market value of their redundant internal organs. The fifth condition regards justice in allocation of organs as a scarce resource, which is a morally distinct concern. One could, for example, utilize a variety of insurance and charitable schemes to ensure that all who need organs would be equally able to purchase the necessary organs.

References

Alora, A., and J. Lumitao. *Beyond a Western Bioethics: Voices from the Developing World.* Washington, DC: Georgetown University Press, 2000.

Aquinas, St. T. *Summa Theologiae.* New York: Benziger Brothers, 1947.

Ashley, B. M., and K. O'Rourke. *Ethics of Health Care: An Introductory Textbook,* 2nd ed. Washington, DC: Georgetown University Press, 1994.

Bay, W. H., and L. A. Herbert. "The Living Donor in Kidney Transplantation." *Annals of Internal Medicine* 106 (1987): 7.

Bia, M. J., E. L. Ramos, G. M. Danovitch, et al. "Evaluation of Living Renal Donors: The Current Practice of US Transplant Centers." *Transplantation* 60 (1995): 322–27.

Beckley, H. "Social Sciences and Theological Ethics." *Journal of Religious Ethics* 25, no. 2 (1997): 343–50.

Boyle, J. "The Principle of Double Effect: Good Actions Entangled in Evil." In *Moral Theology Today: Certitudes and Doubts.* Braintree, MA: The Pope John Paul Center, 1984.

Boyle, J. "Personal Responsibility and Freedom in Health Care: A Contemporary Natural Law Perspective." In *Persons and Their Bodies: Rights, Responsibilities, Relationships,* ed. M. J. Cherry, 135. Dordrecht: Kluwer Academic, 1999.

Cahill, L. "Contemporary Challenges to Exceptionless Moral Norms." In *Moral Theology Today: Certitudes and Doubts.* Braintree, MA: The Pope John Paul Center, 1984.

Connery, J. "Notes on Moral Theology." *Theological Studies* 15 (1954): 603.

———. "Notes on Moral Theology." *Theological Studies* 17 (1956): 561.

Cummings, M. "Gene Therapy: Actualities and Possibilities." In *The Twenty-fifth Anniversary of Vatican II: A Look Back and a Look Ahead.* Braintree, MA: The Pope John Paul Center, 1990.

Finn, D. "Monologue and Dialogue in Christian Economic Ethics." *Journal of Religious Ethics* 25, no. 2 (1997): 335–42.

Finney, P., and P. O'Brien. *Moral Problems in Hospital Practice.* St. Louis: B. Herder, 1956.

Finnis, J. *Natural Law and Natural Rights.* Oxford: Clarendon Press, 1980.

———. *Moral Absolutes: Tradition, Revision, and Truth.* Washington, DC: The Catholic University of American Press, 1991.

Finnis, J., J. Boyle, and G. Grisez. *Nuclear Deterrence, Morality, and Realism.* New York: Oxford University Press, 1989.
Fletcher, B. "The Epidemiology of Occupational Stress." In *Causes, Coping and Consequences of Stress at Work*, ed. C. L. Cooper and R. Payne, 3–50. New York: John Wiley & Sons, 1988.
Fox, R., and J. Swazey. *Spare Parts: Organ Replacement in American Society.* New York: Oxford University Press, 1992.
Gallagher, J. "The Principle of Totality: Man's Stewardship of His Body." In *Moral Theology Today.* Braintree, MA: The Pope John Paul Center, 1984.
Goldstein, D. *Stress, Catecholamines, and Cardiovascular Disease.* New York: Oxford University Press, 1995.
Grisez, G. *Living a Christian Life.* Quincy, IL: Franciscan Press, 1993.
Haas, J. "The Sale of Human Organs." *Ethics and Medics* 15, no. 2 (1990): 1–2.
Healy, E. F. *Medical Ethics.* Chicago: Loyola University Press, 1956.
Hobgood, M. "Poor Women, Work, and the U.S. Catholic Bishops: Discerning Myth from Reality in Welfare Reform." *Journal of Religious Ethics* 25, no. 2 (1997): 307–34.
Hoose, B. *Proportionalism.* Washington, DC: Georgetown University Press, 1987.
Howard, J. "Philosophical and Moral Issues of Organ Transplantation at the Close of the Twentieth Century." *Linacre Quarterly* 61 (1994): 57–64.
Iglehart, J. "Canada's Health Care System Faces Its Problems." *New England Journal of Medicine* 322, no. 8 (1990): 562–68.
John XXIII, Pope. "Address to the Italian Association of Voluntary Blood Donors." *The Pope Speaks*, March 8, 1959, 334.
John Paul II, Pope. "Blood and Organ Donors, Aug. 2, 1984." *The Pope Speaks* 30, no. 1 (1985): 1–2.
———. "Examination of Questions in Greater Depth." *Dolentium Hominum* 3 (1992).
Kelly, G. *Medica-Moral Problems.* Dublin: Clonmore & Reynolds, 1960.
———. "Notes on Moral Theology." *Theological Studies* 24 (1963): 628–29.
Kenny, J. P. *Principles of Medical Ethics.* Westminster, MD: The Newman Press, 1962.
Locke, E. A., and M. S. Taylor. "Stress, Coping and the Meaning of Work." In *Stress and Coping*, ed. A. Monat and R. S. Lazarus, 140–58. New York: Columbia University Press, 1991.
MacIntyre, A. *Whose Justice? Which Rationality?* Notre Dame, IN: Notre Dame University Press, 1988.
Marmot, M. G., H. Bosma, H. Hemingway, E. Brunner, and S. Stansfeld. "Contribution of Job Control and Other Risk Factors to Social Variations in Coronary Heart Disease." *The Lancet* 350, no. 9073 (July 1997): 235–39.
Marmot, M. G., and M. E. McDowall. "Mortality Decline and Widening Social Inequalities." *The Lancet* 328, no. 8501 (August 1986): 274–7.
Marmot, M. G., G. D. Smith, S. Stansfeld, C. Patel, F. North, J. Head, I. White, E. Brunner, and A. Feeney. "Health Inequalities among British Civil Servants: The Whitehall II Study." *The Lancet* 337, no. 8754 (June 1991): 1387–92.
McCormick, R., and P. Ramsey. *Doing Evil to Achieve Good.* Chicago: Loyola University Press, 1978.
McFadden, C. *Medical Ethics.* Philadelphia: F. A. Davis, 1961.
McHugh, J., and C. Callan. *Moral Theology.* New York: Joseph F. Wagner, 1960.
Michejda, M. "Transplant Issues." In *The Interaction of Catholic Bioethics and Secular Society*, ed. R. Smith. Braintree, MA: The Pope John Paul Center, 1992.

Monat, A., and R. S. Lazarus. "Stress and the Environment." In *Stress and Coping*, ed. A. Monat and R. S. Lazarus, 81–86. New York: Columbia University Press, 1991.

Moraczewski, A. S. "A Sour Note in Organ Transplantation: Are Human Organs Saleable?" *Ethics and Medics* (January 1984): 2–3.

Najarian, J. S., B. M. Chavers, L. E. McHugh, and A. J. Matas. "20 Years or More of Follow-Up of Living Kidney Donors." *The Lancet* 340, no. 8823 (October 1992): 807–10.

Nicodemus and Agapius, Sts. *The Rudder*. Chicago: The Orthodox Christian Educational Society, 1957.

Nolan, M. "The Positive Doctrine of Pope Pius XII on the Principle of Totality." *Augustinianum* 3 (1963): 290–324.

Office of Technology Assessment. *New Developments in Biotechnology: Ownership of Human Tissues and Cells*. Washington, DC: Government Printing Office, 1987.

O'Rourke, K., and P. Boyle. *Medical Ethics, Sources of Catholic Teachings*. Washington, DC: Georgetown University Press, 1983.

Pius XII, Pope. *Papal Teachings: The Human Body, The Monks of Solesmes*, selected and arranged ed. Boston: The Daughters of Saint Paul, 1960.

Radcliffe-Richards, J. "Nepharious Goings On: Kidney Sales and Moral Arguments." *The Journal of Medicine and Philosophy* 21 (1996): 375–416.

Reddy, K. C., C. M. Thiagarajan, D. Shunmugasundaram, R. Jayachandran, P. Nayar, S. Thomas, and V. Ramachandran. "Unconventional Renal Transplantation in India." *Transplantation Proceedings* 22, no. 3 (1990): 910–11.

Regan, A. "The Basic Morality of Organic Transplants between Living Humans." *Studia Moralia* 3 (1965): 320–61.

Robb, C. "The Work of Welfare Ethics." *Journal of Religious Ethics* 25, no. 2 (1997): 351–60.

Ross, L. F., D. T. Rubin, M. Siegler, M. A. Josephson, J. R. Thistlethwaite Jr., and E. S. Woodle. "Ethics of a Paired-Kidney-Exchange Program." *The New England Journal of Medicine* 336, no. 24 (1997): 1752–55.

Shiners, J. *The Morality of Medical Experimentation on Living Human Subjects in the Light of Recent Papal Pronouncements*. Washington, DC: Catholic University of America Press, 1958.

Taylor, S. "Health Psychology: The Science and the Field." In *Stress and Coping*, ed. A. Monat and R. S. Lazarus, 62–80. New York: Columbia University Press, 1991.

Thiagarajan, C. M., K. C. Reddy, D. Shumugasundaram, R. Jayachandran, P. Nayar, S. Thomas, and V. Ramachandran. "The Practice of Unconventional Renal Transplantation (UCRT) at a Single Centre in India." *Transplantation Proceedings* 22, no. 3 (1990): 912–14.

Varga, A. C. *The Main Issues of Bioethics*, rev. ed. New York: Paulist Press, 1984.

Wilkins, R., O. Adams, and A. Brancker. "Changes in Mortality by Income in Urban Canada from 1971 to 1986." In *Health Reports*, no. 1. Ottawa: Statistics Canada, 1989.

Wilkins, R., G. Sherman, and P. A. F. Best, "Birth Outcomes and Infant Mortality by Income in Urban Canada, 1986." In *Health Reports*, no. 1, 3. Ottawa: Statistics Canada, 1991.

Wright, I. "This Type A Behavior Pattern and Coronary Artery Disease: Quest for the Active Ingredients and the Elusive Mechanism." In *Stress and Coping*, ed. A. Monat and R. S. Lazarus, 275–300. New York: Columbia University Press, 1991.

Wuthnow, R. *Acts of Compassion: Caring for Others and Helping Ourselves.* Princeton, NJ: Princeton University Press, 1991.

15 The Commercialization of Human Body Parts
A Reappraisal from a Protestant Perspective*

LARRY TORCELLO, PhD
State University of New York at Buffalo

STEPHEN WEAR, PhD
State University of New York at Buffalo

Contents

Introduction	227
The Essential Secular Case against Commercialization	229
Exploitation	230
Coercion	231
Protestant Arguments for and against Human Body Part Commercialization	232
Greed	233
The Protection of Altruism	235
Human Sanctity and Autonomy	236
Conclusion	241
Discussion Questions	241
Endnotes	242
References	242

Introduction

Human organ transplantation has grown from a once quite experimental and often lethal procedure to the currently preferred treatment in many cases of organ failure. This success has been largely due to improvements in transplant immunology, as well as surgical and postoperative methods. Yet, while such therapeutic progress has been quite impressive, the procurement rate for transplantable organs has remained frustratingly insufficient. Despite the high survival rate of organ recipients, the shortage of organs continues to

---

* First published in *Christian Bioethics* 6 (2) 153–169, 2000.

mean that many will die before an organ becomes available to them and that many more will receive their organs only in markedly less advantageous circumstances, their disease having progressed during extended waiting periods. In 1997 alone there were 4,327 people who died with their names on a transplant waiting list.[1]

Various attempts to address this shortage have occurred. These include (1) expansion of the class of acceptable donors from solely living donors to cadavers, brain dead patients, and recently to non-heart-beating donors; as well as (2) the use of organ donor cards and other mechanisms, routine requests to patients upon admission to hospitals, and to families of dying patients, toward increasing the number of people who are given the option of becoming potential donors.

Despite such efforts, the demand for organs continues vastly to exceed the supply. This has led some to reconsider the possibility of commercial forms of organ procurement, including financial reward for living donors. Such an option has generally been met with widespread rejection over the years since organ transplantation became a real therapeutic option. Further, in the name of safeguarding individuals from coercion and exploitation, as well as to insure that donations were made on voluntary and altruistic bases, federal legislation has explicitly banned the commercialization of human organs (Arnauld et al. 1996, 31). However, as the organ shortage problem persists, arguments and advocates in favor of commercialization are beginning to emerge. In this chapter, it is our intention to examine the possibility of human body part commercialization and further to contribute to the growing call to reconsider the current ban on human organ sales in this country.

Our more specific purpose and strategy is to consider the possible acceptability of organ sales from a Protestant Christian perspective. This strategy arises in part from our sense that many of the basic arguments that are typically offered in support of a ban on organ sales are of a quite strange character and lineage. That is, many of the arguments seem to be of a straightforward secular character, without any particular appeal to theological or religious perspectives. But these same arguments do not fare well as secular arguments (where at most one gets to appeal to what rational persons as such should affirm, condemn, or allow), but still have the stridency of unargued taboos far beyond the apparent discomfort and concern that such a commercial practice would usually produce. Or, more simply, the objections often do not have much, if any, secular force; are easily countered; and do not seem to be sufficient to the strident rejection of organ sales that they are intended to support. The intensity of the conclusion is just not matched by the force of its supporting argument.

At first glance, such strident but philosophically anemic objections thus appear to be more the product of cultural taboos and aesthetic discomforts than a rational examination of the issue. If this is all that they are, then such cultural taboos and aesthetic discomforts should hardly be allowed to discredit a practice that might lead to the salvage of many otherwise dying patients.

This chapter represents our conviction that matters are not quite this simple. More specifically, it represents our sense that serious theological concerns may well be behind the antagonism to organ sales and that such underlying concerns should be identified and engaged, lest matters of importance be missed, rather than take the simple philosophical tactic of showing that seemingly secular arguments do not have any decisive secular force. Clearly American and Western European culture has strong Protestant roots, and the secular world has no doubt absorbed and been cross-fertilized with Protestant moral beliefs. Therefore, it is not enough for philosophers simply to dismiss these vague discomforts and taboos as nonphilosophical.

To attempt to state what a generic Protestant view of organ sales might be, however, quickly generates its own serious problems. On the other hand, most Protestant thinkers are steadfastly against organ sales (e.g., Paul Ramsey and James Childress). But this clear fact immediately becomes problematic in that most of these thinkers offer *little or no theological* arguments for their opposition.[2] The few arguments they do offer are similar to the secular arguments just mentioned in that they are long on condemnation and short on even philosophical or secular justifications. Once again, it seems that we are in the land of taboo and vague aesthetic discomfort.

Intent on making sure that there is not a baby hidden away in all this bathwater, we will attempt to pursue the more modest goal of showing why Protestantism (like secular reasoning) does not preclude the possibility of human organ sales as a viable option for increasing the availability of transplantable organs. To pursue this goal, we will first present what we take to be the core secular arguments against organ sales, an argument we suspect is more theological in lineage but still should be dispatched as quite inadequate as a *secular* argument. Second, we will proceed to unearth, or at least to speculate, as to what sorts of Protestant concerns and principles this core secular argument, and others, might appeal to in support of the abhorrence of organ sales that can be found among Protestant thinkers.

The Essential Secular Case against Commercialization

The premier and essential objection to the sale of human body parts on secular grounds is that commercialization would tend unavoidably to harm sellers. More specifically, the basic concern here is that due to the supposed inevitability of exploitation and coercion, the sale of human body parts cannot be contained in a just health care system. We will address this core secular argument in terms of its two separable, primary elements: exploitation and coercion.

Exploitation

The primary impetus offered for the maintenance of an altruistic system of donation is the concern that a commercialized system of procurement would likely lead to the unethical exploitation of the poor. Part of the fear here is that while it is possible that a market for human body parts might well increase the overall availability of transplantable organs, such a system would insure that the donors of the organs would tend to be poor while the recipients would tend to be wealthy (or at least better off than other candidates). As David Thomasma formulates it,

> Prices may escalate far beyond the ability of all but oil sheiks to pay. Poor recipient candidates would have no means available to purchase organs. There would be a maldistribution of organs, just as there is a maldistribution of other goods and services in society. (1988, 22)

Concerning this major fear that organ sales would actually compound already existing problems of social injustice, some philosophers have argued (e.g., Radcliffe-Richards 1996; Annas 1984; Wear et al. 1999) that there is no reason to assume that human body part sales need take place in the context of a radical free market. As Wear et al. write,

> [W]e do not see this issue as usefully approached as if it was all or nothing. Rather, we submit, it seems clear that some forms of commercialization will (and should) be allowed, some should absolutely be forbidden, and the real issue is which forms of commercialization, *between these extremes*, will be allowed or forbidden, and according to which principles of consideration. (1999, 375)

A government program funding the purchase of organs should be able to avoid any problems associated with radical commercialism through proper policy and regulation. Under such a program, the distribution of organs need not necessarily operate under capitalistic principles. There can perhaps be a regulated base payment for organs and a distribution system based in theory on the same principles regulating the commercial procurement of blood and bone marrow, which are already in place. There's no reason why a flat rate could not be imposed, assuring that potential sellers are not motivated to hold out for the highest price. These concerns clearly run into matters of policy rather than issues of whether or not selling organs in itself is right or wrong. As George Annas writes,

> The argument that sale will only sanction the transfer of organs from the poor to the rich can be at least partly answered by having a governmental agency be the sole purchaser and distributor of organs, with distributions based on a criterion other than wealth or social worth. (1984, 23)

Also, one should keep in mind that blood, sperm, and bone marrow are already being procured according to monetary incentives. One can also bring in the issue of artificial organs and other prosthetics. Such products are produced by manufacturers out to make a profit, and yet the capitalism inherent in such practices has not made it so that only the super wealthy can obtain prosthetic body parts. In fact, as experience instructs us, capitalistic forces commonly tend to drive down prices in market situations rather than drive them up. In any case, any regulations that one may wish to impose on in vivo procurement could also apply to cases of cadaveric donation as well.

Coercion

It is inherent in the fear that capitalistic forces would insure that the poor are to be the primary donors, while the wealthy will be the only group capable of benefiting, that the sale of human body parts would involve substantial coercion of the poor. The idea here seems to be that the situation of many poor people precludes a truly autonomous choice to sell one's organs. It is thought that the decision to sell one's organ is such an extreme and desperate act that anyone who would make such a decision must be incapable of the required autonomous rational consent. If this claim is true, then such sales must be rejected as unavoidably coercive. According to Janet Radcliffe-Richards's thorough analysis of this objection, such individuals are thought to be (1) incompetent by ignorance, (2) coerced by poverty, or (3) coerced through unrefusable offers.

Under such assumptions, opponents of commerce in human body parts conclude that commercialization could never be an ethical option to pursue (Radcliffe-Richards 1996, 379–84). This objection is also what George Annas claims to be the single major argument from a legal perspective. As he writes,

> [T]here is really only one major argument against permitting a competent adult to sell his or her nonvital organs: sale is an act of such desperation that *voluntary* consent is impossible. (1984, 23)

As troublesome as the issue may seem, the objection of coercion carries with it a host of unwarranted assertions. First, to charge coercion because an individual is thought to be ignorant is not a telling objection. When faced with ignorance, the best option is always education rather the than removal of options. This brings into play issues of informed consent. It is the medical professional's responsibility to make sure the patient is well informed regarding any given medical procedure; organ donation is no exception. Most laypeople are ignorant of many issues in health care; this, however, is no argument against health care. In sum: if the patient otherwise has the capacity to give informed consent, then this objection collapses into a simple need to assist such donors to accomplish this; it in no way rules out the practice.

Likewise, it is not reasonable to ban the sale of human body parts on the claim that donors would be coerced by poverty. This claim, however, is reducible to absurdity by stretching it to its logical ends. If this were supportable, we would also have to ban many dangerous and unsavory jobs that people are now engaged in. We would be resigned morally to ban most if not all forms of commerce and employment. How many people are currently in the job market working jobs that make them unhappy simply because they are being unjustly "coerced by poverty"? We venture that there are many. However, by rushing to save these people from exploitation, we would certainly be making their circumstances much worse. Janet Radcliffe-Richards formulates the issue well when she argues, "The worse we think it is to sell a kidney or an eye, the worse we should think the situation in which we leave these people when we remove that option" (Radcliffe-Richards 1996, 377).

It is also dubious to assert that autonomous choice can be composed of unrefusable offers. To begin with, like most objections against organ sales, this assumes an unregulated open market. However, as we have already argued above there is no reason to insist on such a market. It is simply a matter of policy to regulate prices in order to assure that coercive "unrefusable offers" are not a factor. In any case, as Radcliffe-Richards points out, it is debatable that one can be accused of coercion by widening an individual's options. The original options are still available: altruistic donation, certain poverty, and the like. However, an individual may come to the conclusion that, all other options considered, sale is the best possible option. As Radcliffe-Richards points out, "It would be convenient to be able to show consideration for the poor by paying less for what they had to sell" (1996, 384).

Such arguments represent what we and others view to be the fundamental secular positions against organ sales. We contend that secular thinkers have already efficiently dealt with these arguments to be extent that a continued ban on human body part sales is no longer warranted on secular grounds. In addition to the above arguments, there are often other miscellaneous arguments that are presented in secular form which involve such issues as altruism and greed. It is our position that these arguments are quite weak and without warrant on secular grounds. It is our belief that such concerns point to an often unnoticed religious influence into secular matters. Therefore, we submit that such issues are more properly addressed in a religious context, which secular thinkers have often tended to ignore.

Protestant Arguments for and against Human Body Part Commercialization

As stated, this section of the chapter will be discussed in terms of Protestant views. The reason that Protestantism can be presented fruitfully as representative is found within the spirit of the reform itself. As James T. Johnson observes regarding the nature of Protestant theology,

> To do theology in the Protestant tradition (or in a specific Protestant tradition, like the Lutheran) one attempts to re-think and redefine the core doctrines for one's contemporaries. This method puts a great deal of stress on the central doctrines of the reformation, upon the Reformers who enunciated them, and upon the concerns and problems of one's own culture and the modes of thought fashionable among one's contemporaries. Intermediate figures in Protestant history are, for this methodology, primarily or only useful as object lessons in relating the pertinent doctrines to a particular historical milieu. (1978, 1365)

With this view in mind, the soil is rich for a fresh discourse to take place in light of Protestant principles. Indeed, contrary to what some secular thinkers may imagine, it is not a matter of dogma that Protestant theologians should automatically be against a practice, such as human body part sales, by virtue of their religious affiliation. Evidence of this is found in the work of James Childress, who has rejected the sale of human body parts, but not on the grounds that it is intrinsically immoral; rather, he has argued that such sales would be problematic and ineffective on secular grounds (1978). However, as we have argued, such concerns are without significant merit.

Since it is our contention that a large part of the distaste some individuals hold for the sale of human body parts is rooted in religious sentiments concerned with things such as greed, the protection of altruism, and human sanctity, we will take these issues up from a Protestant perspective in what follows. Although we will primarily focus on theological concerns, we will begin by briefly identifying the secular form of each concern and showing why it is not decisive as a secular argument.

Greed

It has been suggested from a secular point of view that the knowledge on the part of family members that they can be reimbursed for the use of a deceased loved one's organs may promote the practice of demanding reimbursement before potentially transplantable organs are removed. As R. A. Sells argues, "To encourage the incursion of greed in people suffering from grief would be morally difficult to defend" (1992, 2199). This seems to be an inconsequential argument. All things considered, the possibility of some greed occurring does not outweigh the reality that many people will die for lack of organs if we do not overcome our squeamishness toward ideas such as organ sales. In any case, the worry over greed can be curbed through careful regulation. It is not an unsolvable problem. Furthermore, greed is clearly a religious vice. From a secular point of view, it should have no currency at all. By secular standards, what some may call greed can just as easily be defined as good business sense, or respectable self-interest no different from any other. Nonetheless, "greed" could be curbed through policy regulation, which could be implemented to resolve other concerns (e.g., exploitation, autonomous consent, and coercion). However, though we can deal with this objection on secular grounds easily, it is better answered from a Protestant perspective since it is very likely a product of religious influence.

First, it is important to realize that capitalistic practices are not in and of themselves objects of Protestant condemnation. This is important because it sheds light on the concern that human body part sales might encourage greed. While greed is a vice that one might expect theologians to condemn, it is important not to view capitalism as a sufficient cause of greed. Many professions carry the risk of greed but are nevertheless respectful vocations.

If we were to condemn the sale of human body parts because it might encourage greed, then all sorts of other activities and professions should be likewise condemned for the same reason. However, according to Protestantism any number of secular professions can be seen as "callings" from God regardless of the potential for greed inherent in them. From the perspective of fundamental Protestant principles such as "universal priesthood" and "godly callings," one may argue that the potential to cause greed is not an adequate objection to organ sales. Clearly, commercial activities can be seen as legitimate ways by which to fulfill one's calling. Capitalization itself, even the capitalization of human body parts, is not condemned in Protestant theology. Nor is a desire for financial success itself to be condemned. As Max Weber wrote in his classic study, *The Protestant Ethic and the Spirit of Capitalism*,

> It is true that the usefulness of a calling, and thus its favor in the sight of God, is measured primarily in moral terms, and thus in terms of the *importance of the goods produced in it for the community*, but a further, and, above all, in practice the most important criterion is found in private profitableness. For if that God, whose hand the Puritan sees in all the occurrences of life, shows one of His elect a chance of profit, he must follow the call by taking advantage of the opportunity. If God shows you a way in which you may lawfully get more than in another way (without wrong to your soul or to any other), if you refuse this and choose the less gainful way, you cross one of the ends of your calling, and you refuse to be God's steward, *and to accept His gifts and use them for him when He requireth it:* you may labor to be rich for God, though not for the flesh and sin. (1958, 162; emphasis added)

Commercialization in itself cannot be held as immoral. Insofar as it has the potential to cause greed, it is given another value: insofar as one may avoid the temptation of overzealous greed, and through it the faithful are given a valuable opportunity to test and demonstrate their sanctity. In light of these factors, the argument that sale of human organs should be avoided on the account that they may encourage greed is seen to be no more valid in Protestant theological terms than it was in secular terms.

However, having come to this conclusion, the question remains: can one truly interpret the donation of organs as a divine calling? It is difficult to come up with a reason why one may not be called to such an act, especially when one considers the nature of such a momentous decision. Though some may argue that such a decision can never be autonomous, it may also be argued by the religious that such a decision can only be come upon in earnest through a profound sense of divine intent. However, when considering the nature of such a calling, it might be asked whether or not commercialization could contaminate such a call by obscuring altruism.

The Protection of Altruism

The need for altruism in order to preserve the true purpose of one's call would seem unnecessary if one were to consider, as pointed to in this chapter, that there are many professions that may be subject to a godly calling that do not operate on the basis of altruism. Further, it is simply narrow-minded to suppose that capitalism is incompatible with altruism. As Max Weber has argued, even capitalistic endeavors can be tied to the notion of a godly call. The wealth, which comes with capitalistic endeavors, should not be rejected rashly. Weber wrote,

> Wealth is ... bad ethically only in so far as it is a temptation to idleness and sinful enjoyment of life, and its acquisition is bad only when it is with the purpose of later living merrily and without care. But as a performance of duty in a calling it is not only morally permissible, but actually enjoined. The parable of the servant who was rejected because he did not increase the talent that was entrusted to him seemed to say so directly. To wish to be poor was, it was often argued, the same as wishing to be unhealthy. It is objectionable as a glorification of works and derogatory to the glory of God. (1958, 163)

The parable mentioned by Weber seems particularly relevant to our topic, and we might further remember that in that parable the master reacted to his servants who had made wise financial decisions by adding to their responsibilities. This brings us to our next point. Those who reject the idea of receiving financial reward may be acting analogously to the servant who was chastised by his master for making no investments and failing to increase the master's estate. One may look upon the money entrusted with each servant as a calling to service by God. By wisely administering to their task, the servants who invested were able to bring added glory to their master.

By the same token, it may be reasoned that those who are called to aid others through their donation of an organ, and in doing so obtain financial reward, may likewise be adding to the glory of God. Like the shrewd servants who were given added responsibilities, so might those who obtain financial rewards for their donation also realize an added responsibility. Such individuals may then choose to make an added donation of their payment to charity or find some other way by which their profit could benefit others. By doing so, they not only preserve and enhance altruism, but also create an added means of expressing the grace of God. In addition, it can, therefore, be seen how the commercialization of human body parts might actually encourage charity rather than greed. On these grounds, from a theological view, as from a secular view, altruistic concerns may actually provide greater reason for allowing human body part sales than forbidding them. However, although altruism and charity may stand to increase from commercialization, even if some individuals who "donated" simply decided to keep the financial reward for themselves, the fact remains that they mercifully provided a much-needed item that nevertheless will benefit others in a tremendously meaningful way: "It isn't your sacrifices and your gifts I want—I want you to be merciful" (Matthew 9:13).

Human Sanctity and Autonomy

From a secular perspective, sales of human body parts are sometimes argued against on the grounds that such commodification is repugnant. Repugnancy, however, fails to be a significant argument from a secular perspective. In fact, from a rational point of view, "body part commodification" can have some strong benefits aside from the obvious benefit of increased organs for transplant. By placing property rights on our bodies, we would also give ourselves increased control over them from a legal perspective. R. A. Sells has suggested that surgeons may actually treat a purchased organ less carefully than they would a donated organ (1992). While we do not think such a worry possesses any warrant, one can nevertheless counter it by noting that physicians may be more careful dealing with our bodies in general if we had property rights that would allow us added reimbursement for any accidental damages. This form of property right may conceivably have benefits in other areas as well. As L. B. Andrews points out,

> In our market-based society, our laws are often more protective of property than person. By calling body parts property, there is a legal basis for a remedy when actions are taken with respect to our bodily parts that may not exist under themes of privacy, autonomy, assault, or infliction of emotional distress. (1992, 2151)

Again, it requires no stretch of the imagination in order to place this "secular" objection in its proper religious context. Christians believe that the body is a sacred temple. From a Christian point of view, the commodification of the body would be a great assault upon its sanctity and a repugnant suggestion.

However, perhaps such repugnance is misguided even from a religious perspective. First, if we are to assume that creation is an unbridled good, then it (including humans, despite the fall of humans as interpreted by Christians) is bestowed with sanctity, which for the believer is reflective of God's grace. This sanctity may be felt as jeopardized when we begin to treat human body parts as commodities. This is, we believe, at the base of the religious repugnance over the sale of human body parts. Even if it could be admitted that we make commodities of each other in various ways already, this observation surely does not justify yet another means of tarnishing what a theologian might mean when discussing human sanctity.

However, though we may at first be put back by the idea of human body part commercialization simply due to its uniqueness, it is questionable that anyone can forcefully demonstrate to a tangible degree the ways in which such a practice would actually denigrate human sanctity. If human sanctity is placed upon individuals by God, no earthly activity could truly corrupt such a gift. To assume that sanctity is harmed is to betray a belief that it is fragile, as well as a hubris regarding man's potential to corrupt what God sanctified. Further, there is no reason to believe that such sales need to be conducted in less than an extremely professional and respectful manner. The fact that human beings can be said to possess "interchangeable parts" in the first place does not threaten the sanctity of human beings or the value of such parts. If a token of reward in the form of financial payment is introduced, that is no reason to imagine that sanctity of any kind is necessarily harmed. After all, monetary concerns are already existent in areas such as education and medicine. Yet the sanctity of education and healing cannot be doubted. One may still question whether or not we are free to accept financial reward for the donation of bodily organs. If such organs are viewed as gifts, then it can be questioned as to whether we have the right to expect any reward for them ourselves. This objection is concerned with the allied notion of autonomy.

David C. Thomasma, for example, argues that from a theological perspective we are the creative expressions of a deity. Being such, it is thought that we are entrusted with our bodies yet do not own them in the same sense as something that we may place property rights upon. Thomasma writes,

> All living beings derive their dignity from the gift of life from God. This belief is the source of reluctance to commit suicide, even rational suicide (active euthanasia). If God did create our lives, then we do not have ultimate, absolute

control over them. Applied to the transplant question, this vision prohibits the level of control assumed by the buying and selling schemes. Life and the body are gifts to be enjoyed and for which we are responsible. Just as it wrongs the gift giver to sell a gift one receives, so, too, it is wrong to sell (and buy) organs. (1988, 23)

This sort of objection sounds good *prima facie*; there is, however, a problem. If it is true, as Thomasma claims, that we do not have ultimate control over our lives, then that is no less a detriment to donating our organs than it is to selling them. Thomasma seems to elude here that commercialization would give too much freedom to individuals in regard to their bodies, but it is unclear as to what practical freedom is increased through sales as opposed to donations. If concern over bodily freedom is a real issue, then perhaps one may not have the right to sell organs, but then it seems one would also have no right to donate them. If Thomasma is correct, one would also have no right to donate sperm, ova, or even blood. Of course, Thomasma wants to retain donation as a right, as do most thinkers, but it remains to be seen whether or not such a move is consistent. Surely, if it would wrong the gift giver to sell a gift one receives, so too it could be claimed that giving away a gift is just as unjustified.

For example, Paul Ramsey has argued that for a Protestant it should not be necessary to appeal to the spiritual benefits of charity in order to justify organ donation, since any gift should not be given with the intent of aiding oneself in any way. However, the importance of embodied identity may cause one to pause in consideration of how far one should go in condoning the mutilation of one's own body, even when another individual's earthly life would be extended. He writes,

[A] possible moral justification of organ transplantation from living donors that might be developed within the ambit of Protestant Christian ethics would not need to resort to any "sticky (psychological or spiritual) benefits theory." A reasonable secular transcription of this is the appeal solely to a free and informed consent on the part of the donor. A demerit of this outlook should also be noted. A justification of the self-giving of organs developed on Protestant grounds, precisely because of its freedom from the moorings of self-concern, is likely to fly too high above concern for the bodily integrity of the donor, higher than one finds in even the most liberal Roman Catholic thought. (1970, 186–87)

It is unclear whether such a "demerit," as Ramsey calls it, should be taken as a reason to avoid donation altogether or simply as a cautionary issue reminding us that organ donation should not lightly be entered upon. Ramsey cautions against a Cartesian-like outlook that downplays the value of the human body in terms of personal identity and urges us to remember the importance of human embodiment. The question now becomes whether such embodiment is reason enough to shun the idea of human body part donation all together. We clearly think it is not. There is no denying that human beings are embodied creatures. Nevertheless, from a Christian point of view, and in contrast to Ramsey's way of thinking, it would certainly seem misguided to place a value on the flesh over and above issues of spirituality.

This is not to endorse what Ramsey would call a "sticky benefits theory."[3] Rather, it seems that Ramsey is placing an emphasis on physical embodiment that places the flesh as more essential to identity than the soul. Indeed, it may be a form of reverse Cartesianism that merits just as much caution as its opposite. Clearly, there are many individuals who live with artificial body parts, be they hearts or limbs. However, such a state does not reflect any defect in their identity as a person regardless of the state of their embodiment. Similarly, it is odd to imagine that by donating or selling a kidney to another that we are harming our embodied identity in any way that could be condemned in and of itself.

To recognize identity in embodiment is not to imply that we cannot take measures to alter embodiment and identity as we see fit. After all, the entire field of health care aims to do this at some level when one is ill. Our embodiment as human beings is by nature deeply involved with change. Our embodiment changes drastically with the passage of time; moreover, we can seek rationally to alter it through diet and exercise. Surely, there is a much deeper center of self, more essential center of self, which is not diminished by the sacrifice of one's organs. Furthermore, too strong a focus on individual embodiment loses sight of the communal embodiment we all partake in as human beings. It might be argued that a parent who is forced to watch a child die is suffering a far worse mutilation of their identity than a parent who is permitted to sacrifice a kidney to preserve their child's life. After all, parents invest a great deal of themselves in their children. The same argument can be made for a variety of relationships that people have with others that are more essential to their identity than one of their kidneys. Furthermore, one's embodiment within a larger community of humanity is recognized when one sacrifices an organ for a stranger. Such a practice is in itself reminiscent and in step with the biblical teaching that we are all unified as different parts of a larger and transcendent body. This sacrifice and inner connection is not, therefore, degraded just because money changes hands!

The bodily sacrifice of oneself for another is in itself analogous to the sacrifice that Christians credit Christ as making for the sake of humankind. Insofar as a Christian would like to emulate the life of Christ, it would seem that donation of one's organs for another is beyond reproach. For all these reasons, it seems odd for one seriously to argue against organ donation or organ sales from some vague principle of bodily identity. Ramsey also goes so far as to provide a hypothetical example of a father who decides he would like to donate his heart to his son, thus sacrificing his life for the boy. Indeed, such an extreme case is not beyond the bounds of imagination, given the strong bonds of affection typical between parent and child. However, if such a practice is upon ultimate analysis found to be unjustifiable, we once again need only defer to matters of regulation and policy to ensure that such practices are to be avoided.

In addition, Courtney S. Campbell has suggested that the donation of one's organs may be all the more justifiable if our organs are meaningful to our sense of identity. He argues,

> The self-expressive character of gifts also suggests that central to the notion of gift is the creation of community. The self through the gift extends an invitation of relationship to the recipient. The sharing of self—physically, emotionally, spiritually—displays a profound sense in which the fullness of who we are as persons is realized only in and through relationships with others. (1993, 77)

In any case, we may ultimately turn to the Protestant principle of a "godly calling" to answer such objections as Ramsey's and Thomasma's. If we are to take seriously the notion of a calling, we must take seriously the idea of autonomy. It is up to the individual to make an autonomous choice as to whether or not they wish to answer a call or not. This is why individuals can be said to have the freedom to donate, and it is also foundational to why human beings have the freedom to sell. The fact that Protestant theology embraces the ability of the individual to interpret theological matters in light of their own reflection bears witness to the crucial role that autonomy plays in Protestant theology. It is up to individuals to interpret their own call. Reason may dictate that it is as likely that one may be called to sell an organ as it is that one may be called to donate an organ, and perhaps more likely. In Protestant theology, the freedom of the individual Christian is of the utmost importance. All Christians are called to be "priests" to those around them, but they are also crucially free to interpret their particular callings and interpret for themselves how best to serve God and others. In dealing with Thomasma's concerns, it may be helpful to once more remember the parable mentioned in this chapter. If a Christian were to allow unease over commercialization to blind him or her to the possibilities that money may bring to further serve God and others, then such a Christian may risk making a similar mistake as the one made by the unwise servant of the parable.

Objections such as those that Thomasma and Ramsey raise ignore what Protestant thought holds as the important need of the individual authentically to make his or her own decisions regarding how to serve others. Perhaps an individual would after consideration of the issue still deem human body part sales, or even donations, to be theologically offensive. If so, then emphasis on individual interpretation of theological principles in Protestantism, along with the autonomous responsibility of the individual before God, suggests that it remains a personal choice for the believer whether or not they are to engage in such a practice. If such sales were legalized, it would remain an individual choice. No one could be forced to accept any money, nor could anyone be forced to use it in any particular fashion. Protestant valuations of autonomy are compatible with secular values of freedom. Both should be respected.

Conclusion

It is not our intent to pretend that the sale of human body parts is the ultimate answer to the current organ shortage. However, considering the plight of those who wait for organs and the potential for commercialization to improve the situation, we suggest that a continued ban on human body part sales is ill advised. Alternatively, an investigation into the best means by which to introduce just and effective policy regarding the potential sale of human body parts is most appropriate at this time. We have tried to show that from both secular and Protestant viewpoints there is no justification for a ban on such sales. Although many of the secular objections to the proposal seem to be based in vague "religious" concerns, we have hoped to show that such concerns, when placed in a proper theological rather than secular framework, are nonetheless far from being decisive. In contrast, we have argued that organ sales can be positively defended on both secular and Protestant foundations, and we invite the continued exploration of this issue in theological realms by both secular as well as nonsecular thinkers in order to balance and complement this important ethical debate.

Discussion Questions

1. What is the premier and essential objection to the sale of human body parts?
2. What is meant by the assertion that the primary impetus offered for the maintenance of an altruistic system of donation is the concern that a commercialized system of procurement would likely lead to the ethical exploitation of the poor?
3. What was suggested as a means to avoid problems associated with the radical commercialization of organs?
4. What are the body parts already being procured according to monetary incentives?
5. What has the author asserted regarding the element of coercion as it relates to the poor voluntarily selling their organs?

6. What do the authors assert as it relates to the secular point of view on greed when it comes to the sale of transplantable organs?
7. According to the author, is capitalism incompatible with altruism?
8. In what ways have the authors suggested that from a rational point of view "body part commodification" can have some strong benefits aside from the benefit of increased organs for transplantation?

Endnotes

1. This number was taken from the United Network for Organ Sharing (UNOS) website (http://www.unos.com). It has many of the current statistics one may wish to find concerning the topic of organ transplantation.
2. Paul Ramsey does propose a theological style argument against human organ sales, but as we hope is evident in this chapter, it is not enough to justify a dismissal of such commercialization on Protestant grounds alone. James Childress argues against human organ sales, but does so for what he claims to be secular reasons. However, current secular arguments against human organ sales in general are, we argue, largely unconvincing.
3. What Ramsey calls "sticky benefits" is taken here to refer to benefits that provide a motivation for donation that excludes the possibility of pure altruism. Such benefits may be a psychological satisfaction one may receive through donation, or the hope for spiritual blessings to be bestowed upon one as a result of earthly sacrifice.

References

Annas, G. "Life, Liberty, and the Pursuit of Organ Sales." *The Hastings Center Report* (February 1984): 22–23.

Andrews, L. B. "The Body as Property: Some Philosophical Reflections—A Response to J. F. Childress." *Transplantation Proceedings* 24, no. 5 (1992): 2143–48.

Arnauld, R. M., L. A. Siminoff, and J. E. Frader. "Ethical Issues in Organ Procurement: A Review for Intensivists." *Critical Care Clinics* 12, no. 1 (1996): 31–48.

Campbell, C. S. "The Selling of Organs, the Sharing of Self." *Second Opinion* 19, no. 2 (1993): 69–79.

Childress, J. F. "The Body as Property: Some Philosophical Reflections." *Transplantation Proceedings* 24, no. 5 (1992): 2143–48.

D'Alessandro, A. M., R. M. Hoffman, and F. O. Belzer. "Non Heart-Beating Donors: One Response to the Organ Shortage." *Transplantation Reviews* 9, no. 4 (1995): 168–76.

Johnson, J. T. "History of Protestant Medical Ethics." *Encyclopedia of Bioethics* 3 (1978): 1364–73.

Radcliffe-Richards, J. "Nephrarious Goings On: Kidney Sales and Moral Arguments." *The Journal of Medicine and Philosophy* 21, no. 4 (1996): 375–416.

Ramsey, P. *The Patient as Person: Explorations in Medical Ethics.* New Haven, CT: Yale University Press, 1970.

Sells, R. A. "The Case against Buying Organs and a Future Market in Transplants." *Transplantation Proceedings* 24, no. 5 (1992): 2198–2202.

Thomasma, D. C. "The Quest for Organ Donors: A Theological Response." *Health Progress* (September 1988): 22–28.

Wear, S., J. Freer, and B. Koczwara. "The Commercialization of Human Body Parts: Public Policy Considerations." In *Persons and Their Bodies: Rights, Responsibilities, Relationships,* ed. M. J. Cherry, 363–68. Dordrecht: Kluwer Academic, 1999.

Weber, M. *The Protestant Ethic and the Spirit of Capitalism,* trans. T. Parsons. New York: Charles Scribner's Sons, 1958.

Index

A

ABO incompatible transplantation, 122
abortions, 77
aesthetic discomfort, and organ sales, 228–229
aid-based argument, organ market, 152–155, 164, 165
AIDS, from blood transfusions, 75
almsgiving, 216
Alora, Angeles Tan, 213
altruism
    and capitalism, 235
    and charity, 236
    and organ donation, 38, 40, 82–84, 118, 132, 133, 166, 174, 203, 235
    and organ market, 217
    and presumed consent, 81
    protection of, 235–236
American Medical Association (AMA), 131–133
American Red Cross, 74
American Society of Transplant Surgeons (ASTS), 131–132
amputation
    morally licit, 208–209
    and totality principle, 208–210
Amsterdam Forum, 121–122
Anderson, Elizabeth, 177
Andrews, L.B., 236
Annas, George, 230, 231
antigen typing
    and kidney transplants, 98, 104
    paid for by organ broker, 103
antitrafficking legislation
    Europe, 35–37, 40
    lack of, 32, 36
    victims *vs.* criminals, 40–41
appendectomy, elective, 211–212, 220n9, 221n10
Aquinas, Thomas, 205, 206, 208–212, 219n3, 220n7
Ashley, Benedict, 219n1
Austria, presumed consent, 81
autonomy
    and collective good, 193
    of donors, 144–148
    and human worth/dignity, 175–176, 198–199
    and organ market, 144, 145–155, 162–166, 198–199, 236–241
    personal physical, 49, 82–84, 145
    and poverty, 145–155, 162–168
    and Protestant theology, 240
    -undermining constraining options, 148–155

B

"baby organ snatchers," Tijuana, Mexico, 7
Bangalore, India, kidney trade, 59, 60
Belgium, presumed consent, 80–81
Bilirakis, Michael, 79
biomechanical organ replacement, 73
Biomedical Tissues Services, Ltd., 4–5
black market
    for illicit organs, 32–35, 86
    and organ shortage, 50
    and organ theft, 50, 52
    and poverty, 86, 119–120
    price of organs, 55
blood donation, 38–39, 74–75
    as charity, 211
    motives of seller, 195
blood transfusions, safety of, 74–75
blood typing, and kidney transplants, 98, 103
body, *See also* autonomy
    objectification of, 133–134
    as property, 132–133, 138, 236–237
    as self, 132–133, 137, 138, 173, 238–241
    stewardship of, 209, 220n8, 237–238
    totality principle, 205–212
    value of, 172
body parts
    commodification, 236–241; *See also* organ market
    dealers, 5; *See also* organ brokers
    global market, 9–10
    stolen, 50, 52
    value of, 5
bone, 10, 76
bone banks, 9
bone marrow donation, 38–39, 76
brain death criterion
    China, 18–19
    Japan, 118
    and organ transplantation, 99–100
    Transplantation of Human Organs Act, 64–65, 66
Brazil, transplant tourism, 119
Brimm, Dianah, 126

Bristow, Lonnie, 132
Buddhism, and organ harvesting, 16
Bulgaria
    lack of antitrafficking legislation, 32, 36
    organ trafficking, 30

C

cadaveric organ transplantation, 72, 99–100, 122
    and Aquinas' totality principle, 210
    body-as-self view, 134
    Catholic Church on, 189–190
    financial compensation for, 131–132
    kidney, 72, 99–100
    market, 5–6, 87–88, 133–135, 157n3
    and next of kin, 135
    tax credits for, 131
cadavers, 5–6
    commodification, 133–135
    nationalization of, 81–82; See also China
    as property, 135
Callan, Charles, 216
Campbell, Courtney S., 240
Canada
    infant mortality, 215
    life expectancy, 214
Canon of the Apostles, and self-mutilation, 206–207
capitalism
    and altruism, 235
    and escaping poverty, 198
    and lower organ prices, 231
    and Protestantism, 234–235
cardiovascular disease, and low job control, 214
caritas, 203
castration
    Catholic Church on, 206–207
    Chrysostom on, 220n7
    voluntary, nonmedical, 206–207
Catholic Church
    on cadaveric transplants, 189–190
    on castration, 206–207
    charity and organ markets, 215–217
    on consent, 192
    on organ transplantation and sales, 189–192
    and totality principle, 205–212
    on xenotransplantation, 189
Catholic transplantation agencies, 192–194, 195–200
Cebu Province, Philippines, 120
Center for Organ Recovery and Education, 99–100

charities
    government and, 193
    private medical, 192–194
charity
    and altruism, 236
    blood donation as, 211
    organ donation as, 203–204
    and organ market, 215–217
    and totality principle, 208–217
Chennai, India, "Kidney-vakkam," 149
child kidnapping, 7
Childress, James, 233
China
    brain death criterion, 18–19
    execution process, 17–19, 82
    families of condemned prisoners, 14
    kidney transplants, 16, 120
    legal definition of death, 18
    medical professionals role in organ procurement, 17–18
    organ procurement from executed prisoners, 13–15, 82, 86, 119, 120
    organ recipient ranking, 14–15
    prisoners executed for religious/political beliefs, 19
    secrecy in harvesting prisoners' organs, 15–16, 82
    unidentified prisoners, 14
    "voluntary" consent of prisoners, 14–17, 30, 81–82
Chinese Communist Party, 19
Christianity, *See also* Catholic Church; Protestantism
    charity and organ markets, 215–217
    and commodification, 236–241
    and totality principle, 205–212
Chrysostom, on castration, 220n7
cloning, 182–184
coercion
    and organ markets, 132, 192, 231–232
    and poverty, 231–232
collective good, *vs.* common good, 193
Colombia, transplant tourism, 119
commercialization, and Protestantism, 234–235
commercial living donors (CLDs), 119; *See also* vendors
    Egypt, 120, 121
    organ sales from, 124
    preexisting health conditions, 121
    reimbursing for expenses, 124
commodification
    body parts, 236–241
    cadavers, 133–135
    Christian perspective, 236–241
    of human gametes, 170

Index

kidneys, 107–109
  and legal rights, 236
  non-biological products, 169, 170
common good, *vs.* collective good, 193
compassion, and organ donation, 203–204
condemned prisoners
  and consent, 14–17, 30, 81–82
  kidneys from, 120
  organ procurement from, 13–19, 81–2, 86; *See also* China
confidentiality, and secrecy, 15–16
Confucianism, and organ harvesting, 16
consent
  Catholic Church on, 192
  condemned prisoners and, 14–17, 30, 81–82
  expressed, 38
  and financial compensation, 40
  presumed. *See* presumed consent
conspiracy law, 8–9
constraining option, 148–155
Convention on Human Rights and Biomedicine, 30, 36
Cooke, Alistair, 4
cornea market, 137
corruption, and organized crime, 26
Cosa Nostra, 25
Council of Europe (COE), 30, 35–36
Council of Nicaea, 206–207
crimes, classifying, 26–27
criminals, organized, 26
Cruzan vs. Director, Missouri Department of Health, 82
Cuellar, Hector Ramirez, 7
cultural taboos, and organ market, 228–229
current market. *See* organ market
Cyclosporin-A, 72, 143, 215

D

Davis vs. Davis, 76
death, and identity, 135
death row, and free consent, 14–17, 30, 81–82
deceased, rights of, 134
DeGowin Blood Center, 75
Dergaus, Alex, 126
dialysis, and kidney transplant waiting list, 35
dignity. *See* human dignity/sanctity
DNA donation, 38–39
documents, falsification of, 4
donor registration, 50–51, 83
donors, *See also* commercial living donors; kidney donors; living organ donation; vendors
  advertising for, 69
  autonomy of, 144–148

"close association," 67
coercion of, 231–232
despair of, 31–32
emotional attachment, 65, 67
exploiting, 31–32, 146–148, 197–198, 230–231, 232
financial incentives, 31, 38–40, 51–52, 54–55, 122–123, 131–133, 134
life expectancy, 213
motives of, 195
"near relatives," 64
poverty and, 31, 33, 34–35, 38–40, 51–52, 54–55, 121, 122–123, 131–133, 134
recruitment of, 32–35
reimbursing for expenses, 79–80, 124
risks to, 213
tax reduction/credits for, 194
"unrefusable offers," 232
unrelated living, 118
as victims, 35–36
dura mater, 76
Dworkin, Gerald, 143–144, 145–148, 154, 161, 162–166
dying patients, as "sources," 216

E

eBay, kidney auction, 84, 98
economic status, and health, 214
Egypt, transplant tourism, 119, 120, 121
embalmers, tissue harvesting/selling, 4–5
embodiment
  communal, 239
  of identity, 132–133, 238–241
embryos, frozen, as property, 76
emergency situations, and Uniform Anatomical Gift Act, 78–79
end-stage renal disease (ESRD), 59, 118
English medical schools, 19th century, 84
Estonia, organ trafficking, 30
Europe
  antitrafficking legislation, 35–37, 40
  kidney transplant waiting list, 31
  Mafia organizations, 25
  organ shortage, 30–32
  presumed consent, 80–81
  transplant tourism, 29–32
  transplant waiting list, 31
  unrelated living donors, 118
Euro-Transplant, 122
Evans, Richard, 137
execution
  by gunshot, 18
  by lethal injection, 17
  and organ removal, 82, 86
  prolonging to obtain viable organs, 17–19, 82

exploitation
  defined, 197
  of donors'/recipients' despair, 31–32
  of poor donors, 146–148, 197–198, 230–231, 232
expressed consent, 38
extortion, 26

F

false information, providing, 9
"Falun Gong: Organ Harvesting and China's Ongoing War on Human Rights," 19
Falun Gong, 19
families. *See* next of kin
fascia, 76
felony crime, failure to report, 9
fetal egg/ovary transfer, 170, 179–181
fetus, respect for, 180–181
financial incentives to donors
  AMA proposal, 131–133
  arguments against, 54–55
  arguments for, 38–40, 51–52, 122–123, 134
Finnis, John, 220n5
First and Second Regional Synod, 207–208
First Council of Nicaea, 206–207
Florida, sale of anatomical matter, 8
Food and Drug Administration (FDA), organ market and, 88
foreign trade zones, 9
forward markets, 101–102, 106
France, presumed consent, 80
free consent, and death row, 14–17, 30, 81–82
free markets
  arguments against financial incentives, 54–55
  and escaping poverty, 198
  kidneys, 96–101
  organ donation, 52–53; *See also* organ market
  and organ prices, 231
Frist, Bill, 79
Frontline Karnataka kidney trade investigation, 59–69
funeral homes, tissue harvesting/selling, 4–5
futures market, 101–102, 106, 107–109, 157n3, 161, 210

G

gambling, 26
gametes, commodification of, 170, 176–179

Georgia, organ trafficking, 30
German Federal Criminal Office (BKA), 25
Germany
  Central Commission on Ethics, 37
  kidney transplant waiting list, 31
gift giving, 203–204
"godly callings," 234, 240
good, notion of, 219n3
government
  ban on sale of organs, 49–52, 228
  control of organ transplantation, 192–194, 198
  dehumanizing policies, 205, 215–216
  fraud and, 198
  imposing flat rate for organs, 230
  and private charities, 193–194
greed, and organ markets, 233–235
Greene, Rex, 132

H

hair, selling, 171–172, 174
Hass, John, 204
Health and Human Services (HHS), 78, 83
health insurance companies
  Catholic sponsored, 200
  joint venture with organ brokers, 104–105, 106–107
  kidney dialysis/transplant coverage, 96
  as resellers or brokers, 105
"healthy lifestyle" bonus, 88
heart transplants, 72
heart valves, 76
Hema Care, 75
hemophilia, 74–75
hepatitis virus, 75
Hindu, The, 63–64
Hobbes, T., 173
homeless persons, unexplained disappearances, 6
hospitals, and Uniform Anatomical Gift Act, 78–79
Howard, Reverend Father Joseph, Jr., 219n1
Hughes, Paul, 144, 148–149, 150–152
human dignity/sanctity, 172–176
  and organ sales, 198–199, 204, 236–241
  "reductive materialist" conception, 192
  and selling reproductive tissues, 185
"human flourishing," 52
human immunodeficiency virus (HIV), 75
Human Organ Transplants Act, 155
human rights, and organ trafficking, 123–124
human trafficking, 26
Human Transplantation Act, 120

Index

I

identity, embodiment of, 132–133, 238–241
illicit organ market, 32–35, 86; *See also* black market
illicit services and goods, 26
immunosuppressants, 72–73, 215
India
    economics of organ trade, 68–69
    "kidney colonies," 119
    live unrelated transplants, 214
    organ trade, 59–60, 68–69; *See also* Karnataka kidney trade
    transplant tourism, 29–30, 119
informants, offenders as, 28
International Kidney Exchange, 86–87
International Society of Nephrology, 123, 125
in vitro fertilization, 180–181
Iran, kidney vendors, 68
Iranian model, 121–122, 123
Ireland, lack of antitrafficking legislation, 32, 36
Israel, transplant tourists from, 30, 120, 121
Istanbul Declaration, 123
Italy, kidney waiting list, 118

J

Jacobs, H. Barry, 86–87
Japan
    brain death criterion, 118
    kidney waiting list, 118
    non-heart-beating donation, 122
Jayasri, Alladi, 63–64
job status, and health, 214
Johnson & Johnson Company, 6
Johnson, James T., 233

K

Kant, Immanuel, 172–175
Karnataka Appropriate Authority
    complaints against, 63–64
    failure of, 61–67
    improving, 66–67
    role of, 64, 66
Karnataka Authorisation Committee, 59–61
    complaints against, 63–64
    failure of, 61–67
    improving, 66–67
    role of, 64
Karnataka Health Task Force, 67
Karnataka kidney trade
    broker networks, 63, 64, 65–66
    economics of, 68–69
    failure of legislative bodies, 61–67
    features of, 60–61
    investigation of, 59–60
    role of physicians, 67–68
Kelly, Gerald, 210
Kempana, H.S., 62
Kennedy, Edward, 79
kidney brokers, Mandya district, 63, 64, 65–66
kidney buyer, expenses, 105
kidney dialysis, 73
kidney donors
    "affection and attachment," 65, 67
    cadaveric, 72, 99–100
    kidney failure in, 100–101
    living, 72, 100–101, 118
    price paid to, 33, 105
    risks to, 213
    survival rates, 100
kidney market, 86–87, 96–101
    forward, 101–102, 106
    futures, 101–102, 106, 107–109
    laws against, 172
    options, 101–102, 106
    Philippines, 119, 120, 121
    price discrimination, 103
    prices, 33, 105–106, 107
    purchaser, 104–105
    spot, 102–105
    tracking system, 105–106
kidneys
    as commodities, 107–109; *See also* kidney market
    eBay auction of, 84, 98
    economic shortage, 96
    illicitly donated, 32–35
    mechanical, 73
    medical shortage, 96
    sources of, 99–101
    supply/demand, 96–101
kidney transplantation
    antigen typing and, 98, 104
    blood typing and, 98, 103
    cadaveric, 72, 99–100
    China, 16
    cultural barriers to, 118
    fraud and, 125–127
    history of, 72–73
    India, *See also* Karnataka kidney trade
        cost of, 68–69
        live unrelated, 59–61, 67–69
    living donors, 72, 95–96, 100–101
    price for, 106
    primate-to-human, 73
    and rejection, 98
    risks to donor, 213

unrelated living donors, 118
waiting list, 95–96
xenogenic, 73
kidney transplant waiting list
and dialysis, 35
Europe, 31
Germany, 31
U.S., 56n1, 57t, 118–119, 124
"Kidney-vakkam," 149, 165
Kumar, Sanjay, 149, 165

L

Lakeside Hospital, 65
lethal injections, 17
Lithuania, lack of antitrafficking legislation, 32, 36
liver slice transplantation, 213
liver transplants, xenogenic, 73
living donor organ market, 85–86; *See also* kidney market; organ market; vendors
Catholic Church on, 191, 192
kidneys, 100–101
"near relatives," 64
objections to, 86
unrelated donors, 118
living organ donation, *See also* donors; kidney donors; organ donation
Catholic Church on, 190–191
permissible conditions, 221–222n14
risks of, 213
and totality principle, 210
London Renal Transplant Centre, 126
Lumitao, Josephine, 213
Lupron, 85
lymphocytic choriomeningitis virus (LCMV), 6

M

MacIntyre, Alasdair, 220n4
Macklin, Ruth, 171, 176
Madras, India, 165
Mafia organizations, Europe, 25
Maharashtra, India, kidney trade, 69
mail fraud laws, 9
maiming, morally impermissible, 209
"Making an Ass of the Law" (Mani), 69
Malta, lack of antitrafficking legislation, 32, 36
mammary cells, sales of, 170, 181
Mandya district
brokers network, 63, 64, 65–66
kidney trade, 60, 61–63
Mani, M.K., 69

"Markets and Morals: The Case for Organ Sales" (Dworkin), 145, 154
Mastromarino, Michael, 4–5
McFadden, Charles, 212
McHugh, John, 216
Medicaid, 96
medical device manufacturers, buying illegal body parts, 5–6
medical ethics, and execution process, 17–18
medical industries, buying illegal body parts, 5–6
medical professionals
body-as-property view, 138
and live unrelated transplants, 67–68
next of kin and organ donation, 50–51
objections to organ markets, 196–197
role in illegal kidney trade, 67–68
medical tourism. *See* transplant tourism
Medicare, 96
Metrodin, 85
Mexico, child abduction for organs, 7
Moldavia, transplant tourism, 119, 120
Moldova
living standards, 31, 33, 40
organ trafficking, 29, 30
M.S. Ramaiah Hospital, 65
multi-organ explantation, 38
"murder by gangs," 54–55
Murray, Tom, 171
mutilation, morally licit, 208–209

N

Nagaraj, G.V., 62
narcotic trafficking, 26
National Health System, 122–123
National Organ Transplant Act (NOTA), 78, 79, 96, 106, 131
Negrete, Michael, 6
Nelson, Ernest, 5
nerves, 76
next of kin
as "access barrier," 216
body-as-self view, 138
and cadaveric donations, 135
and organ donation, 99
and Uniform Anatomical Gift Act, 78–79
nonregenerative tissues, legislation, 77–80
nonvital organs, 73–74
nucleic acid amplification (NAT), 75

O

obligation to rescue, 136–137
offenders, as informants, 28

Index

Oklahoma Blood Institute, 75
OKT-3, 143
oocyte donation/sales, 75–76, 170, 176–179
   for cloning, 181–184
   open market, 85–86
   students, 86
options markets, 101–102, 106
oral statements, false, 9
organ(s)
   defined, 73–74
   demand/supply, 10, 49–50, 83, 228; *See also* organ shortage
   lymphocytic choriomeningitis virus-infected, 6
   nonvital. *See* nonvital organs
   regenerative. *See* regenerative organs and *individual tissues*
   vital. *See* vital organs
organ brokers, 30; *See also* kidney brokers
   antitrafficking legislation, 41
   donor recruitment, 32–35
   expenses, 105–106
   fees, 103
   and forward market, 101–102
   governmental regulation of, 104–105, 106–107
   Mandya district, 63, 64, 65–66
   insurance companies as, 105
   joint venture with insurance companies, 104–105, 106–107
   profits, 119
   spot markets, 102–105, 106–107
organ donation
   for "affection and attachment," 65
   and altruism, 38, 40, 82–84, 118, 132, 133, 166, 174, 203, 235
   cadaveric. *See* cadaveric organ transplantation
   Catholic Church on, 189–192
   as charity, 203–204
   coercive, 132, 192, 231–232
   and compassion, 203–204
   financial incentives, 31, 38–40, 51–52, 54–55, 122–123, 131–133, 134
   free markets, 52–53
   ideal public policy, 192–194
   illicit, 32–35
   inter vivos, 132, 134; *See also* commercial living donors; donors; kidney donors; living organ donation
   and next of kin, 99
   open market approach, 84–87
   poverty and, 31, 33, 34–35, 40, 121
   private medical-charitable agencies, 192–194
   reasoned ideal argument, 135–136
   registering as, 50–51, 83
   rescue obligation, 136–137
   single-purchaser system, 122–123
   state legislation, 77–78
   tax reduction/credits for, 194
   unemployment and, 40
Organ Donation Trust Fund, Pennsylvania, 83
organ donors. *See* donors; kidney donors; vendors
organized crime
   and corruption, 26
   defining, 24–27
   documenting, 27–29
   informants, 28
   and organ trafficking, 24–27
   and violence, 26
"organ mafia," U.S.-Mexican, 7
organ market
   aid-based argument, 152–155, 164, 165
   and altruism, 217
   arguments against, 54–55, 143
   and autonomy, 144, 145–155, 162–166, 198–199, 236–241
   benefits to vendors, 213–215
   and body part commodification, 236
   cadaveric transplants, 5–6, 87–88, 133–135, 157n3
   Catholic Church on, 195–200
   Catholic transplantation agencies, 192–194, 195–200
   changing laws against, 49–52
   and charity, 215–217
   and coercion, 132, 192, 231–232
   cultural taboos, 228–229
   dehumanizing aspects, 204
   differential pricing, 195
   ethical concerns, 171–176
   FDA and, 88
   flat rate for organs, 230
   fraud in, 199
   futures, 157n3, 161
   global, 9–10
   government controlled, 192–194, 198
   and greed, 233–235
   and human dignity, 198–199, 204, 236–241
   illicit, 32–35, 50, 52, 55, 86, 119–120
   India, economics of, 68–69
   kidneys, 86–87, 96–101; *See also* Karnataka kidney trade
   living donor. *See* living donor organ market
   moral issues, 52, 162–166
   and organ shortages, 51
   physicians' view of, 196–197

posthumous, 87–88
and poverty, 145–148, 162–168, 197–198, 213–214, 230
price discrimination, 103
private, 195
Protestant arguments for/against, 229, 232–241
secular arguments against, 228–232
and totality principle, 210
value of organs, 194
organ procurement, Chinese prisoners, 13–19
Organ Procurement and Transplantation Network (OPTN), 78, 79
organ recipients. *See* recipients
organ replacement, biomechanical, 73
organ shortage, 143, 161, 216, 227–228
and black market, 50
Europe, 30–32
and organ market, 51
possible solutions, 228
organ snatching, stories of, 24, 39, 84
organ tourism. *See* transplant tourism
organ trafficking
business of, 29–32
communication devices and, 9
criminalization of, 40–41
demand/supply driven, 30–32
documenting, 27–29
extent of, 120–121
fraud and, 125–127
greed and, 3
and human rights, 123–124
and international community, 123–124, 125
investigating, 9
Istanbul Declaration, 123
lack of legislation against, 32, 36
laws against, 8–9
and organized crime, 24–27
and poverty, 86, 119–120
and transplant tourism, 118–119
organ transplantation
ABO incompatible, 122
brain death and, 99–100
control of by medical professionals, 198
expense of, 137
government control of, 192–194, 198
and human dignity, 198–199, 204, 236–241
increasing number of, 37–39
legalizing payment for, 38–40
non-heart-beating donation, 122
rejection and, 72
sacramentalization of, 199–200
success rate, 143
survival rates, 137
waiting list. *See* transplant waiting list

organ vendors. *See* vendors
O'Rourke, Kevin, 219*n*1

P

Pakistan, transplant tourism, 119, 120, 121
Panday, Amar Kumar, 62
Pavicevic, Borko, 125–127
Pennsylvania, Organ Donation Trust Fund, 83
People's Liberation Army (PLA), 19
Pergonal, 85
pharmaceutical companies, buying illegal body parts, 5–6
Philippines, transplant tourism, 119, 120, 121, 213
physicians
body-as-property view, 138
and live unrelated transplants, 67–68
next of kin and organ donation, 50–51
objections to organ markets, 196–197
role in illegal kidney trade, 67–68
Planned Parenthood vs. Casey, 82
Pop, Pera, 125–127
Pope John XXIII, 211
Pope John Paul II, 192, 196, 219*n*1, 221*n*11
Pope Pius XII, 190–191, 211, 216–217
Portugal, unrelated living donors, 118
posthumous organ market, 5–6, 87–88, 133–135, 157*n*3
poverty
aid programs, 152–155, 164, 165
and autonomy, 145–155, 162–168
and birth outcomes, 215
and coercion, 231–232
free market economy, 198
and organ donation, 31, 33, 34–35, 38–40, 51–52, 54–55, 121, 122–123, 131–133, 134
and organ market, 145–148, 162–168, 197–198, 213–214, 230
and organ trafficking, 86, 119–120
and voluntary consent, 231
presumed consent, 38, 80–81
and altruism, 81
Catholic Church on, 192
condemned prisoners and, 81–82
price discrimination, kidney market, 103
price-to-antigen test result ratio, 103
Prince, Dennis, 98
prisoners, condemned
kidneys from, 120
organ procurement from, 13–19, 81–82, 86, 120; *See also* China
and "voluntary" consent, 14–17, 30, 81–82

Index

prostitution, 26
Protestant Ethic and the Spirit of Capitalism, The, 234
Protestantism
    autonomy and, 240
    and commercialization, 234–235
    and organ market, 229
    secular professions as callings, 234, 235–236
public policy, ideal, 192–194

R

Radcliffe-Richards, Janet, 231, 232
Radin, Margaret, 135, 174
Ramsey, Paul, 238–240, 242n2
Rau, G.V. Krishna, 62, 63
reasoned ideal argument, organ donation, 135–136
recipients
    body-as-self view, 138
    exploiting despair of, 31–32
    survival rates, 227
    as victims, 35
Recommendation 1611, 37
regenerative organs/tissues
    donation/sale of, 74–77, 171
    and donor autonomy, 144–148
    and principle of totality, 210
Reid, Henry, 5–6
rejection
    transplanted kidneys, 98
    transplanted organs, 72
    in transplant tourists, 119
rent seeking, 104
reproduction
    paradigm of and selling fetal parts, 180, 182–184
    significance of, 184–185
reproductive tissue
    animal to human transplants, 191
    sales/donation of, 75–76, 170, 180, 182–184
rescue obligation, 136–137
"resurrectionists," 84
Roe vs. Wade, 82
Romania, organ trafficking, 30, 119
Russia, organ trafficking, 30

S

Saint Basil the Great, 195
secrecy, and confidentiality, 15–16
self-mutilation
    Apostolic canons on, 206–207
    Thomas Aquinas on, 208–210, 220n7

Sells, R.A., 233, 236
semen donation, 38–39
Serbia, organs from executed prisoners, 82
single-purchaser system, 122–123
Skid Row, 6
skin donation/sales, 76, 137
"slayer provisions," 88
Spain, organ donation program, 122
sperm
    as property, 76
    sale of, 75–76, 176–179
spot markets, kidneys, 102–105, 106–107
stem cells, 76–77
"sticky benefits theory," 238, 239, 242n3
students, unexplained disappearances, 6
Sudarshan, H., 61, 64, 66–67
suicide clauses, 88
surrogate motherhood, commercial, 134
surveillance, 28

T

Tadd, G.V., 155
Tamil Nadu, India
    "kidney colonies," 119
    kidney trade, 59, 69
tax credits/reductions, 194
tendons, 76
Thomas, Philip, 62, 66
Thomasma, David, 230, 237–238, 240
Thomists
    and totality principle, 206
    view of Aquinas, 220n4
Thorne, Emmanuel, 161
Tijuana, Mexico, "baby organ snatchers," 7
tissue-processing companies, 4
tissues
    banks, 9
    demand/supply, 10
    donation, 76–77
    lymphocytic choriomeningitis virus-infected, 6
    nonregenerative, 77–80
    regenerative. *See* regenerative tissues
Titmuss, Richard, 74
totality principle, 205–212
    and amputation, 208–210
    and cadaveric transplants, 210
    and charity, 208–217
    and futures market, 210
    and living organ donation, 210
    reinterpretation of, 211–212
    and self-mutilation, 208–210, 220n7
tracking system, kidney market, 105–106

transfer expenses, 105
Transplantation of Human Organs Act, 59, 61, 64–65, 66, 69
transplant technology, 72–73
transplant tourism
  Americans, 121
  defined, 119
  Europe, 29–32
  fraud and, 125–127
  and human rights, 123–124
  India, 29–30, 121
  internet and, 9
  Israelis, 120, 121
  Istanbul Declaration, 123
  kidneys, 118–119
  and organ trafficking, 118–119
  Pakistan, 121
  Philippines, 119, 120, 121, 213
  public health risks, 119
  and rejection, 119
  risks to recipients, 119
  Turkey, 29, 30, 34, 155
transplant waiting list
  buying way up, 41
  and economic status, 137
  Europe, 31
  Italy, 118
  Japan, 118
  kidneys. See kidney transplant waiting list
  manipulating, 41
  U.K., 156n1
  U.S., 83, 88, 228, 57t, 83, 88
  and value of life, 50
Turkey, organ trafficking, 29, 30, 34, 155

U

UCLA Medical Center, sale of body parts, 5–6
Ukraine, organ trafficking, 29, 30
undercover observation, 28
undertakers, tissue harvesting/selling, 4–5
unemployment, and organ donation, 40
Uniform Anatomical Gift Act, 72, 77–79
United Kingdom
  living donor transplantation, 122
  19th century medical schools, 84
  single-purchaser system, 122
  transplant waiting list, 156n1
United Network for Organ Sharing (UNOS), 79, 131–132
United States
  child kidnapping, 7
  kidney shortage, 119

kidney transplant waiting list, 56n1, 57t, 118–119, 124
organ demand/supply, 10, 49–50, 83, 228
transplant tourists from, 121
transplant waiting list, 57t, 83, 88, 228
unrelated living kidney donors, 118
U.S. Public Health Service Title 42, 8–9
Universal Declaration of Human Rights, 123–124
"universal priesthood," 234
urban myths, organ-snatching, 24, 39, 84

V

Valesians, 206
"valuable consideration," 79
vendors, See also commercial living donors
  autonomy of, 144–155, 162–166
  dehumanizing, 204
  economic benefits, 213–215
  economic necessity, 145–155, 162–168
  exploiting, 31–32, 46–48, 146–148, 197, 230–231, 232
  health benefits, 214
  Iran, 68
  motives of, 195
  preexisting health conditions, 121
  risks to, 121
Venkatachala, N., 63
victims
  defined, 34
  donors as, 35–36
  recipients as, 35
Villivakkam, 149, 151, 165
violence, and organized crime, 26
Virginia, donor registration, 83
vital organs, 73–74, 174–176
vivisection, 18
voluntary consent
  and condemned prisoners, 14–17, 30, 81–82
  and poverty, 231
voluntary donation. See donors; kidney donors; living organ donation; organ donation

W

waiting list. See transplant waiting list
Weber, Max, 234, 235
white-collar crime, 27, 41
Whitehall II study, 214
Willed Body Program, 5–6

wire fraud laws, 9
World Health Assembly, 125
World Health Organization (WHO), prohibition against buying/selling organs, 123–124
World Medical Association, 17
World Organization Against Torture, 7

X

xenotransplantation, 37, 73, 189

Z

Zutlevics, T.L., 144, 147–148, 149, 151, 152–155

A Call for Authors
Advances in Police Theory and Practice

AIMS AND SCOPE:

This cutting-edge series is designed to promote publication of books on contemporary advances in police theory and practice. We are especially interested in volumes that focus on the nexus between research and practice, with the end goal of disseminating innovations in policing. We will consider collections of expert contributions as well as individually authored works. Books in this series will be marketed internationally to both academic and professional audiences. This series also seeks to —

- Bridge the gap in knowledge about advances in theory and practice regarding who the police are, what they do, and how they maintain order, administer laws, and serve their communities
- Improve cooperation between those who are active in the field and those who are involved in academic research so as to facilitate the application of innovative advances in theory and practice

The series especially encourages the contribution of works coauthored by police practitioners and researchers. We are also interested in works comparing policing approaches and methods globally, examining such areas as the policing of transitional states, democratic policing, policing and minorities, preventive policing, investigation, patrolling and response, terrorism, organized crime and drug enforcement. In fact, every aspect of policing, public safety, and security, as well as public order is relevant for the series. Manuscripts should be between 300 and 600 printed pages. If you have a proposal for an original work or for a contributed volume, please be in touch.

Series Editor
Dilip Das, Ph.D., Ph: 802-598-3680
E-mail: dilipkd@aol.com

Dr. Das is a professor of criminal justice and Human Rights Consultant to the United Nations. He is a former chief of police and, founding president of the International Police Executive Symposium, IPES, www.ipes.info. He is also founding editor-in-chief of *Police Practice and Research: An International Journal* (PPR), (Routledge/Taylor & Francis), www.tandf.co.uk/journals. In addition to editing the *World Police Encyclopedia* (Taylor & Francis, 2006), Dr. Das has published numerous books and articles during his many years of involve-ment in police practice, research, writing, and education.

Proposals for the series may be submitted to the series editor or directly to –
Carolyn Spence
Acquisitions Editor • CRC Press / Taylor & Francis Group
561-998-2515 • 561-997-7249 (fax)
carolyn.spence@taylorandfrancis.com • www.crcpress.com
6000 Broken Sound Parkway NW, Suite 300, Boca Raton, FL 33487